بسم الله ٱلرَّحْمَـٰن ٱلرَّحِيم

A Doorway in Tunis

Memoir of a Fugitive Family in Muslim Lands

Aisha F. Saidi

Cover design: Kate Winter and Karen Lee
Front cover image: Through the Arches of Tunis Medina. 100203287 | © Evgeniy Fesenko | Dreamstime.com
Back cover image: Hamsa or Hand of Fatima. 156893354 | © Itstatulya | Dreamstime.com
Base map: North Africa and Middle East political map. 96996889 | © Peter Hermes Furian | Dreamstime.com
Routes overlaid on base map: Jubair Saidi and Karen Lee
Image for chapter head: Black and white round symmetrical arabesque, decorative mandala. 149931262 | © Olesya Klivenkova | Dreamstime.com
Floral decorations: 176136444 © Flossstudio | Dreamstime.com

Redpoll Media

Cornish, Maine

Library of Congress Cataloging-in-Publication data available upon request.

Paperback ISBN: 979-8-9880061-0-7
Ebook ISBN: 979-8-9880061-1-4

DEDICATION

To my extended family and friends, I thank you for your love and your support of my many revisions of this book. May your days and nights be blessed with connection to the beautiful creation and to the One that is All.

CONTENTS

PREFACE

Why does a young, white woman from a middle-class family reject American culture, become Muslim, marry an incarcerated Black American man, and then — with her three young children — follow him to North Africa after his escape from prison? This memoir is my effort to answer these questions and tell the story of my family's fugitive life in the Muslim world.

Emerging from a difficult youth, I deny the existence of love. Then, as an adult, I fall in love with a convicted criminal. Living with him and our children in the developing world, I take refuge in my spiritual life, nurture my children, and face the hardships of our life on the run. Along the way I encounter the kindness of strangers, but also the torment of a collapsing marriage.

Traveling by car and camper trailer from 1980 to 1993, my family's travels cover thousands of miles across a dozen countries. We settle down in a place for a year or two, make friends, learn the local language, become acculturated, and then move on with endless restlessness.

These constant travels arise partly from our fear of discovery by the U.S. authorities and partly as a response to the dangers we inadvertently stumble upon in turbulent countries. In this account, I use pseudonyms and change some details of people who befriend us. However, I haven't changed my and my children's names or those of most westerners we encounter.

Driven by an insistent urge to explore the unknown and willing to take serious risks because of my vision for our future, I get on a plane in New York with my children, headed for a very different world from the one I know. By the mercy of God, we survive to tell this story. Sheer luck plays a part, but even more important is the help given us by generous people we meet as we explore Muslim lands.

Aisha F. Saidi
2026

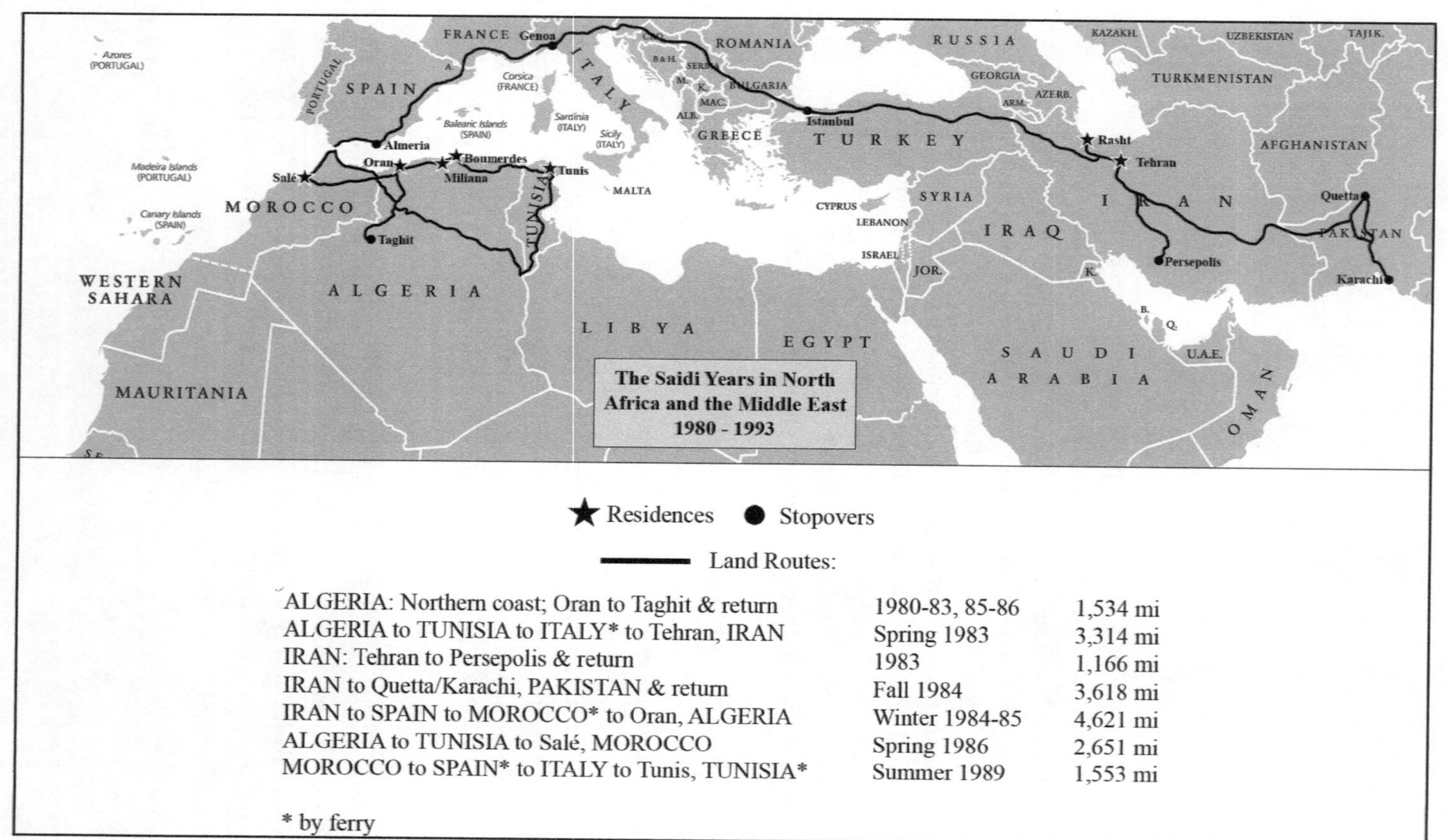

The Saidi Years in North Africa and the Middle East 1980 - 1993
Residences
Stopovers
Land Routes:
ALGERIA: Northern coast; Oran to Taghit & return — 1980-83, 85-86 — 1,534 mi
ALGERIA to TUNISIA to ITALY* to Tehran, IRAN — Spring 1983 — 3,314 mi
IRAN: Tehran to Persepolis & return — 1983 — 1,166 mi
IRAN to Quetta/Karachi, PAKISTAN & return — Fall 1984 — 3,618 mi
IRAN to SPAIN to MOROCCO* to Oran, ALGERIA — Winter 1984-85 — 4,621 mi
ALGERIA to TUNISIA to Salé, MOROCCO — Spring 1986 — 2,651 mi
MOROCCO to SPAIN* to ITALY to Tunis, TUNISIA* — Summer 1989 — 1,553 mi
* by ferry

I

DAWN PRAYER
1980

"Every new beginning comes from some other beginning's
end."

Seneca

Feeling the hollow pit in my stomach, I realized how little I understood this
new world to which I had come with my three young children. Far from
friends and family in America, we had just landed in Tunisia, a small, sunny
country in North Africa perched on the shores of the Mediterranean Sea. I
held my sleeping, eight-month-old infant, Jubair, against my chest and
uttered a silent prayer. Yusuf and Jamal squirmed as we sat on the hard
plastic seats in the Tunis-Carthage International Airport, and I reassured
them their father would be coming soon. At ages five and six, they trusted
me completely. But we had been waiting two hours, and he hadn't come to
get us. I knew nothing about Tunisia, and I knew no one here. For the
children, I tried to stifle my rising anxiety.

The Tunisian customs officer had spoken to me in Arabic, examining
the Arabic name on my passport and seeing my head scarf, long coat, and
loose pants. When I replied that I spoke English, he switched to English
and half-jokingly chided me for not knowing any Arabic. Again, he spoke
to me in Arabic, but I could only stammer a reply, "Salaamu alaikum." This
wasn't exactly what he was hoping for. He urged me to learn Arabic and
stamped my passport. My children and I moved on.

As we waited, we passed the time watching people exit from airport
customs and rush downstairs to the embrace of jubilant relatives, all
exclaiming in Arabic and French — languages that were incomprehensible

to me. Hours passed. We had removed our winter coats, but still, sweat streamed down my forehead and my shoulder muscles ached with tension.

Scanning the crowds for his father, Jamal asked, "Where is Abu?" I wondered the same thing. He should have been here long before now.

"Ummi, I'm thirsty," cried Yusuf. I fumbled in my backpack for the water bottle and cookies for the kids. Jubair woke up and I nursed him discreetly under my waist-long head scarf…

> *He's not here*
> *In this strange land,*
> *People of unknown tongue:*
> *I swallow a lump,*
> *I'm on my own.*

Remembering Abdullah's last, brief, overseas telephone call before the children and I left the States, I searched my wallet for the scrap of paper on which I had written the address he had given me. My only option was to find my way to that place, but I didn't know who or what I would encounter there.

After loading our luggage onto a cart and changing some traveler's checks, I strapped Jubair into the baby sling on my chest and led the children outside to the street. It had been a bitterly cold, windy day when we left New York, but here the dry, dusty heat blasted us and began baking us. I smelled the ancient air of Tunis and knew with even greater certainty that I was in a totally foreign land.

Walking to the long line of taxis waiting at the curb, I asked one driver if he spoke English. No. Yelling down the line he asked the other drivers if any of them spoke English. None. The empty ache I felt became even more acute, but I forced myself to think clearly. I pulled out the scrap of paper and showed the address to the driver. He scratched his chin and shook his head. He said something to the other taxi drivers, and they emerged from their cars to examine the piece of paper. There was a lot of shaking of heads, and I felt a twinge…

> *Address unknown.*
> *There's nowhere to go,*
> *Only this slip of paper.*
> *He's not coming*
> *To bring us home.*

Oh, Allah help me
And my helpless children.

A driver from the end of the line of taxis approached to confer with the others. He held the paper in his hand, tilting his head as he read the words. He pursed his lips and shrugged. Then he maneuvered our luggage cart to his taxi and began loading the suitcases into the trunk. We piled into the taxi, and he wheeled away from the curb with our wide-eyed American family in the back. I wasn't sure that he knew where to take us.

"It's a donkey!" cried Yusuf as we passed a donkey pulling a cart along the road.

Jamal's eye was caught by an airplane taking off from the airport. "Is that our plane?" he asked.

Numbly, I also wondered if it was our airplane, returning to the familiarity of the U.S. The taxi drove down a scruffy, broad, grey asphalt road surrounded by a barren landscape of packed dirt, pale desert plants, and trash blowing in the hot wind. In the un-air-conditioned taxi, the breeze through the open windows provided absolutely no relief from the smothering heat. Trying to remember the way, in case I needed to retrace our steps, I focused on the area through which we were driving.

Presently, I saw palm trees alongside the road and some buildings the same color as the dusty earth. The buildings grew more numerous and taller, and the street became more populated with people, animals, and vehicles. Then, as the taxi sped along, we plunged into the city on a wide airy avenue sheltered by rows of palm trees and adjoined by narrow streets packed with cars, donkey carts, children playing, women dressed in sheet-like wraps, and noisy vendors hawking their wares.

The driver looked again at the address on the paper and turned into the first of many twisting alleys barely wide enough for a car. After countless turns, I knew that I would never be able to find my way out of the maze by myself. The taxi slowed as it inched along a footpath just wide enough for one vehicle. Pedestrians flattened themselves against the baked mud walls on either side to let the taxi pass.

The whitewashed sides of the path stretched two or three stories high above the grimy street, with only an occasional door at street level or a solitary window far above the clatter of the street. I felt pressed into a nearly featureless tunnel with no roof. The slice of sky I could see above seemed far away. At the bottom of the tunnel, the taxi moved slowly. The driver said something to me and drove a few more feet and stopped. He turned and spoke once more and handed me the piece of paper that contained the valuable address. We were here. He hopped out, quickly unloaded our luggage, and opened the back door of the taxi.

Clumsily, I exited the taxi. I saw no apartments or houses, no windows, except for one at the top of the high, naked wall. There were no faces looking down from above, no plants adorning window boxes. Nothing. I didn't understand…

> *Only sky above.*
> *And a single heavy wooden door by the taxi.*
> *No doorbell, no number, no name,*
> *Not even a doorknob or handle,*
> *Only one large keyhole: no key.*

I looked at the driver and he pointed to the sturdy wooden door, nodding his head in a friendly way. Noting my bewilderment, he went over and pounded on the door a few times. Soon, a tall, heavy woman wearing a long dress and head scarf opened the door. She said something in Arabic, but I could only show her my ticket, the paper with the address. Silently she read it, nodded, and proceeded to haul our luggage up long, dark stars into the interior of the building.

I turned to pay the taxi driver and realized I didn't know how much the fare cost. I held out my hand to give him a few of the smaller bills and he shook his head no, it was too much. He reached into my palm and took only the money that was due him, smiled in welcome, and went on his way. I was grateful for the honesty of the taxi driver.

The woman did not return down the stairs to invite us into the house. Pausing at the doorway I wondered whether it was appropriate to enter the house without her. I decided to follow her footsteps up the unlit, narrow stairwell. I straightened my scarf, hitched my bag over my shoulder, and patted Jubair's back. Saying "Bismillah, in the name of God," I took the hands of Jamal and Yusuf and passed through the doorway.

The woman led us into her apartment, where it appeared she lived with a petite, dark-haired, friendly woman. Both wore long, simple dresses and soft head scarves. The women served us tea and pastries, which the children devoured a bit too enthusiastically, eliciting smiles from the ladies. The smaller woman tried to communicate with me in French as well as Arabic, but I could neither understand nor communicate anything. I tried using English and even my high school Spanish, but both languages were useless. The only communication that worked was non-verbal, and my cheeks became fatigued with the constant smiling that was my only way to express myself…

> *Where are you?*
> *Why'd you change the plan*
> *And not tell me?*
> *We're safe, I think,*
> *But do you know we're here?*

Our first day in Tunis passed slowly for me. As the day wore on, I began to feel less apprehensive. To keep my mind from spinning into fits of worry, I turned my attention to the children, who depended so completely upon me. I kept Jamal and Yusuf busy reading their books, drawing pictures, or playing with a rubber ball in the courtyard at the center of the apartment.

The courtyard measured about twenty by thirty feet, with tall concrete walls, a couple of access doors, windows high up on the walls, and the bright blue sky up above. In the middle of the area was a concrete basin and a water pipe topped by a faucet. Jamal and Yusuf laughed as they bounced the ball to each other and off the walls, happy at last to run and play after our long trip. However, after a few minutes of fun, the large woman came and beckoned us to come back inside the apartment. I got the impression that the kids' noise might disturb the other, unseen occupants of the building.

The apartment itself had well-scrubbed concrete walls and floors, whitewashed but poorly lit by an occasional light bulb. The high ceilings gave a sense of spaciousness to the home and helped maintain the cool temperature, which was a great relief after our heat-blasted taxi ride. A long hall reached from the kitchen at the back of the apartment, past a small dining room off to one side, followed by a bedroom, and then a room at the front of building, which was for our use during our stay. The simple, undecorated room had a double bed and two couches, along with a crib that the women brought in for my baby.

From this bedroom, two wide windows overlooked the alley below and the nondescript front door where the taxi had deposited us. This outlook was to become my favorite place, for I longed to see the outdoors, even if I was in the middle of a city. Jamal and Yusuf loved watching the continuous action in the alley below — children kicking a small ball up and down the narrow thoroughfare, the clamor of a man selling vegetables piled high in his wooden cart, and occasional cat fights surging up the walls and down the street. We all watched for the arrival of Abdullah, whom we thought must be arriving shortly.

In the late afternoon, I heard a man's voice in the hall. He was speaking Arabic to the large woman. Turning, he saw me and spoke.

"Salaamu alaikum! Welcome! I'm Muhammad. You must be Aisha. Your husband told me you might be coming. Please, come have tea. The children too!"

Relief floods me, cool, healing,
Layers of worry fall away.
Oh my God thank you.
We're safe,
Abdullah is coming to us.

We all filed into the dining room, a space sufficient only for a table and cushioned seating all around it, like a large booth. On the walls were pictures displaying Arabic calligraphy — most likely passages from the Qur'an, I thought. Muhammad was wiry and middle-aged, with wavy black hair, a trim beard, and a warm, open face.

Turning to Jamal and Yusuf, he asked, "How was your plane ride?"

"High up, over the ocean!" exclaimed Yusuf.

"We saw a movie," said Jamal.

Muhammad smiled and offered the children cookies that his wife had set on the table. "And how is your family in America?"

"Good," Jamal offered. "Nana and Pop Pop moved to another house."

"Karen takes us to the playground," added Yusuf.

Trying not to seem impatient, I asked, "How did you meet Abdullah? Where is he?"

Turning to me, Mohammad replied, "One day at the mosque, I met your husband and got to know him. He told me he couldn't find a job here in Tunisia, so he decided to go to Algeria and seek work there. He asked me to look after his family if he wasn't here when you arrived."

"Thank you for your kindness," I said, feeling a bit less awkward.

"My home is your home!" he exclaimed. "Let my wife know if there is anything you need." I later learned that his sincere offer was traditional Arab hospitality.

I felt relieved at the news, and yet worried that Abdullah had not contacted me. Was he safe? I did not have an answer to this question, and evidently, Muhammad didn't either. As time passed slowly, day after day with no word from my husband, I tried to keep Jamal and Yusuf busy with reading and math lessons, as well as our daily prayers in Arabic. When Jubair wasn't sleeping or nursing, he was happy to practice kicking, babbling, and sitting up in his crib. He had a keen interest in the activities of his brothers, and I put him on my lap to watch as they made pictures and practiced writing their English alphabet.

After lessons, lunch, and quiet playtime, Jamal and Yusuf asked if we could go outside to play. But I was uncertain about taking them into the chaotic scene on the street below, even for a few minutes. It certainly wasn't a good place to play, and if we ventured far from the nondescript doorway of the apartment, I was sure we'd get lost.

When I tried to help the two women in the kitchen at dinner time, they shooed me out immediately. I wondered why I wasn't allowed to assist them, but I guessed it was a cultural practice of some sort. Without enough to do and unable to communicate with the women, I felt bored and isolated…

Achingly distant
My tongue knows no common words.
My ears hear only noise.
My heart feels so alone.

One of the women called my name, and as I came out of the front room into the hall, she seemed to wave me back, with her hand palm down and outstretched fingers pushing away from herself in the gesture that means "go away" in the U.S. I backed up, puzzled. Then she repeated the gesture vigorously, speaking Arabic to me. I backed away some more. Finally, she came and took my arm to guide me down the hall toward the dining room. Then I understood that the actual message was the second movement of her outstretched hand as it quickly moved back toward her body, indicating "come toward me." I wondered what else I was misinterpreting due to cultural differences. I had never felt more like a stranger in the world than I did then.

Without the ability to communicate, I had to rely solely on observations. Wafa, the tall, heavyset woman, was quiet and calm. I thought she was somewhat distant, though it was difficult to tell with the language and cultural differences. Khadija was short and trim, with a lovely smile and friendly manner. Often there was loud shouting between Wafa and Khadija. To me it sounded as if they were having a disagreement. However, their faces did not reveal the anger I expected to see. Were they used to arguing with each other? Or were they just discussing something loudly? I couldn't tell. I also didn't know their relationship to each other. I knew that Wafa was Muhammad's wife, and I thought she had indicated that Khadija was her sister. But the two women seemed so different.

Days turned into a week, and then another week, as I waited for word from Abdullah. But even if he had been able to call, there was no telephone in Muhammad's apartment. Not being able to call my parents in the U.S. weighed on me, as I knew they would be worried that their daughter and grandchildren had disappeared without a trace into North Africa. I had no option, however, but to keep waiting for my husband and caring for the children.

When I could no longer delay doing the children's laundry, Wafa showed me how to fill the tub in the courtyard with water and scrub the clothes by hand. My hands ached with the cold, and my skin turned red from the harsh laundry detergent. Then I hung the clothes to dry on a thin clothesline near the tub. Fortunately, I still had some disposable diapers for the baby, but they wouldn't last forever, and I didn't know where or how to buy more.

Three weeks had gone by when Khadija came to me and used sign language to tell me she would take me shopping with her. I had just nursed Jubair, and he was sleeping soundly. Yusuf and Jamal were playing with their small set of Legos, and they promised to be good for Wafa, who would watch them while I was gone. Khadija led me down the dark stairs to the street below and opened the heavy door onto the street.

I suddenly felt lighter under the bright sunlight and open air, dusty though it was. Khadija grabbed my hand and led me firmly along the alley, avoiding obstacles and pushing assertively through crowds of shoppers. Never letting go of my hand, she turned down another alley, which led to a broad empty square. As we walked hand in hand across the square, I felt uncomfortable being led like a child, but Khadija didn't seem to notice. It evidently was a common practice, as I saw other women walking hand in hand, and occasionally two men doing the same.

As we approached the far side of the square, I saw small shops with colorful awnings and bins full of oranges, vegetables, spices, and household goods. Khadija carefully inspected some vegetables and chose only the best specimens while bargaining with the vendor on the price. We stopped in a butcher's shop, where plucked, naked chickens hung over a large chopping block. Khadija purchased a chicken, and we moved on. A little way down the row of stalls, she led me into a shop that had tall walls lined with shelves of canned food and other packaged goods. The only familiar items I saw were cartons of eggs on the lower shelves, and loaves of French bread in a huge basket at the front of the store. Khadija helped me purchase disposable diapers, which looked more like women's sanitary napkins than baby diapers. She also indicated some packets of folded plastic that I should buy for the baby, though I didn't know why...

> *I can't understand. How to act. How to speak.*
> *How to shop. Strange boxes, cans, mysterious brands,*
> *Arabic labels.*
> *How much is it. Is it too much. Which coins, which bills to use.*
> *Shopkeeper is friendly. Khadija is cheerful.*
> *But I'm exhausted, lost, foreignness all around.*
> *I'm a hapless beetle in a colony of honeybees.*
> *I did this. Brought my children here. Oh God.*
> *Almost one month here, no word from Abdullah. No word.*
> *What next? What to do? Oh my God.*

In our darkened room, I awoke to the moving chant of the pre-dawn adhan, the haunting Muslim call to prayer being chanted from the roof of the local mosque. The children were still sound asleep, so I completed my ablutions and performed the first of the five daily prayers. Though as a busy mother, I often found it difficult to wake up before dawn, this was my favorite time to pray...

> *Dark and quiet*
> *The early morning hour envelops me.*
> *Alone I reflect, connect with One.*
> *With each prayer, sleep changes to deep relief:*

The kids are safe, I'm safe.
I give thanks for strangers caring, sheltering us for God's sake.
In the deep realm of prayer, I am content.
First light.
My heart prays: Merciful One, please protect my family and me.
And dawn turns to sunrise.

It was another sunny day in Tunis, and soon Jamal and Yusuf were going stir-crazy, cooped up in Muhammad's apartment on such a fine day. I didn't know where they could play outside, nor did I know how to ask Wafa or Khadija about this. Fortunately, Khadija was perceptive. Using gestures, she offered to take us outside so the boys could play while Jubair napped under Wafa's care. She took us out to a large, dust-blown area of packed dirt that hosted not a single tree or blade of grass.

Jamal and Yusuf ran wildly, kicking a wobbly, cheap plastic ball that they had found. Two rough Tunisian boys tried to enlist my sons in a pick-up game of soccer, but it was a vastly unequal match. Khadija seemed not to trust the Tunisian boys to play nicely, so she kept a tight rein on things. I felt grateful for her sisterly protectiveness.

When we returned to the apartment, we found someone in our room, his back to us as he gazed at Jubair sleeping in the crib. He didn't need to turn around for me to recognize him.

"Abdullah!" I cried as I rushed to him and collapsed into his arms, sobbing with joy. All my anxiety of the past weeks disappeared in our fierce embrace.

Jamal and Yusuf ran up and joined our hug, crying, "Abu! Father!" I had so many questions for him, but now I just melted in the warmth of our family embrace.

"Did you miss me?" Abdullah joked.

"Yes! Yes!" the boys called out. We all laughed.

"Um, whose baby is this?" Abdullah asked. "The woman here told me something but I'm not sure what she said." Like me, he spoke no Arabic, though we had both studied Qur'anic Arabic.

"This is our Jubair!" I exclaimed, picking him up. It had been a long time since Abdullah had seen the youngest member of our family. Meanwhile, the baby, now awake, was confused by this unfamiliar person and all the commotion. His face wrinkled up as he began to cry, and that signaled the unification of our family, both parents tearful, the children either laughing or crying, and all of us reaching out to hold each other.

Suddenly serious, I stepped back, searching my husband's face for unspoken thoughts. He understood and replied, "It's okay."

"No problems?" I asked to make sure.

"No problems."

We never talked about our situation in front of the children. In fact, we didn't talk about it with anyone. For this was no ordinary reunion. Abdullah Khalid was an American convict with a life sentence who had escaped from prison in the U.S. He had fled to North Africa, where he planned to find work, become invisible to U.S. law enforcement, and support his young family.

A highly intelligent, personable Black American, Abdullah was a convert to Islam. I had met him and married him while he was behind bars, when he was called by his Muslim name, Abdullah Khalid, or his birth name, Rick Briar. For five years, we had never been free of surveillance by prison guards within grim concrete walls. We had not been together as a family in our own space with the prospect of a shared future or the hope of many years of growth and love. Now our married life and family life became our own, but we'd have to carefully hide our past from others' scrutiny.

I hadn't realized how heavy a burden I'd been carrying in the past month. I felt immensely relieved now that Abdullah was by my side. My heart expanded with love. And he brought good news too,

"I got a job teaching English to Algerian engineers at the Institute of Petroleum in Boumerdes. It includes an apartment, which will be ready by the time we arrive."

"Alhamdulillah! Thank God! When do we leave?"

"In a couple weeks," he replied. "The semester begins in January."

"Amazing. How did you find this job?"

"Well, someone recommended me."

I saw that Abdullah was being deliberately vague, and I knew not to pursue details that he wouldn't give me. I guessed he had met someone in Algeria who had used their influence to obtain work for him. Regardless of the source of the job, it was the vehicle for beginning our new life together as a family…

We will be free.
Facing the dawn of this new, strange world
We will build our lives
Forge a new path
And leave our past
Melting away.

2

SEIZE THE DAY
1957-1974

"Seize the day, for you never can tell when you'll have another chance."

Horace

Angry mobs of people were yelling abuse at the soldiers who surrounded the entrance to a large, impressive building. Surging, the crowd erupted, screaming at two black teenagers who were being escorted up the stairs toward the door of their high school. I had never seen news like this on television. At nine years old, I usually paid no attention to the evening news hour, which was a ritual for my parents. I was much more interested in the latest adventure story I was reading. However, this evening in September 1957, I was riveted to the images being broadcast into my home and countless other homes throughout the U.S. The somber, frightened faces of the Negro students disturbed me. They were just trying to go to school.

"Why are those people yelling at the kids?" I asked. My mother didn't reply. Her silence told me that this was one of the many forbidden subjects in our white family.

But my father's reddened face was agitated, like it was when my brother or I did something really, really bad. Raising his voice, he exclaimed, "Beverly, you have to understand. Negroes should go to their own schools! They have no business mixing where they don't belong."

Though I wanted to ask about this, I understood I would only earn punishment for contradicting my father. But I wondered. I had given much thought to the story of the Good Samaritan and other moral themes, which I encountered at Sunday School and in the books I was reading.

The news broadcast shifted to Arkansas Governor Faubus, who was saying something about the Supreme Court and the people of Arkansas. He was angry, too, like Dad, who grew up in Arkansas. Then, Faubus's face was replaced by the serious but familiar image of President Eisenhower, to whom I had written a letter a couple of years earlier. Someone in his office had even written me back, wishing me happy birthday on his behalf…

I like the President's kind face.
Those kids. I hope they're OK.
They're so brave.
But the people yelling, they look awfully mean.
Why do they want to hurt those kids?

This event, my first conscious exposure to the violence of racism, was one of many that impacted my thinking during the Civil Rights era of the 1950s and 1960s. It helped me understand what happened eight years later at a public pool in my hometown in New Jersey, where I got my first real job at the age of seventeen. Having earned Red Cross certifications in lifesaving, water safety instruction, and advanced first aid, I was hired as a lifeguard at Mountwell Pool in Haddonfield.

Over the years, white families had abandoned going to the large, stream-fed pool as more black kids came from Camden to swim. These urban teens and children were often rough, and no parents accompanied them. When I worked there, the pool employees were the only white people. Experienced lifeguards didn't want to work at Mountwell, but I was happy to have a full-time job for the summer. I was determined to protect the people who came to the pool.

Evidently, I was the only conscientious employee there. The manager, a grizzled, older man who was often absent, advised me to relax and not worry about the people in the pool. The assistant manager spent most of his time in the mysterious pump house, and he was never available when one of the lifeguards had a problem.

One hot day in July, the pool was crowded with kids, but I was the only lifeguard watching the pool. The rule was that there should always be at least two of us on duty, or three if the pool was crowded. But the other two lifeguards, older teenage boys, were nowhere to be seen. I was steaming…

Where are those jerks?
I'm the only one guarding for hours!
Gotta pee but can't leave my post.
Scan the pool for halting, gasping, rough play, dunking.
Scan for anything not right.
Scan the deep water, though it's too deep to see the bottom.

Finally, I saw one of the lifeguards slip out of the pump house, and I waved him over vehemently. "What were you doing in there?" I yelled. "Rob, you were supposed to relieve me two hours ago!"

He grinned but didn't reply.

I smelled booze on him. "Where's Dave?"

Still silent, he nodded at the pump house.

"Your turn," I said abruptly, jumping down from the lifeguard chair and rushing off to the bathroom.

A few weeks later, I returned from my day off to find that the pool was closed, and the water had been emptied. Rob and Dave were getting ready to clean the pool, which we usually did every two weeks.

"Hey, what's happening?" I asked. "We just cleaned the pool."

Rob and Dave looked down.

"What?"

"A guy died. Drowned," said Dave.

"Beverly, we were both watching the pool!" Rob defended himself and his buddy. "But we didn't see anything!"

I looked at them, stunned. "Drowned? What happened?"

Dave sighed, "The guy's friends came and told us they couldn't find him. They had looked everywhere. Said he wouldn't have gone home without them."

"Where was he?" I asked softly.

"We had to keep diving down in the deep part. Over and over. It's fifteen feet deep and it's dark, you can't see anything. He was down there. It took both of us to haul him up."

When they described the man, I knew who he was. I used to watch him as he entertained his friends with jumps and dives off the board. He was a tall young man with dark skin and a nice smile. His friends, sitting on nearby bleachers, would make comments and joke with him as he climbed the ladder out of the pool...

The rest of the summer passed quietly as I struggled inwardly with the young man's death, the pervasive racism in my world, and my uncertain future. I prepared to go off to college, but I wasn't enthusiastic. All I had ever wanted to do was to join the Navy, go to sea, and travel the world. But my father put his foot down and forbade me from doing that. He said that only immoral women went into the Navy, and anyway, women weren't allowed to serve on ships. The main reason I should go to college, in his view, was to find an educated man to marry.

Although my mother had a master's degree and was a firm believer in the benefits of education, she didn't contradict my father. My mother struggled with mental illness and was emotionally remote from me, my brother, and our two younger sisters. As a child, I had learned not to expect her attention let alone support. Never knowing when her mood would shift from subdued to enraged, I tried to avoid her as much as possible. The forest and swamps bordering the Cooper River were my refuge from my mother's violent episodes and my father's demands. Whenever I was depressed or lonely, the tall, ancient trees and the soft forest floor comforted me.

I was determined to leave home as soon as I could, so at the age of seventeen, I gave the appearance of obeying my father's wishes. Instead of following my seafaring dreams, I went to college, but not with the intention to "catch a man." I would begin to live my life on my own terms and figure out where I was headed.

Goucher College, a women's college outside of Baltimore, was unfortunately a complete mismatch for me. It was a haven for young women who hadn't managed to get into Ivy League colleges. I hated the competitiveness and superior attitude of many of the students. The carefully manicured lawn and the boring brick buildings were the opposite of the messy, living forests, swamps, and mountains that I loved.

Worse, I discovered that the Goucher administration assumed the role of a surrogate parent, enforcing curfews and dress codes. Even dinners were formal sit-down affairs with assigned seats. I noted that on this campus, there were no African American or brown people, no children, no young men my age, no cats or dogs, and no joy.

I decided I would transfer out of Goucher as soon as I could. Meanwhile, I wanted to have some adventures outside of the college. To do that, I needed spending money, so I got a part-time job loading and running dishwashers in the dining hall kitchen. On weekends I explored nearby Baltimore, and it was there that I met Richard Ginsburg, who became a good friend. We shared an interest in opposing racism and the legal inequality of African Americans in the U.S. One evening we attended a speech by Stokely Carmichael at Morgan State University, a historically black college in Maryland. The fiery speech by this radical, black power advocate was electrifying.

Returning to Baltimore by train after several days with Richard at his Philadelphia apartment, I was deep in thought. My visit had been a relief from studying for both of us. We had also taken a break from listening to the alarming news of spring 1968 — the police violence against anti-war demonstrators in the U.S. and the increasingly deadly escalation of the war in Vietnam. I knew three young men who had been deployed to the war. Two came back psychologically damaged. One didn't return alive.

There was another American soldier in Vietnam whom I didn't know during this period. Rick Briar — my future husband — had survived the horrors of that war. But during our marriage, he rarely spoke to me of his experiences in Vietnam. Like a couple of my friends who had served there, he refused to answer my questions about the impact of the war on him. He was proud of his service in the Army and wanted to leave it at that.

As my train pulled into Penn Station on April 6, 1968, I was looking forward to getting back to the dorm and getting some sleep. I would catch a bus from Baltimore to Towson and then get a taxi to the college dormitory before curfew. The train station was abnormally quiet as I ascended the staircase to the cavernous main hall. For the first time in my life, I saw groups of armed soldiers patrolling a public building. Civilians emerging from the trains avoided the soldiers and moved quickly to exit the station. A chill rose up the back of my neck and skull.

Worried, but not comprehending the situation, I carried my luggage out to the street. The bus stop was crowded with people standing in clusters and whispering to each other. Something was wrong, but I didn't dare ask. This was a location known for crime. I thought it was better if I minded my own business. Buses came, picked up passengers, and disappeared, but my bus did not come. Finally, I was alone at the dark bus stop. I waited, feeling increasingly vulnerable and anxious.

A police car suddenly pulled up, and the cop leaned out of the car window yelling, "Get the hell out of here, girl! Don't ya know there's riots three blocks away? The city's burning!"

I flinched. No one had ever spoken to me like that. Words stumbled out of my mouth, "Uh. But my bus. Hasn't come. I'm waiting."

The cop sighed, "There's no more buses. Where ya going?"

"Towson."

"Get in," he grumbled, reaching over to open the passenger door. "I'll drive ya there. It broke wide open when he was killed. There's too many a' them and not enough a' us."

I didn't understand who was killed, but riots and fire were clearly dangerous. The cop was angry and nervous, and I reverted to the habits of my childhood when dealing with irate adults. I refrained from speaking.

When I finally got back to the dorm, I learned that Martin Luther King, Jr. had been assassinated, and serious rioting had erupted in cities all over the country. African Americans who suffered discrimination in all aspects of their lives, and whose hopes were expressed so well by King, were grief-stricken and outraged. I was heartbroken, not only for the loss of this great defender of people who were ignored and oppressed by our society, but also for others who had perished in the fight for equal rights. The loss for our society of such brave leaders as Medgar Evers, President John F. Kennedy, Malcolm X, and Martin Luther King, Jr. had been incalculable...

He taught love, peace, justice.
We need him still,
As we follow his dream.
Why kill the dreamer?
How can I dream with my world falling apart?
If I could pray, would I find answers?
Would my heart be less broken?
Or would I hear only silence?

After dropping out of Goucher and returning home, I worked the summer as a lifeguard, not at Mountwell, but at a well-run pool in the distant suburbs. Then in the fall I took a job as a retail clerk at a department store, where I was bored beyond words. Despite the lack of stimulation, I kept working there to save money for my plan to return to college.

In the spring of 1969, I was happy to learn I'd been accepted for transfer to Boston University. My parents offered to pay the tuition, though I'd be responsible for other expenses. I was excited. But before school started in the fall, I wanted to do something fun. I would spend some of my savings on a vacation. Everyone talked about San Francisco and the hippie culture of love in Haight Ashbury, so I thought I'd check it out. Hopefully Richard would join me there.

My first day in San Francisco, I explored the gritty Market Street neighborhood near my room at the YMCA hotel. The area looked similar to the red-light district of Philly, with its strip clubs, bars, and inevitable drunks passed out on the pavement. Another day, I took the cable car up the steep hills of this beautiful city, where people with money lived in large, stately wood and brick homes carefully painted in pastel shades of blue, green, mauve, cream, or lavender with contrasting trim. Stepping off the cable car, I walked until I found a viewpoint with spectacular views of the deep marine blue San Francisco Bay...

> *Bright sunlit bay, sailboats skimming vast waters.*
> *A golden bridge springing from San Fran*
> *And landing across the bay.*
> *I lean on fence post*
> *Taking it all in. But only briefly:*
> *Cop tells me move on.*

After a couple of days walking around the city, I decided I needed an infusion of green plant life. I filled my canteen, bought bread, cheese, and apples, and walked two miles to Golden Gate Park. There, I was delighted to receive a massive dose of the life I was anticipating — grass, shrubs, flower gardens, trees, and even a grove of old oak trees. Though I found the exotic, tropical plants of the Conservatory interesting and the Botanical Garden's collection attractive, I was looking for something a bit wilder. When I discovered untended, wooded areas in the huge park, I ducked into the embrace of wild trees.

In this forest within a city, I was pleased to encounter no other people. But just in case, I left the trail and went deeper into a thicket of young trees and brambles, looking for a hidden place to rest...

> *Leaves in thick rotting layers*
> *Unruffled by human feet.*
> *Shoes off now, holy ground,*
> *I lay down, receive trees' welcome.*
> *I'm home.*
> *Tears of relief wash my face.*
> *I always forget how much*
> *I need this.*

Upon returning to the hotel, I found a message at the desk from Richard. Having driven across the country on a sightseeing tour with a friend, Richard was going to spend a few days in the city before flying back East.

I called his room, "Hey, I'm in the lobby."

"I'll be right down, Bev!"

It was so good to see his tall, lanky form walk out of that elevator. We shared a long hug and an even longer kiss.

Then Richard eyed me, "You look kinda skinny. Let's go eat."

"Sure! But let's find someplace cheap," I replied. "I'm counting my pennies." I was suddenly joyful. I gave him another hug, feeling how much I had missed him. At dinner, we chatted about our summer vacations and ate our fill.

"What should I see in Frisco, do you think?" Richard asked me. "I've only got three days before I fly home."

"Well, definitely Haight-Ashbury. I haven't been there yet, but it should be cool. Golden Gate Park has nice gardens, lakes, a Japanese Tea Garden. Or we can take a cable car up Russian Hill, where there's great views..."

"Nah, I've seen enough views on that long drive out here. Not another park. Let's go to the Haight and see what's happening. Maybe we can pick up some grass."

In the "Summer of Love" of 1967, up to 100,000 hippies with long hair and brightly decorated clothes had descended on Haight-Ashbury, bringing a culture of art, music, meditation, drugs, and free love. Two years later, drawn by the mystique of that earlier summer, Richard and I arrived in this district of San Francisco. We found plenty of hippies in "Hashbury," but they were grimy, poor, and not too happy. I didn't see much love there either, just young girls selling their bodies on street corners and drug dealers sitting on stoops, selling their wares. There were "head shops" that sold beads, peacock feathers, hippie hats and clothes, and drug paraphernalia, but these catered to tourists. We turned off on a side street, found a guy selling grass, and bought a nickel bag and some rolling papers. Then we went off to Golden Gate Park to enjoy a smoke.

When Richard discovered that the famous soul singer, James Brown, was giving a concert in Oakland, we were excited at this not-to-be-missed opportunity. We couldn't believe our luck that there were still tickets. We took our clothes to a laundromat, so we'd have something clean to wear. And then, we had a special night out.

We were already toked up and mellow when we entered the concert hall, which was packed with enthusiastic black fans. James Brown, the Godfather of Soul pranced out onto the stage to the swelling sound of the swing, jazz, and soul orchestra. When he screamed the first words of his signature song, "I feeeeel good..." the crowd went wild, singing right along with him. I did, too...

> *He sings, dances body and soul*
> *Nobody else like that.*
> *With him we roar, shout, sing, move*
> *We become the soul he sings.*

Brown was funky, soulful, and a genius entertainer. Sweat pouring off his body, he sang what he felt deep down, and we all felt it. Afterward, I was exhausted and emotional, for the music released my mind and opened my heart.

Too soon, it was time for Richard to leave. I had treasured the short time I had spent with him. After he left, I stayed a while longer, wandering around, exploring whatever sites didn't cost anything. But I was suddenly lonely. The city that had previously been exciting was now dull. Running low on money, I used my return trip ticket and flew back to Philly. I had a lot to do before I moved to Boston in September.

Although classes and homework took up most of my time at B.U., the social and political disturbances of those two years are what I remember most. That turmoil, which began in the early 1960s and lasted through the early 1970s, had a lasting impact on me and many people of that era. We saw how deeply rooted inequality of minority groups was in our society, and we discovered that racist attitudes had resulted in grievous harm to people both at home and abroad. In response, we raised our voices in countless protests in every state against injustice in the U.S. and the war in Vietnam.

But most pressing for many young men — and their friends and families — was the military draft, which would send them to a deadly Southeast Asian civil war that the U.S. government had entered without clear and honest justification. Middle class white men could avoid the draft by getting a medical deferment, if they could find a doctor willing to document it. Or they could enroll in college and get an educational deferment. Some young men even moved to Canada to wait out the war. Obviously, money or influence was necessary for these options. But for blacks and poor people, the draft was inescapable.

My brother, unwilling to take an easy college deferment, won an exemption on the grounds that he was morally opposed to war. As alternative service, he worked in a mental hospital for two years. I felt fortunate, as a female, not to be in my brother's position.

But I understood that my gender came with serious disadvantages. In 1969, when I arrived in Boston, it was still illegal for me as an unmarried woman to obtain birth control. I could be denied housing based on my sex. I could be refused a credit card or a loan on the grounds that I was a woman. Employers could legally discriminate against me in hiring and pay, in preference to males. There were even limited quotas for admission of women to graduate schools. And as a woman, I was expected to conform to standards of appearance, clothing, and behavior that didn't apply to men…

> *I'm a woman so I'm less?*
> *So I have to be hobbled*
> *By girdles, bras, shoes?*
> *So, I gotta play weak,*
> *Silly, dumb*
> *Hell No Way.*
> *I'm gonna put on my jeans,*
> *Lace up my sneakers,*

Do what I want,
Be my own self.

Along with many other people, I was angry about injustice toward women and African Americans as well as Hispanics, gays, the poor, and the people of Vietnam. Across the U.S., these issues were fire for the boiling pot of unrest among young people. There were countless demonstrations on college campuses and in major cities of the U.S. A month after arriving in Boston, I participated in a huge, peaceful anti-war demonstration of 100,000 people in the birthplace of the American Revolution.

Although I was outraged by the war and its brutality, I was somehow able to pursue my studies doggedly. During spring break, I even visited Richard in Ann Arbor, where he was in his first year of law school at the University of Michigan. At his apartment, we relaxed, smoke pot, and enjoyed his home-cooked specialty: broiled steak, baked potatoes, and salad. Together, we tried LSD for the first time. Under its influence, I was mesmerized by the continually shifting shapes and colors I saw whirling through the darkened room.

As usual, we discussed politics and our career plans. However, this time, our quiet discussion turned into a heated argument. Richard had always planned to become a criminal defense attorney so he could help the people who really needed it. Now, however, he told me he was planning to go into corporate law, where he could make a lot of money.

Shocked at this, I blasted him. "I can't believe this, Richard! You want to prey off the people for your rich, white, corporate bosses? You always said you wanted to make a better world."

"I still do, Bev," Richard replied. "A corporate lawyer is in a better position to wield influence and achieve change in society."

"Wield influence to benefit your rich, corporate bosses, not the people who are getting ripped off every day by corporations..."

"That's not fair!" he objected.

I continued, "You used to want to help people society neglects — African Americans, the poor, and immigrants. Now you're going to ditch them and turn your back? So you can earn money, lots of money?"

I was not going to back down, and this made him argue his view even more forcefully. I was bitterly disappointed in him. I left the apartment and went for a long walk. My flight left the next day.

Back in Boston, the political atmosphere was charged. Non-violent protests continued, but there was increasing violence from the left-wing Students for a Democratic Society. Even more violent was the Weather Underground, or Weathermen, a small group of several hundred nationally who were an extreme radical faction of the SDS. This notorious revolutionary group was active in bombings of government and corporate buildings.[1]

On April 15, 1970, there was another demonstration in Boston. From my apartment, I took the trolley down to B.U. and joined protesters marching to Boston Common, where 60,000 protestors were rallying peacefully. As the demonstration came to a close, another protest was organized by the November Action Coalition to march to Harvard Square in Cambridge. Without anything else to do, I decided I would take the subway there. If I had known the Coalition was part of SDS, I wouldn't have gone.[2]

As I came up from the underground station at the Square, I smelled tear gas and saw police a block away, their backs to me, charging protestors with raised clubs. From the Harvard dorms I heard Beethoven's Ninth Symphony being played at top volume through an open window facing the Square, a surreal contrast to the violence. As I crossed the street to get a better view, I heard the police loudspeaker broadcasting the order for the protestors to disperse. However, the demonstrators could not comply, even if they had wanted to, because they were surrounded by police forces. When some of the demonstrators threw cobblestones at the police, the latter threw the stones back and used their clubs on the trapped protesters.

Too late, I realized the situation was out of control, and I should leave immediately. The Cambridge City police were now running in all directions, looking for demonstrators to beat. I looked around for escape and saw a nearby office building entrance crowded with twenty or so shoppers and office workers. Quickly, I ran over and slipped through the door into the entrance to join them.

---

[1] https://time.com/4549409/the-weather-underground-bad-moon-rising/

[2] https://www.nytimes.com/1970/04/17/archives/damage-estimated-at-100000-after-harvard-riot.html

As we huddled between the front glass doors of the building and the locked inner doors, few words were spoken. There was only just enough room for all of us to stand. Everyone looked scared, wondering if the police would haul us out of our refuge and start beating us, too. I turned to look toward the block where the battle was going on. The police had closed ranks and were moving toward the protestors. Meanwhile, tired and uncomfortable in the cramped space, I wanted to go back down into the subway so I could go home. I looked carefully around the vicinity of the building and saw no cops. I paused a moment, still scanning for police, and then decided to make a run for the subway entrance, just across the street…

SHIT! where'd he come from! cop on my ass! he turns to club a reporter in a phone booth, poor guy falls curled up to the floor. Cop clubs the guy's crotch. Oooooh. I run fast fast fast… downstairs, down down down… He's right behind me, I leap! BAAAM club comes hard UGHHHH my right arm goes dead. Even faster I leap down the stairs in bounds bigger than me. He swings, misses. At the bottom I turn sharp right. Hide! hide! I pull off my hat, my cape, turn it inside out, ball it up. Thousands waiting for trains. Don't run don't run. Stop stop stop.

Breathing hard I stop, walk up to a woman and man, and I stand real close, like I know them. My eyes speak to their eyes. Help. Me. Help. Me. Their eyes say YES. I make myself invisible, invisible. They speak Spanish. The man turns to me, pretends to talk to me as the cop stalks right behind me, looking for me. I feel his hatred pass behind me, sending a chill through my body. Yet I am invisible, invisible. He scans the platform, can't see me. He disappears into crowds, looking, looking. But he WILL come back.

A train comes, the woman takes my hand, guides me to the train. I don't care where it goes, I need out of here. My arm still dead, can't feel it. I shiver and shake, I know this is shock. The man finds a seat for me, asks me in English where I'm going. Brighton I say. He asks people on the train. One guy says he'll take me. He takes me to his stop and finds another rider to take me further. I don't know where I am. I'm passed from one person to another until I arrive home. Strangers helping a stranger, such love IS possible.

My roommates took me to the emergency room, but fortunately, my arm wasn't broken. However, for the rest of my life the bone in my upper arm had a ridge where that cop had clubbed me. I felt very lucky he had missed my head, for which he was aiming. Within a week, my arm regained its feeling, and I could use it normally, but the damage was much deeper than that.

My sense of security in society was shattered. My sense of order was turned upside down. The cop was a hoodlum in uniform, bent on exercising his power, pouring his hate on whoever happened to be in front of him. I understood that thus far in my life I had naïvely expected cops to be helpful to people. Now I knew that this was false. Ever since that time, I've never trusted a policeman, and I've never felt comfortable around one.

But worse than these permanent changes in my perceptions was the psychological pain that I experienced. For months afterward, I was shaken to the core, emotional and weeping at odd moments, overcome with fatigue, apathetic about my studies, excessively alert to potential dangers, depressed, and feeling hopeless. I couldn't stop thinking about the moment that club slammed into my arm, and about my narrow escape from the predatory policeman. But when I thought about the Spanish-speaking couple who hid me from the cop in plain sight, and the kind strangers who made sure I got home safely, I felt some reassurance that the world wasn't all bad.

Although later I identified my symptoms as those of PTSD, in 1970 there was almost no understanding of the aftermath of trauma. My worst symptoms improved gradually, while others plagued me for many years, especially the hyper-vigilance, anger toward authority figures, and a return of the chronic depression that had characterized my childhood. I was twenty-two and knew only that I felt bad and was not exactly myself. I tried hard to act normally, deny the emotions I was feeling, and "grin and bear it," as my parents had always advised me. I didn't tell anyone how I was feeling, and I felt safer that way.

Two weeks later, the national news reported that soldiers had fired on 2,000 unarmed student demonstrators in Ohio, killing four students and wounding nine. Then, a similar incident happened at the historically black college, Jackson State University in Mississippi, where police fired without

warning on an unarmed group of students, killing two and wounding
twelve…

> *That could have been me, bleeding out on earth,*
> *Me, screaming over my murdered friend.*
> *It was me at Harvard Square:*
> *I escaped*
> *But it's not over.*
> *I gotta go far away*
> *Somewhere safe*
> *If any place is safe.*

The response of American students to the killings at Kent State and
Jackson State was outrage. Four million students at universities, colleges,
and high schools went on strike and spontaneously organized protests.
Most of the demonstrations were non-violent, but there were also bombings
or burnings of ROTC buildings on some campuses. As a result of massive
student unrest in Boston, the administration of Boston University cancelled
classes and final exams, closed dorms, called off undergraduate commence-
ment, and required all students to vacate the campus within 48 hours.[3]
However, four thousand students refused to leave the university grounds
and vowed to continue the strike.

Too emotional and unstable to join the protests, I was relieved that final
exams were cancelled, because I knew I was not in any shape to face more
stress. It seemed pointless to me anyway, with society collapsing, the
hypocrisy and cynicism of politicians exposed, and the future of young
people endangered.

In June, I moved to a more spacious, sunny, corner apartment in a nearby
neighborhood with two other students. The rent cost no more than my
previous apartment but there was more space and privacy — a large living
room with windows on two sides, a bedroom for each of us, a large, eat-in
kitchen, and a small balcony. Like my roommates, I worked a full-time job
during the day as well as a few hours a week at the local food coop. We

---

[3] http://www.bu.edu/articles/2012/1970-revisited/

scrounged discarded furniture and bought used clothes at the army-navy store.

On hot summer nights, we enjoyed cool breezes flowing through the windows of this top floor flat, sitting on the living room floor, listening to music, passing a bottle of cheap wine, and smoking strong grass. Through these recreational activities I met a whole new set of friends. Some were students and some not. Some were truly different, like the MIT student who went barefoot summer or winter. There was also a serious guy who talked in riddles no one could understand. People said that he got messed up on LSD and was never right after that.

Richard came for a month-long visit, but by then, our relationship was fading. I was angry with him — and often with life in general — and didn't hide it. After we broke up, I never saw him again. It was only in writing this memoir that I searched the internet for his name and found his 2018 obituary. Although I was sad to read that he had passed away, I was surprised to learn that he did not go into corporate law as he had planned. Instead, he became a public defender for the state of Michigan. I had underestimated him. He had followed his original impulse to make the world a better place and help the poor through his talents as lawyer.

My life in Boston so far had been tumultuous. I felt the need to relax, but whenever things got too quiet, I was overwhelmed with anger, fear, and flashbacks. I kept these raw feelings at bay by smoking grass or taking LSD, either alone or with a couple of friends. Then, on one momentous acid trip, I experienced a life-changing vision…

> *Big hill rock so beautiful, so alive,*
> *Rough rock comfortable.*
> *I let acid take me*
> *Slowly slowly.*
> *Stories in clouds pass overhead*
> *Stories of many lives and my own.*
> *My soul is connected*
> *With sky, earth, trees, birds*
> *With children playing ball*
> *With this rock holding me in its palm,*
> *Connected with vastness*
> *Greater than the universe,*
> *A vastness in every molecule, every drop, every living being,*
> *In my soul, in my body:*

Tears of joy
So grateful.

The acid trip was much more intense and real than anything I had ever felt. I desperately wanted to feel that bliss again, the sublime feeling of oneness with all of existence, and the direct experience of cosmic consciousness. Unfortunately, on a subsequent trip, I woke up the next morning to find that the left side of my face was numb. The numbness persisted for the rest of my life. Whether it was due to the LSD or to some other substance mixed with the drug, I realized that using acid was not a safe way for me to feed the deep, spiritual longing I had felt. In my studies of Eastern religions, I had learned that mystics often used specific means to achieve an ecstatic connection with all of reality. I hoped that mystical practices might be my way forward, and I decided to delve deeper into spirituality. I didn't realize it at the time, but this moment was the beginning of my quest for oneness with All.

Still struggling with fluctuating emotions, I returned to classes in the fall of 1970 and threw myself into academic work. However, I was again rocked when some Weathermen robbed a bank just three blocks from my apartment. The extreme, armed radicals killed a policeman and stole $26,000. Although three male bank robbers were captured, two female accomplices escaped.

When I saw the newspaper picture of one of the women, Katherine Ann Power, my stomach lurched. A student at Brandeis, she was my age and looked very much like me, with an oval face, smooth pale skin, glasses, and long blond hair pulled behind her ears. I was her double and she was mine. I could have been her, on the run for a bank robbery gone terribly wrong. My double could have been me, always on the alert for imminent dangers. However, she disappeared into the counterculture underground and didn't surface for twenty-three years. Meanwhile, I wandered above ground, always looking over my shoulder.

It was getting harder to focus on my studies, but I felt I had to graduate. After finishing my studies, I didn't know what I would do. I wasn't interested in going to graduate school or getting a permanent job. I thought I might hitchhike around, picking up temporary jobs when I had to. Meanwhile, I plowed through my courses, taking a break only for a long weekend with a friend from New York. I thought it would be good to get away for a bit.

Our drive down to the city was a welcome change from studying, and we were surprised at how good it was to talk together without being stoned. When we arrived at her house, she led the way up the sidewalk to the front door, rang the doorbell, and then squealed with joy when her mother opened the door. Mother and daughter hugged each other, kissed, laughed, and hugged again. I was startled as strong emotions suddenly surged to the surface of my consciousness. I had never experienced or seen what it might be like to have a real, loving relationship with one's mother.

Love. This is love. Look!
They're so happy. But not me. No.
My tears falling, falling, heart wrenched.
This is a mother, a real mother.
Why didn't mommy hug me like that? Oh mommy why?
I thought love was a lie,
But no, it's real, I see love right now.
BAAAM! Help me! Cop's after me! run! run!
Where am I?
Young black man dead in a dark, dark pool, his mother weeping.
Crowds scream no! no! Four dead in Ohio!
I'm wobbling, collapsing, my double smiling at me.
No! I yell at her.
Don't rob that bank! A cop is dead! Run! Hide!
Tears like blood streaming down my shirt,
Deep endless pain, endless weeping,
Grieving forever.
Can't get myself together.
This loving woman. I never met her. She doesn't know me,
But brings me into her home, holds me, comforts me
Like I'm her own child.
Her love embraces me and I'm out of my head.
Moaning, I can't speak. What's wrong with me?
I sob, sob, sniffle, sigh until exhausted.
I'm empty, no more tears come.
Just deep aching.

Once final exams were over, I packed my knapsack and camping gear and gave away anything that didn't fit in the pack. I left Boston, heading for wild, natural places to heal my wounds. As a young teen, I had hiked on the Appalachian Trail with church groups, and at the age of seventeen, I had made a four-day solo AT hike. Now I was going to spend a few weeks hiking in the mountains.

On the trail, I was alone. The crunch of stones under my feet and the sound of my breathing were the only sounds I could hear as I labored up the rocky, tree-shaded trail. A spring burst from the mountain, letting its water trickle downhill. Pausing to taste the cool, delicious liquid, I rejoiced at the earth's bounty. I splashed my sweaty, grimy face with the icy water and shivered happily.

As I approached the top of a mountain, the trail widened out onto a bare, rocky ridge overlooking endless valleys and peaks covered with deep forest. These were the northern Appalachian Mountains. Looking down below, I saw an occasional house roof or church spire peeking out of the trees. But up here on the ridge, I was the only person in sight. I sat on a rock and breathed the sweet mountain air. Lighting a joint, I smoked and absorbed the natural beauty all around me.

Clouds rolled across the sky, darkening the scene before me, and I knew bad weather was coming. It was time for me to move off the ridge. But I was too late...

> *Golf ball hail!*
> *Bending over,*
> *I let my pack take the barrage,*
> *And run back to tree line.*
> *Ow, ow, ice ball hits me!*
> *Safe under trees, I laugh,*
> *Ice balls bouncing*
> *Covering rocky earth.*
> *Hot, hailing day in June!*

Each day my body worked, sweating and muscling over boulders, while my chaotic emotions fell away and my mind went quiet. However, at night my mind revisited places I didn't want to go, and I dreamed of mischievous mountain-dwelling spirits who were chasing me. Eventually they invaded my waking hours…

> *Can't sleep,*
> *Bad dreams,*
> *Spirits chasing me.*
> *Now I'm awake but still*
> *They follow, chase me,*
> *Want me to leave*
> *Their mountain.*
> *I gotta descend to human places.*
> *Spirits won't go there,*
> *I hope.*

My adventure had turned risky with the onslaught of the mountain spirits. The trail map didn't show any trails going downhill from the AT for many miles, west or east. I didn't think I could keep hiking as far as the next trail intersection – a three-day hike – without losing my mind. I decided to leave the ridge and bushwhack downhill, knowing it was a calculated risk.

Fortunately, I safely came off the mountain. I made my way to the summer camp where my brother worked, and I took a job waiting tables. Toward the end of the summer, I heard about a yoga weekend in a conference center nearby. Since I couldn't afford to pay the entrance fee, I just walked in, unobserved. Wandering into a large hall where everyone was seated on the floor cross-legged, I sat down and joined them in meditation.

After a weekend of doing yoga, meditating, and chanting, I wanted to do more. I wanted to do it every day. The yoga asanas stretched my muscles and helped my body relax, giving me a feeling of peace. While I found it hard to control my thoughts during meditation, I discovered that if I could do it for a couple minutes, it helped to calm my anxiety. Best of all, the practice of chanting mantras, along with dancing and eastern music, was healing for me, giving me a sense of joy that I hadn't experienced outside of nature or drug-induced states.

The sponsor of the yoga weekend was an organization called Ananda Marga, or "Path of Bliss." I was attracted by its goal of supporting social and economic change, as well as individual and collective spiritual growth. These broad aims coincided with my own spiritual longing and my dedication to social justice. Ananda Marga, which had an ashram in Philadelphia, seemed to be just what I was looking for. When my job at camp ended, I packed my knapsack and took a bus to that city, looking forward to my next adventure.

At the yoga retreat I had met a curly-haired, deep-voiced young man named Ron. He was serious about yoga and the programs of Ananda Marga and had a leadership role in the local organization. Ron's room in the ashram was sunny and spacious, and I would join him and other ashram residents there for discussions of yoga teachings and the service projects. He performed his social service by visiting inmates in Graterford Prison in Philadelphia and teaching them yoga. Once, I accompanied him to the prison, which triggered me...

> *Smell of caged humans.*
> *No windows no fresh air.*
> *Thick heavy steel doors SLAM shut. I jump.*
> *Massive locks clank behind, my head jerks, chill rises up my spine.*
> *Grim hostile guards, stiff in heavy uniforms emanating*
>   *aggression.*
> *My heart pounds BAM! Run run! Whoa stop.*
> *Wake up! THIS is not THERE.*
> *I'm cold.*
> *Ron leads the way. Uh, yoga class.*
> *Wiping beads of sweat off my face, I slow my breath.*

I could never bring myself to return to Graterford to teach yoga with Ron. Meanwhile, he and I developed a casual relationship marked by mutual attraction and convenience. Our only shared interest was yoga, but we became disillusioned with Ananda Marga when we learned of serious scandals within the top echelons. We distanced ourselves from the organization but continued to meditate and practice yoga asanas when we weren't working.

In my various part-time jobs, I sold local newspapers on the street, gave away free cigarettes in front of department stores, and did library research for a graduate student at the University of Pennsylvania. But the best job was shelving and ordering books at the Penn bookstore. Whenever things were slow, I was permitted to read, and that is where I encountered a book that would be a catalyst for my next transformation. A product of a new photography technique, this book displayed stunning color photographs of the development of human fetuses within the uterus.[4] Returning again and again to this book, I was held captive by each awesome, precious being who was growing inside its mother…

> *Little one floating in inner space,*
> *Peaceful, dreaming,*
> *Safe in divine womb.*
> *I worship, revere, love this,*
> *I long for this.*
> *No! You're crazy,*
> *Not stable.*
> *No money,*
> *No interest in marriage,*
> *To Ron or anyone.*
> *Put that book away!*

My biological urges were alarmingly strong. I was shocked at how I was feeling because I had always hated being female. I had always been angry about the physical, social, educational, and economic disadvantages that being a woman entailed. But here was a gift I hadn't considered: the thrill of growing a new human being in my body, of birthing and loving and raising a child.

This was the beginning of a major change in my self-concept. Trying to integrate this evolving part of me, I experienced a clash of emotions: awe at the miracle of life and resistance to motherhood; embracing my femaleness and running away from it; wanting a serious relationship with Ron and rejecting it entirely.

With no reason to stay in Philadelphia, Ron and I decided to move to Northern California and help a friend build her house. Before we left, I discovered, unsurprisingly, that I was pregnant. While I worried that I was not ready for the responsibility of caring for a baby, I was exhilarated at the

---

[4] *A Child is Born,* by Lennard Nilsson, 1965.

miracle of pregnancy. Together, Ron and I planned a natural childbirth. In August 1973, we packed our stuff into Ron's old car and started on a long road trip across the U.S.

When our work on digging the foundation of our friend's house came to a halt due to lack of equipment and funds, Ron and I moved to a small, two-story rental house on the Russian River in Guerneville. The house was in a residential neighborhood of older, wooden houses, many of which were used as cheap rentals or modest vacation homes. From the back door of our house, a steep, sandy bank, choked with tangled trees and undergrowth, led to the river fifty feet away.

Ron got a job as a laborer on a construction site, while I made our house comfortable with thrift shop finds and prepared for the baby's arrival. One evening a week, Ron and I attended free childbirth classes, where we learned about the stages of childbirth and practiced techniques to prepare for a natural, drug-free birth. I received prenatal care at a local women's health clinic run by certified midwives. My midwife was a warm, caring person with experience in helping hundreds of babies into the world. With her and Ron's assistance, I would deliver our baby at home in late winter.

Five weeks before my due date, northern California experienced a week of torrential, seasonal rains. Looking down the wooded bank behind our house, I could see the rushing muddy waters of the Russian River speeding west toward the ocean…

> *River river what do you see?*
> *How will you feel when you join*
> *The great salt ocean?*
> *My baby floats within me*
> *How will my little one feel*
> *Flowing into the vast world?*

The next morning, we were alarmed to see that the river had risen precipitously, lapping the foundation of our house. Quickly, we gathered food, clothes, and crucial belongings and loaded our car. By the time we left, the water was seeping into the house and showed no signs of retreating. The river would probably remain flooded for a week or two, so we couldn't return to the house any time soon. But we couldn't afford a motel room, and we didn't have the equipment to camp in the cold, rainy winter. I called the one person I knew in the area, the teacher of my childbirth class, and explained our dilemma. She and her husband generously opened their home to us.

Even though we were safe and had a warm, dry place to stay, the catastrophic flood had brought out my deepest anxiety. My hormones demanded immediate action, but there was nothing to do but wait for the waters to recede. Distressed, I was subject to sudden tears at all times of day or night. I must have been a difficult guest for my friend, who tried to comfort me, without success. Ron couldn't help me, either.

After a week, the flow of the Russian River reverted to its normal size, and Ron and I returned to our house. The flood waters had reached a height of four feet inside the house, coating everything in the house with a thick layer of mud. After two days of scraping mud, Ron had to return to work, but I toiled on. I was desperate to make the house ready for the birth of our child.

Finally, the downstairs was as good as I could get it, though it was still gritty and damp. I hoped the stove and refrigerator would continue to function despite the mud on interior parts that I couldn't reach. Standing up, I stretched my aching back and felt a hard pang in my belly. A few minutes later my womb contracted again. My labor had started three weeks early.

The small, clean upstairs room I had prepared for the birth was fortunately unaffected by the flood. It was in that room, with Ron's support and the expert efforts of the midwife, that I delivered a healthy, five-and-a-half-pound boy. Exhausted, I wanted to sleep, but first, the midwife put the baby to my breast and showed me how to position my nipple in his tiny mouth...

> *Perfect little miracle mouth.*
> *Tiny precious fingers and eternal eyes.*
> *Little wise old man.*
> *For the first time in my life*
> *I'm in love,*
> *Completely,*
> *With this beautiful child.*

Honoring the river of life,
The river that touched us but didn't destroy,
Honoring you, we call our son River.

This overwhelming love helped me in the difficult adjustment to motherhood. There was so much that I didn't know about babies, but the midwife, who visited often, answered my questions and offered sound advice. I struggled with fatigue, lack of sleep, frustration, doubts about my ability to mother my child, and most of all, the sense of the awesome responsibility I had assumed...

I'm just a young wandering wild one,
Taming myself for this child.
Oh Love, please help me!

After work one evening, Ron came home from work tired and irritable, but he smiled when he saw that a letter had come in the mail. Reading it, he sighed, commenting on a poem honoring the birth of our son. He handed me the letter, which was written in neat cursive, and signed, Rick Briar.

"Who is Rick Briar?" I asked.

"A black guy I met visiting the joint in New York. He's an incredible person," Ron replied.

"He's a prisoner?"

"Yeah. I wrote him about River's birth. I don't know why he's in that place. I mean, he did something bad to end up in prison, but he just doesn't belong in a place like that. He's a really intelligent, mellow guy. Attended the yoga class I taught. Afterward, we talked about all kinds of stuff. He's knowledgeable and interesting."

"What's he in for?"

"Murder."

"Oh..." I was shocked.

I read the moving and expressive poem. What an exceptional person he must be to write so beautifully while incarcerated in that grim, noxious prison. I don't know what happened to that letter, but when I think of the verses written by Rick Briar, my memory of it is a feeling...

Words tremble with love,
Of newborn life rising from earth,
A sunny daffodil
Shining like a smile.
Words raise a wish
For life fully lived,
Life we watch unfold,
A tight, long, pale bud,
Slowly opening to the world,
A bright hello.

I held the sentiment in my heart and cherished the thought that this man, this poet, was a caring individual who felt deeply and was unafraid to let his feelings spill over the cup of his life, flavoring the world around him with light.

For me, it was easy to love a sweet, pure baby, but much harder to love another adult in the complex web of human verbal and unspoken interactions. My relationship with Ron had begun as a friendship but never progressed to love. We were drifting apart, and neither of us made an effort to reverse that trend. The situation was complicated by the fact that I was pregnant again, adding financial stress to our interpersonal problems.

I knew I needed a stable situation in which to birth my second child and care for ten-month-old River. Despite my uneasy relationship with my parents, I decided to return to the East Coast to stay with them for the birth of the baby.

3

PRISON AND LOVE
1975-1980

"Love is or it ain't. Thin love ain't love at all."

Toni Morrison[5]

Stepping through the door to the prison visiting area, with River on my hip, I scanned the well-lit room. Large windows overlooked a trim lawn and early spring flowers filling a courtyard. Inside, I noted that a few people were seated in chairs, talking to each other in low voices. At the far end of the room a couple of men were coming into the visiting room. Since I'd never seen Rick Briar before, I didn't know how I would identify him. I stood still, uncertain. River craned his neck to look at his surroundings and began to wiggle restlessly. One inmate, dressed in brown pants and shirt, came toward me.

"Beverly Lee?" he asked quietly. He was a medium height black man with trim build, a calm and open face and friendly brown eyes. He wore a finely crocheted white cap on his head.

"Yes, are you Rick?"

"Yes, I am. Please call me Abdullah. That's my Muslim name. Abdullah Khalid. And who is this?" he smiled at River.

River responded by babbling and holding his arms out to Abdullah, who gathered him up, laughing. My little son immediately turned around and held his arms out to me, "Mum mum!"

On returning East, I had written Abdullah a short letter of thanks for the poem he had sent us, beginning a stream of correspondence that con-

---

[5] *Beloved*, Toni Morrison, 1987.

tinued for years. Through his expressive, reflective letters I learned he was politically radical and an avid reader. Meeting him in person now, I felt he was even more impressive, with grounded, warm eyes, a mellow voice, and a respectful manner.

River, a friendly toddler, had wandered off to explore the room and meet people. "Hey River, come on back here," I called. "Look, here's your ball. Let's play!"

River and I sat on the floor and played catch while Abdullah told me how he had arrived at this point in his life. Born in North Carolina, Abdullah was raised by his grandmother because his mother was very young. He didn't get along with his grandmother's husband, who was often abusive.

"I wished I could fight back, but I was too small," he said. "Things got better when I was in high school, and after graduating I left home to go to The Citadel."

"The Citadel?" I asked. I was unfamiliar with it.

"A military college in South Carolina," he said. "After that, I entered the army as a lieutenant and served in Vietnam." His voice trailed off, his face reflecting a shadow.

Seeing a glimpse of discomfort in his face, I changed the subject. "And what did you do when you got out of the army?"

"Well, I moved to New York, where some friends of mine lived. I was pretty angry about everything, and I became active with the Black Panthers. That's how I ended up here," he added wistfully.

I waited for him to continue. In his face, I saw sadness but acceptance of his past, and a desire to move forward with his life.

"I was guarding a Black Panther daycare center there when police attacked it," he began. "There were children there. There were women there. Civilians. I defended the center, and a policeman was killed. That was 1972." He paused, looking at me and considering his next words, "I was convicted of a capital crime, killing a police officer. My lawyer convinced the court that during the crime, I had a PTSD flashback to the war, so the death sentence was reduced to life in prison."

I swallowed and looked toward the garden beyond the window. If his sentence hadn't been reduced, I wouldn't have met him. Not knowing how to respond, I was silent. Growing up in New Jersey, across the Delaware River from Philadelphia, I was aware that such an event was unfortunately frequent there and in other cities in the late 1960s and early 1970s. During that period, police under commissioner Frank Rizzo clashed repeatedly and violently with local African American citizens, the Black Panther Party, and other civil rights organizations. The black community was outraged by police brutality and lack of neighborhood control over police presence.

I found it impossible to imagine Abdullah as a dangerous murderer, a prison "lifer" who for the rest of his life would be confined behind bars, not permitted to redeem himself in society. In his intelligent face and mild demeanor, I saw no indication of a hardened criminal.

Finally, he broke the silence, shifting the conversation. He told me how he had met Ron and asked me how I met him. As I talked about events in my life and my return to my parents' home, I realized Abdullah had the ability to make me feel completely comfortable with him. He truly listened to me, which was an attribute I hadn't often encountered among other men I had met. As Ron had told me, this man was remarkable.

Our visit was over too soon, and I had a long drive ahead of me, from upstate New York to southern New Jersey. Before starting out, I nursed my son, put him to sleep in the baby seat on the floor of the car, and ate the cold supper I had brought from home. Then I found some rock music on the radio and drove, reflecting on my new friend, a gentle, kind companion. I had never met anyone like him.

Over the next months, our letters to each other were a window into each other's lives as we shared our views, experiences, feelings, and poems. There seemed to be no end to the topics we covered in these long, written conversations with each other. I valued him as an increasingly central part of my life and realized I was falling in love with him.

My occasional visits to Abdullah stopped as my due date drew near. I had chosen to give birth at a maternity center in Philadelphia that was staffed by trained midwives. In late July, with my mother at my side, I delivered a healthy baby boy, whom Ron and I named Forest...

Little one, hello!
Wrinkled little face illuminates,
Gazing long into my eyes.
I meet you at last, you sweet little being,
Joy and love surrounding my heart.

Abdullah: Congratulations on the birth of little Forest! I hope the baby is healthy and you are recovering well.

Bev: Forest and I are well, and he's nursing well. River loves his little brother, but I have to watch him — he gets a little too enthusiastic when he hugs the baby! Abdullah, one thing I wanted to ask you. You've told me how important your religion is to you. How did you come to Islam?

Abdullah: I was raised in a church going family. Mom — that's what I call my grandmother — had a wonderful voice and used to sing in the church choir. I enjoyed the services mostly because I loved the music and Mom's singing. But after I left home and went into the army, I stopped going. It just didn't have much meaning for me anymore. When I came back from Vietnam, I met some Muslims and I started attending a local mosque. After I ended up here, I got serious about studying Islam and reading the Qur'an. It gave me something I really needed.

My relationship with Abdullah stirred me to explore Islam. Early on in my reading I was surprised to learn that Muslims believe in and revere all the prophets of Judaism — Abraham, Moses, and more — as well as Christianity's Jesus and his mother, Mary. In fact, Muhammad is believed to be the last in a long line of prophets sent by God though the ages to all of humanity. Islam does not oppose Christianity or Judaism but continues those strong religious traditions.

Raised in a Christian church, I was taught that God was divided into the trinity of Father, Son, and Holy Ghost, but I never quite understood how that worked or why it was a necessary article of faith. In contrast, Islam strongly emphasized the oneness of God, which was closer to my own belief...

> *This is what I feel: One God,*
> *One cosmic consciousness,*
> *Holding sky, sea, mountains, trees, birds, animals – and me,*
> *Many names – God Allah Yahweh Jehovah Brahman,*
> *Only one Reality.*

Bev: I've started to re-read *The Autobiography of Malcolm X*. But I wanted to ask you about him. As a "Black Muslim," he poured all his energy into the Nation of Islam. He was devoted to Elijah Muhammad, earned his respect, and moved up in the ranks. His voice was a beacon to oppressed black people. Why did he give that all up to accept Islam?

Abdullah: Well, for one thing, there were activities going on in the Nation that he strongly disagreed with — immoral and illegal activities. But the real reason he accepted Islam was a change in his heart that came about during his pilgrimage to Mecca. I believe Allah put a seed of love in Malcolm's heart and showed him truth during that journey. Malcolm couldn't deny his own heart, he couldn't deny the truth that he experienced. I guess it was something like that for me, too, when I became Muslim.

I understood that the brotherhood Malcolm X experienced in the Hajj was an important principle of Islam:

"O men! Behold, We have created you all out of a male and a female, and have made you into nations and tribes, so that you might come to know one another. Verily, the noblest of you in the sight of God is one who is most deeply conscious of Him. Behold, God is all-knowing and all-aware." (Qur'an 49:13)

As I studied the foundations of Islam, I learned that the central practices are daily connection with the One through prayer, fasting, empathy for and support of the poor, and performing the pilgrimage to Mecca. For me, these pillars of Islam offered both a spiritual path and a way of life to which I could wholeheartedly ascribe.

But an equally important factor in my acceptance of Islam was an inner certainty, a feeling from deep within my heart that gave me the final push. In my frequent visits to a mosque in West Philadelphia to study Islam, my heart was touched by the members of that community...

Light in their faces, peace in their eyes
These sisters and brothers – black, brown, white,
Ordinary people like me. But,

In response to all of this, both my heart and mind expanded, pointing the way. At the mosque, in late 1975, I accepted Islam, repeating in Arabic the simple words of faith: "I testify there is no god but Allah, and I testify that Muhammad is His Messenger."

With my change in religion, I also chose to change my name to Aisha Farid, meaning "alive" and "unique." I felt I now had a name that reflected who I was and who I hoped to be on this path. I was glad to abandon my former name, Beverly Gail Lee, which had reflected my parents' hopes, but not my own dreams.

From the beginning, my practice of Islam was not easy for me. I struggled especially with conservative interpretations of Islamic law. For many of my questions, the answers of scholars could vary widely, and I realized that the practice of Islam was influenced by cultural, historical, and political circumstances. I decided I would reserve judgment on the various legal interpretations, instead adhering to the pillars of Islam, continuing to study, and trying to understand the breadth and depth of this religion.

Abdullah and I followed a moderate vision of Islam, like the majority of Muslims worldwide, both then and now. But if I had been a young woman now rather than 1975, I think my acceptance of Islam would have been much more difficult. The extremists who now claim to wage war, commit murder, and spread devastation in the name of Islam were not yet born when I accepted Islam. Although these deviants are a tiny percentage of the 1.8 billion Muslims in the world today, they unfortunately command attention on the world stage. Still, some Americans are not deterred from becoming Muslim. Of the roughly 3.45 million Muslims in the U.S. in 2021,[6] nearly a quarter (23%) are converts to the faith,[7] like Abdullah and me.

---

[6] https://www.pewresearch.org/fact-tank/2021/09/01/muslims-are-a-growing-presence-in-u-s-but-still-face-negative-views-from-the-public/

[7] https://www.pewresearch.org/fact-tank/2018/01/26/the-share-of-americans-who-leave-islam-is-offset-by-those-who-become-muslim/

Aisha: Women everywhere continue to suffer legal and cultural discrimination. I just can't accept the second-class status that some Muslims prescribe for women. I recently read that Islam brought to 7th century Arabia a definite improvement of women's status and rights. Shouldn't Muslims continue the progress up to the present? The 20th century is a different world from the Arabia of Muhammad's time!

Abdullah: You're right about changing with the times. Islam has adapted to many cultures and eras, and will continue to do so, but some people are attached to the cultural habits of their ancestors. We should follow the example of Muhammad, who is the prime role model for Muslims. His respectful behavior toward women was noted by his companions and recorded in the hadith. Also, the Qur'an is clear in describing women and men as equal partners:

> "And as for the believers, both men and women — they are close unto one another: they all enjoin the doing of what is right and forbid the doing of what is wrong, and are constant in prayer, and render the purifying dues, and pay heed unto God and his Apostle. It is they upon whom God will bestow His grace: verily, God is almighty, wise!" (Qur'an 9:71)

As a new Muslim, I felt ambivalent about hijab, the modest attire of a Muslim woman. When I first put on a head scarf, I felt awkward and self-conscious. In an instant, the scarf changed the style of my clothing — my loose, embroidered shirt and flowing, long skirt — from carefree hippy to proper Muslim woman observing hijab. I made a pact with myself to give hijab a good try before deciding whether I would commit to it.

Learning the Islamic prayers, first in English and then in Arabic, required discipline, but I persevered. The ritual prayer, salah, is composed of declarations of faith and recitations from the Qur'an, accompanied by physical postures of standing, bowing, and prostrating. I initially experienced resistance to the prostration, which is a position of absolute submission of the ego. But as in Buddhist or Yoga meditation, salah gives one an opportunity to let go of ego, and as I continued to perform the daily prayers, I began to feel a sense of peace and surrender…

Prayer, a refuge from harshness,
Nest for my fledgling self.
My heart grows in the warmth of Allah's love,
My feet meet the path of Islam.

LETTERS, NOVEMBER 1975

Abdullah: Habiba — that means beloved — on Thursday I had this dream of you. I had been meditating for quite a while and went into a dreamlike state when I saw you buying material for a dress. You were looking at rich blue material with white dots. I knew you were going to make a beautiful dress with it. Then I woke up and my meditation ended. It was very powerful, but I'm not sure what it meant.

Aisha: Wow, Abdullah, this is incredible! On Thursday I went shopping for fabric at the department store. I've been thinking of making a long dress and matching head scarf. I stopped to look at some silky, smooth fabric, deep blue with white polka dots!!!! I pulled the bolt out so I could feel the fabric and imagine it made into a dress. I couldn't make up my mind and then moved on. But you dreamed exactly what I experienced!

Abdullah: Amazing! We were connected at the soul level. In my dream I saw you clearly at that exact moment. You've got to buy that material and make a dress with it!

This psychic experience was the first of several such occurrences that convinced us that we were deeply connected to each other. I had had similar episodes throughout my life, including unconsciously receiving another person's thought or image and transmission to someone else. I had also tried to consciously transmit with some success. Since Abdullah was always on my mind, perhaps I had been unconsciously sending my thoughts to him at the fabric department. But Abdullah's dream painted such a detailed picture of what was in my mind that I realized he might be psychic, too. I'd never been so close to anyone that we shared thoughts with each other without even being in the same location. From this moment on, our love only grew.

Aisha: When we're apart, I miss you so much. You mean so much to me, Abdullah. I've never experienced such a deep spiritual connection with anyone.

Abdullah: I'm sure we will be together one day. I miss you every day and want to be with you and River and Forest. But I want to be fair to you. You deserve a Muslim husband who can support you and care for you and the kids. I can't do that right now.

Aisha: I want you as my husband, Abdullah. Only you. I want to be your wife, your partner in life.

Abdullah: I want so much to be your husband and father to the children. I'm still awaiting word on the judge's ruling on my appeal. My lawyer is hopeful, and I'm sure that our situation will improve. But there's no need to rush. Let's talk more about it.

Our situation often seemed hopeless to me. When he told me he was sure we would be together, I wanted to know when and how this would come about. I was in love with a beautiful man who was imprisoned under a life sentence. Emotionally, I couldn't just stop loving him. But neither could I imagine the two of us being in this situation for the rest of our lives, him on the inside and me and the kids on the outside of prison walls. To resolve this inner conflict, I chose to believe his optimistic assessment of the outcome of his legal appeal and move forward with our relationship.

I was at a turning point in my life. Throughout my childhood and youth, I had denied that love was real, but now I had found deep love not only with my children but also, incredibly, with a unique, thoughtful man. Not only that, but I had long been searching for a spiritual path that spoke to my innermost heart, and I had found it now in Islam. I felt I was becoming a new, more fulfilled person.

But there were other things that hadn't changed in my life. In most ways, I was still as radicalized as I had been during my student years. Much later in life, I understood that my anger toward racism, sexism, and the abuse of authority was stoked from within by an inner fury that resulted from the traumas I had experienced in my life. But at this point, I didn't make that connection at all. In fact, I thought I had put my past behind me.

Also unchanged was my lifelong urge to travel and seek adventure. I didn't know it yet, but this dream would soon begin to unfold. An upheaval was coming, and it would plunge me and my family into an odyssey that I never could have imagined.

Early in 1976, Abdullah was granted a transfer to a state prison in North Carolina so he could be near to his grandmother and family members. Although he suggested that I continue to stay with my parents, I was determined to live close to him, so he arranged for me, River, and Forest to stay with an American Muslim family in a nearby community. Amin and Fatira were kind and generous people who welcomed me and my children as family.

As I arrived at the prison, I was surprised to find that the white guards were polite to me, even though they knew Abdullah was black. The visiting room was clean, spacious, with plenty of light. There were few visitors there at the time, so Abdullah and I were able to talk quietly.

"It's so good to see you! Finally!" exclaimed Abdullah with a broad smile. "At least now we're in the same state! How are the kids adapting?"

"They love playing with Fatira's little boy. River took a little nap so he's full of energy now." I released my toddler's hand and he climbed up in Abdullah's lap. Then, restless, he got down and wandered off to say hello to a guard, who crouched down to reply. Forest snoozed in my lap.

"Did you think about what I said in my last letter?" Abdullah asked me, gazing intently at my face.

"Yes," I felt my face radiating love. "I agree."

He returned my smile, "I was hoping you'd say that." His eyes flickered toward the guard on the other side of the room. He continued, speaking slowly and with emphasis. "I want you to know. I'm sure something good is going to happen. I can feel it," he squeezed my hand. "We will make a life for ourselves beyond these walls."

Abdullah and I were joined in marriage at a simple Muslim ceremony at the prison, officiated by a Muslim imam from the local mosque. I moved into a small wooden house in a poor neighborhood and became active in the Muslim community there. Both children were open with and curious about our new friends.

Meanwhile, Abdullah and I petitioned for our Muslim names to be legalized through the courts. He had long used his Arabic name – Abdullah Khalid – but I had to do some thinking. Eventually, I chose the first name of Aisha which means "alive"; my last name would be Saidi, or "happy".

Although we didn't legally change the children's names, we also began calling them by Arabic names: Jamal (or "beauty") for River, and Yusuf ("Joseph" in Arabic) for Forest. Joseph is the name of a prophet mentioned in both the Bible and the Qur'an.

Within the past two years, my world had changed rapidly. I had given birth to Forest, become a Muslim, developed a relationship with a convicted murderer, moved away to North Carolina, gotten married in a prison ceremony, and changed my name legally. I had met diverse Muslims, black, brown, and white, with whom I now shared a way of life. I observed hijab and dedicated myself to my spiritual path. But then, on May 4, 1977, Abdullah escaped from the Correctional Institution…

Muslim sister pops in with big news:
They say your husband escaped!
Prison lock down. Police looking for him.
What? Legs wobbling, I sit down, thump.
He escaped! Tears well up, drip. What to do.
She sits quiet, hand on my shoulder.
"A life beyond these walls," he said.
He got out! Tears of joy and fear.
Will he reach safety?
No contact. Until he's safe. Somewhere.
God help us.

I wondered how he'd escaped. According to a local newspaper, the prison warden said that Abdullah was a model prisoner who just walked out of the prison. He apparently joined a group of prisoners leaving with relatives after appearing before the Parole Board.

It wasn't long before the Muslims in my neighborhood came under pressure from state and federal investigators, so I decided it was best for the community that the children and I return to Philadelphia, where we would stay with my friend, Nadira.

However, when I arrived, I learned that authorities were searching for Abdullah throughout the city. There were reports of federal surveillance of mosques in Philly and of Abdullah's family. There was evidently a sighting of Abdullah in the fourteen-square-mile Fairmont Park, but he disappeared before he could be apprehended. I had seen men loitering on the street where I was staying, and the neighbors told me they were not locals but police. I was tense and worried for my husband. To calm my nerves, I focused on cooking, cleaning, caring for the children, and praying. I didn't dare go to the mosque. Nadira did the food shopping, while I laid low.

In the three months I stayed at Nadira's home, I had received no news about Abdullah and no word from him. I was increasingly hopeful that he had made a successful escape. Then, in mid-August, he called me.

"Habiba, it's me."

"Wait! This phone isn't secure."

"It's ok. I want you and the kids to come to Montreal. Take the train. Someone will meet you at the station."

"Abdullah my movements are being monitored," I explained. "There are people continuously watching the house. They'll follow me."

"That's not a problem. I'm safe. You can try to shake them off, but it doesn't matter if they follow you."

Abdullah was confident in his plan, but I couldn't imagine how he would be safe if the feds followed me to the border. Canada and the U.S. were friendly nations and had a mutual extradition treaty. But if he felt it was safe, I would take the risk. "All right. I'm worried about this though," I cautioned him.

"There's only one train a day from Philly to Montreal," he said. "Can you take the train the day after tomorrow?"

"Yes."

"See you soon, then. I love you!" Abdullah was upbeat.

"I love you too. See you in Montreal." I trusted he had a plan to avoid the feds, and now it was time for me to act. I would need to steel myself for whatever came.

Hurriedly, I cashed out the contents of my very small bank account. I washed the children's and my clothes and packed two suitcases to the brim. Nadira helped me pack meals for the long train ride ahead. After a fitful night's sleep, we piled into Nadira's car and she drove us to 30th Street Station, where we said tearful goodbyes.

As I was buying tickets for the fourteen-hour Amtrak ride to Montreal, I realized Jamal had wandered off and approached a man who had squatted down to his level.

"Can I give him a piece of candy?" the man asked me.

"No," I responded curtly. Who was this guy to offer my child candy? I called Jamal to me, getting a strong feeling that the man was an undercover policeman. I turned away and led Jamal and Yusuf downstairs to the platform.

On their first train ride, the children were excited by the speed and clattering noise of the wheels on the tracks as they watched Philadelphia roll past, soon to be replaced by the vast city of New York. My mind was as chaotic as the ever-changing, never-ending urban scenery…

> *Plain clothes cop at far end of rail car,*
> *Another two rows behind,*
> *Watching me. I see their eyes shift. Creepy.*
> *Hope your plan works Abdullah,*
> *I'm coming to you, mile by mile, hour by hour.*
> *Farms spread over the hills,*
> *Steep forested mountains,*
> *And rocky ridges like giant turtles:*
> *Walk on the land, they say, come to safety.*
> *But I go on and on to Montreal.*
> *Merciful God protect us.*

Despite the constant tension I felt, I encouraged the children to play a game of naming things that whizzed by our window — house! car! cow! bicycle! I was relieved that Jamal and Yusuf enjoyed the ride and didn't complain at being confined to our seat. I didn't let them walk up and down the aisle alone past our shadowy watchers. As darkness approached, I fed the boys and put them to sleep. Then I pulled my scarf over my face and tried to get some rest.

Finally, I felt the train slowing as it approached Canada. The border crossing was seamless, with an official examining my U.S. driver's license and giving a friendly nod to me and the kids. When the train pulled into the station in Montreal, I fetched our luggage, wondering how I would find the person who was going to pick us up.

Suddenly, there appeared before me a man with brown skin and a kufi on his head, "Sister Aisha?" I nodded. "Abdullah sent me. Let me take the luggage. I'm here to pick you up." He guided us to his car, loaded the luggage into the trunk, and started driving. "It's not too far," he said.

Shortly afterward, he pulled up in front of a tall building. As we took the elevator up several floors, he explained that he was taking us to an apartment where we should wait and relax until he brought Abdullah to us. Once in the apartment, I let the children explore the sparsely furnished two-bedroom unit.

We were just sitting down to eat the last of our food when there was a knock at the door. I looked through the peephole of the door. There was Abdullah smiling widely. Opening the door, I rushed into his arms, relieved after weeks of worrying about him.

"Oh my God, Abdullah you're really here!" I cried. "It's so good to see you. You look well. How are you?"

"I'm good! Especially now that you're here," he replied. "How was the trip?"

"Really long. But the kids were fine."

Abdullah knelt to hug Jamal and Yusuf, who were confused and surprised to see him. "I hear you guys were good on the train ride and took care of your mother."

The boys nodded solemnly, then Jamal exclaimed, "The train went really fast!"

"Fast!" repeated Yusuf.

Abdullah laughed and gave them another hug.

I felt joy rising in me, "Are we really here together now? I can't quite believe it!"

Abdullah smiled and gave me a warm hug and a long kiss.

The man who had helped Abdullah returned to drop off hot food, which the children and I consumed with relish.

"This is delicious. Do you want some?" I asked Abdullah.

"I've eaten already. Any problems with being followed?"

"Actually," I said, looking up at him, "There were undercover cops watching me in the train car. The whole trip here."

Suddenly, the door slammed open. "Police! Don't move!" Instantly, cops swarmed into the apartment, grabbing Abdullah and me and hustling us into separate rooms. A cop pushed me into a chair and hovered over me.

I couldn't see the children, but I heard them crying, "Mommy! Ummi!"

Instinctively, I rose to go to my kids, but the cop shoved me back into the seat, shouting "Sit! Sit still!" He peppered me with questions, which I ignored.

Then it was over. A group of cops pushed Abdullah, handcuffed, out the door, and my captor turned away from me to join them. As he exited the apartment, wordlessly closing the apartment door, the children and I rushed to each other…

Tightly I hold my scared kids,
Trying not to cry.
I feel my own fear:
Abdullah's gone,
I'm alone,
My tender children weeping.
I hold them in my arms, saying it's OK now.
But it's not.
From my grief rises anger at Abdullah's bad plan,
Rage at those who terrorize children.

But I knew these volatile emotions were not what I needed now. I had decisions to make, so I closed the fear and anger off in some inner compartment. Then, I turned to God, praying for guidance and protection of my husband, children, and me.

I sat for a moment. As I pondered all that had transpired, I was startled by the ring of the telephone. It was Abdullah's friend, the one who had driven the children and me to this building.

"Sister Aisha," he said. "I'm so sorry this happened. Are you all right?"

Quickly, I replied, "I'm OK. The children are OK." It was true, at least physically.

"Have you thought about what you want to do? You could stay as long as you want with sisters in our community," he offered.

Pausing, I considered. For me, there was only one option. "I have friends in Philadelphia. I'll take the train back," I said. "Hopefully tomorrow."

"I'll find out what time the train leaves and buy your tickets," he replied.

"Thank you so much, brother. You've been very kind." I struggled not to break down in tears.

"Mashallah, as God wills, sister. The believers are protectors of each other."

I had just enough strength to put the kids to sleep and climb into bed with them. We were all exhausted. I did not awaken until the phone rang the next morning. It was Abdullah's friend, "If it's all right with you, I'll pick you up in an hour and take you and the children to the train station."

On the train ride home – wherever home was – my mind was in a haze of random thoughts weaving in and out of consciousness, alternating with periods of numbness. When I could bear it, I ran through all the events of the past couple days, trying to understand what went wrong and what I should or should not have done. I refused to cry in front of the children, but my heart was awash with tears.

Later, a newspaper in the county where I grew up published the news of Abdullah's escape from the prison in North Carolina and the FBI agents tracking me every step of the way from Philadelphia to Montreal. The article printed my full birth name, Beverly Gail Lee, and the Haddonfield residence where my parents still lived. I was sure my parents had read the article.

After his capture in Montreal, Abdullah was taken by U.S. federal agents on a seventeen-hour drive to North Carolina, handcuffed and shackled in the back seat of a car. Meanwhile, my heart was heavy and full of regret and anxiety as I arrived in Philadelphia. My ill-fated decision to follow Abdullah to Montreal had exposed me and my children to danger…

Heartache and loss
Dread stretched taut:
They could take me away,
My children bereft,
Oh God no!
Yet, still
I love this man.

Following Abdullah's capture, the prison system in North Carolina sent him back to prison in upstate New York, where he was put in solitary confinement for a few months. Although he couldn't call me and I wasn't permitted to visit him during that time, we wrote long letters to each other, strengthening our relationship. Meanwhile, I found a two-bedroom apartment in Woodlynn, New Jersey, not far from my parents' home.

My middle-class parents were terribly worried about the direction of my life, not only for me and their grandchildren, but also for their own reputation among their neighbors and relatives. They didn't understand my change of religion and they couldn't accept my living among African Americans. They were angry that I had married a convicted prisoner. Worse, they were mortified my name had appeared in local newspapers in connection with the arrest of Abdullah in Canada. At the behest of my parents, my siblings Gerry, Judy, and Karen, visited me.

"Hey welcome! Come on up! Watch your step, don't mind the toys. Jamal! Yusuf! Come see who's here," I called to the kids.

Judy had a pained look on her face at my use of Arabic names for the children. Gerry looked down abashed, then brightened and called to the kids, "Hi fellas!"

"Jamal, Yusuf, say hello to Uncle Gerry," I said. "And Aunt Karen and Aunt Judy." The kids excitedly skipped from one adult to another and then ran into their room to fetch their toy trucks. So many people to play with!

"Have a seat," I gestured to pillows on the floor and brought a couple more.

"Nice apartment!" said Gerry. "Who lives downstairs?"

"The landlord. He's a nice guy. I'm lucky to have found this. Rent's not bad."

"We heard you got married," Gerry began.

"Yeah, Abdullah's a wonderful person. I hope you can meet him."

Gerry was reluctantly coming to the point of the visit, and I saw that Karen and Judy were letting him do all the talking. "Well, Mom and Dad are pretty upset about Abdullah."

I felt my face flush. "I'm sorry Mom and Dad are upset, but it was my decision."

"They, you know, everything is so hard for them," Gerry continued. "Abdullah's escape was in the news, and your name was in the news. When you changed religion…"

"A cult!" Judy exclaimed, unable to hold her tongue.

"You know," Gerry cut her off too late, "they worry you're not making the best decision…"

"So, they don't like him because he's black?" Now I was angry. "And they want me to divorce my husband?" Gerry looked down and didn't reply. Karen remained silent.

"Well maybe not because he's black," Judy equivocated. "Because he's in prison."

"You don't know Abdullah," I said, raising my voice. "You don't know anything about him, and you dare to come here and judge him? To my face?"

"But he's a Black Muslim!" cried Judy, "They hate white people!"

"He's Muslim and our religion is Islam. It's a worldwide religion with millions of people of all races. So-called 'Black Muslims' or the 'Nation of Islam' are different." I emphatically distinguished between Islam and the separatist black religious organization of Elijah Muhammad.

"No difference, it's all the same," Judy replied. "They'll treat you like dirt!"

I stood up. "I'm Muslim. I've accepted the religion of Islam." Outraged that they would try to dissuade me from my marriage and my religion, I felt my adrenaline surge. "I've married the man I love. I've accepted the religion I love. And you will LEAVE my home NOW!"

"Bev, no, come on," Gerry tried to calm me.

"No, you are going to LEAVE. ALL OF YOU. NOW!" I threw the door open for them and pointed to the exit. I had never been so enraged with my siblings, even though I knew that my parents had put them up to this. They had never heard me raise my voice to one, let alone all of them. They filed out the door silently.

The disturbing visit playing over and over in my mind, and my body still vibrating with adrenaline, I needed to get some fresh air. Perhaps a walk would help. I tried to make my voice sound cheerful, "Hey boys, let's go to the park!"

"Yaaayy!" Jamal cheered. Yusuf enthusiastically tried to imitate him.

"Bring the ball," I suggested, and Jamal rooted through his closet.

Off we went to the park, where the children kicked the ball here and there, giggled, and ran after it. Three-year-old Jamal was trying to share the ball with Yusuf, who made valiant attempts to kick it.

To soothe my nerves, I leaned back on an old oak. My breathing slowed as I looked up at the sky through the broad spreading branches. The leaves quivered as a faint breeze sifted through the limbs, giving me reassurance of the persistence of life that goes on despite whatever happens in my life. I breathed out, "Praise Allah." My anger slowly dissolved.

When Abdullah was finally released from "the hole," or solitary confinement, he was able to have visiting privileges. The prison was old enough that the smells of caged humans permeated the concrete and could neither be smothered by layers of paint nor scourged by disinfection. It reminded me of the prison in Philadelphia which Ron and had I visited to teach yoga. That had been six years ago, but it seemed like a century. My first visit to Abdullah was harrowing…

> *Every voice, every footfall, every clanging gate echoes wall to*
> * wall.*
> *Cacophonous yelling, banging, unending ear-blasting.*
> *Harsh. Stinking. Maximum security.*
> *Concrete visiting room, grimy chairs,*
> *Air humid with human sweat.*
> *Inmates and visitors yelling to be heard.*
> *Deafening, exhausting noise.*
> *Nowhere sunlight, nowhere sky, nowhere trees, nowhere bird*
> * songs.*
> *Abdullah smiles, sunshine erupts.*
> *How does he keep his soul alive*
> *In this dungeon of souls?*

LETTERS, MARCH 1978

Aisha: It looks like spring is coming. It feels good to get out of the apartment and go for long walks in the park. I saw crocuses blooming today and it cheered me up. Jamal and Yusuf played with the whiffle bat and ball. They're getting pretty good at it. I miss you so much, Habib. I wish we could walk under spring skies together, through fields of flowers.

Abdullah: I never really notice the seasons in here. It's always the same, except in winter this place is really cold, and in summer it's sweltering. Some guys get to work in the fields around the prison growing vegetables, so I guess they notice the seasons. But inside the joint, even sunlight is rare. I'm so glad I have you babe. I'm keeping hope alive for us.

LETTERS, DECEMBER 1978

Abdullah: Merry Christmas! Though we don't celebrate it, it's hard to escape the "holiday spirit," even in here. Mom sends me pictures of her and the family in North Carolina. I miss her and worry about her… she's getting older. Sometimes I get a visit from the family here in Philly. But our relationship is rocky a lot of the time.

Aisha: We went over to visit my parents. They wanted to give the kids gifts and I didn't object. They're so proud of their grandchildren and wanted to celebrate the holiday with them. And the kids haven't forgotten Santa Claus. We had a nice dinner together. But Christmas is getting more and more like a foreign holiday to me.

Through our correspondence we expressed the joys, worries, and tedium of our daily lives apart and our dream to live in an Islamic society. But it was our regular visits that made our relationship feel real. In early summer of 1979, I asked a friend to babysit the kids, and I visited Abdullah by myself. Fortunately, on this weekday, the visiting room was not crowded and the noise level was reduced to a low murmur. Even better, Abdullah had received permission for us to sit in a small outside patio along one side of the visiting room. The blank concrete walls and floor of the patio corralled us, but the beautiful, blue, free sky overhead was tantalizing.

There were four or five other couples in that small space, kissing and hugging, oblivious to the fresh air and promising sky. The guards could watch prisoners there, but their attention was focused on patrolling the main visiting room, which held a hundred or so visitors. Abdullah and I took full advantage of the situation. Sitting on his lap with my black jellaba flowing around us, we joined in a deep, passionate embrace.

Three months later, a pregnancy test verified what I already knew — I was pregnant with Abdullah's baby, a miracle child conceived in the most unlikely of circumstances. With our pregnancy, my husband became energized to develop plans for our future. We never discussed his efforts in our correspondence or telephone calls, which were monitored by the prison authorities. However, if we had a chance during visits for a relatively quiet exchange, Abdullah would tell me what he was thinking.

"I've been in contact with someone in Libya. I'm hoping they will offer to exchange an American in Libyan prison for me," Abdullah explained. "And if that doesn't work, Iran might be interested in a similar trade."

"So, you'd be safe from the feds in Libya?" I wondered. "Or Iran?"

"Yeah, neither one is friendly with the U.S. And after I get settled, you and the kids can join me there."

"Oh Habib, I really hope that will work out for us, inshallah."

I wondered why either Libya or Iran would be concerned with helping an American Muslim prisoner. I couldn't see how such an action would benefit them. And I was sure the state of New York would never agree to exchange Abdullah, regardless of the U.S. citizen they might free from a foreign prison. Still, I held out a faint hope that somehow this could come about.

Engineering a prisoner swap was not the only thing Abdullah was considering in his efforts to free himself. When he began talking about a plan to escape from the correctional facility, I worried about his mental state. Such an effort seemed beyond reality, considering the heavy fortifications of the prison and the captors' knowledge that he was a flight risk. But I didn't share my misgivings with him, for I knew that hope was how he survived in that forbidding place.

I thought that legal avenues might be a more realistic approach. Perhaps Abdullah's sentence could be shortened, or he could be transferred to a less restrictive setting. In one visit, he told me he was working with his lawyer on this approach.

"My lawyer says we have a good chance of getting my sentence reduced," he said. "Or even nullified."

"Wow that would be great!" I exclaimed.

"Yeah, the lawyer said we would focus on the fact that I was trying to return the money."

"What? What money?" I was confused.

"It was some Muslim brothers who robbed the bank, not me," he explained. "I persuaded them it was forbidden in Islam to steal, so they gave me the money to return. I was on the way to the bank to give it back when the police arrested me."

With a sinking feeling, I wondered how this story could be resolved with his previous story about defending the Black Panther daycare center. I couldn't merge the two stories and convince myself they were versions of the same story. Nor could I forget either story. It was likely that both were lies. The most painful realization was that I had married him based on a lie. I wondered what other falsehoods he had told me.

Lies
Twist my trusting heart.
Yet I'm so in love,
My soul so connected to his.
I never dreamed

I could find such love,
On a spiritual path.
But now this blow,
And our child is coming.

Absorbing my hurt and confusion, I never confronted him. Instead, I fell back on what I had learned as a child about family relationships. I tried to avoid contradicting Abdullah, and I denied to myself that anything was wrong. My parents' mantra might have been, "Everything is fine, just fine." That was the way we lived, and it seemed normal to me back then. Now, thinking of my years with Abdullah, I understand that I didn't know how to have a healthy relationship with him, or anyone for that matter. Perhaps Abdullah didn't either.

I was tangled in conflicting emotions, and I didn't have the maturity to resolve my dilemma by walking away. I still believed in him. Although I had caught him in a lie, I didn't perceive him as a devious liar, and I couldn't conceive of him as a callous murderer. I knew him as an intelligent, soft-spoken, decent person who tried to live according to the religious code of Islam. I believed his lies must have come from a place of shame and regret.

But even worse than my denial and rationalization was my failure to consider the murdered policeman's loved ones, who were forever deprived of his presence in their lives. Abdullah's rash act, however it happened, had caused irreparable harm to that family and their community. But I was too wrapped up in our love to see that.

Back at my apartment, I kept busy home-schooling Jamal and Yusuf. In 1979, teaching one's children at home was nearly unheard of, but I had researched the issue and found that I had the legal right to do so. To me, teaching the kids was fun, and I took to it naturally. We went regularly to the public library, where Jamal and Yusuf chose books to take home. We also took field trips to the Philadelphia Zoo, the park along the Cooper River, or to the mosque in West Philly.

Midway through the school year, I received word from the local school that I was required to register Jamal, who would have been in first grade. In response, I visited the principal and explained what I was doing, showing him the syllabus and lesson plans I had developed and some of the books I was using. Surprised, he acknowledged that I was allowed by law to teach my kids and asked that I bring Jamal for testing to make sure he was at grade level. Without any special preparation, Jamal did very well on the tests.

Meanwhile, I was growing bigger, rounder, and heavier as my pregnancy progressed, and I arranged to deliver at Booth Maternity Center in Philadelphia, where Yusuf had been born. This time, my sister Karen accompanied me and helped me through the labor. On a full moon during a terrific thunderstorm, a beautiful, healthy baby boy was born. His full head and facial features reminded me of early pictures of Abdullah when he was a skinny kid with a large head. Abdullah and I named him Jubair, which means "one who mends," in Arabic.

When the baby was a few weeks old, I took him with Jamal and Yusuf to visit Abdullah. Carefully, I placed Jubair in his father's arms.

"He's wiggling!" Abdullah smiled with pride and joy. "And look at that big head!" Jubair gazed into his father's face for the first time and slowly drifted into sleep.

"Jubair poops a lot!" exclaimed Yusuf.

"Ummi lets me hold him sometimes," said Jamal. "I think he likes me."

Yusuf cried, "He likes me too!"

Abdullah laughed and turned to the boys, "One day you'll be able to play with your younger brother."

"Yeah, we'll teach him soccer!" predicted Yusuf—accurately, as it turned out several years later.

"How about you Jamal? What will you do with your brother when he gets older?"

"I'll show him how to climb a tree, Abu!" Jamal was already an enthusiastic climber. "And maybe I'll read stories to him."

Abdullah and I smiled at each other and at our children, but then his expression turned from happiness to consternation. "Habiba," he spoke tenderly, "I want so much to take care of you and the children. I want to, I have to be the father these children deserve, the husband you deserve."

"I know, I know. I want that so much, too, Habib. One day, inshallah," tears sprang to my eyes.

"Inshallah," he replied, choked up. His gaze turned inward, and he was quiet.

A month later – on May 16, 1980 – Abdullah disappeared from his cell at the upstate facility. The authorities were unable to find him in the prison or surrounding area and had expanded the search to New York City. They also alerted authorities in Philadelphia, where he had been sighted on his previous escape. I received word of his escape when a friend from the mosque in West Philadelphia called me. She let me know that the police were searching everywhere, including the mosques. The prison authorities noted that he had been visited in prison by friends dressed as Muslim clergymen. They speculated that he had been given a Muslim robe as a disguise, and he walked out of the prison undetected.

When Abdullah was not immediately found, the state and federal authorities launched a large manhunt. Federal agents interviewed my neighbors to get information about me. They harassed my parents and siblings. Meanwhile, two federal agents came to my door to question me. When they asked if they could come in, I refused. While Jamal and Yusuf stood behind me, watching, I answered the cops' questions. There was not much to say, for I didn't know where he was or where he was going, and I hadn't seen him since the last time I visited him at the prison.

Outwardly, I may have exuded a stoic calm, but inwardly, I was in a state of agitation. I hadn't believed him when he talked about escaping, and now he was gone. How could he have escaped from behind those forbidding maximum security walls? I worried about his safety, but even more I worried about my security and the impact on our children. Mindlessly, I went through the motions of everyday life while my heart clenched…

> *My inner earth's shaken,*
> *The walls waver,*
> *Yet I shore myself up*
> *For our little ones.*
> *Wherever you are, my love,*
> *Fly, fly, don't look down,*
> *Don't fall.*
> *Flee to safety,*
> *Stay free,*
> *And I'll dream safe haven.*

I didn't hear from Abdullah for months, and slowly, my state of panic receded. I stayed close to home, assuming I was under surveillance. I continued with my routine, teaching the kids and taking them outside for exercise. Karen, who was living in an apartment nearby, occasionally came to visit me and the children. I didn't see much of my parents, who had quickly sold their home in New Jersey and retired to New England. My Muslim friends in the next town were a good source of support and help to me, and we often visited with each other. It was a quiet life, until one day I received a brief letter from Abdullah.

LETTER, OCTOBER 1980

Abdullah: Habiba, I'm safe in Libya now. I miss you so much and long to hold you and take care of you. I've been looking for a job. It's not certain yet, but there are some possibilities that may open up. Inshallah we will be together soon. I'll let you know as soon as I have news. Give my love to the boys. With so much love for you, Abdullah.

Pausing for a minute, I wondered whether my watchers had missed the letter or read it and let it pass. But it didn't matter, I realized. Abdullah was beyond the reach of U.S. authorities. Jumping up, I laughed, whooped, and danced around the apartment. Jamal and Yusuf stared in astonishment, not understanding. Then they joined me, wiggling, hopping, and laughing.

My heart lightened as I experienced a sunbeam of hope for the future. Abdullah and I would finally be together, living with our children in a Muslim society. Still a leftist, I was looking forward to leaving the U.S. with its rampant materialism, oppression of African Americans, acceptance of endless foreign wars, and abuse of the environment. Americans had just elected right-wing politician Ronald Reagan as president, and I was angry at his disparagement of the poor, opposition to improved opportunities for minorities, and encouragement of anti-environmental policies. But leaving America was more than a political statement. I saw in my next steps the realization of my childhood dreams. Very soon, my family and I would be traveling and living in foreign lands.

The following weeks were busy as I prepared for our emigration, getting medical checkups and vaccinations for us all, obtaining a family passport, choosing which belongings we would take with us, and quietly notifying my closest friends, my brother, and my sisters.

The phone conversation with my parents was difficult. I knew how they felt about my husband and the direction of my life. Their hearts must have been filled with sorrow and concern for the welfare of their grandchildren, but they said little. My mother asked me to write them when I arrived in Libya, and the brief exchange came to an end.

As I write this, I cringe at my youthful lack of sympathy for my parents. But I know that my relationship with them had been fractured in my childhood, and the damage had never been acknowledged or repaired. If I was rough with their feelings, it was because I was determined to choose my own path as opposed to the path that they had planned for me. And, unfortunately, it was because they and I had no language to discuss our feelings.

A few weeks later, there was a very brief and cryptic phone call from Abdullah. I assumed he was being cautious because my phone was probably tapped. I was to fly with the children to Tunis, the capital of Tunisia, where we would be picked up. Also, I should bring extra Muslim attire for his new wife. He'd explain later. He told me he loved me and couldn't wait to see me and the kids. He ended the call. I processed what I had just heard. My anguish and rage hit all at once…

> *WHAT new wife?*
> *You escape, find new love, marry NEW WIFE?*
> *I wait. Patiently. Five years.*
> *Our life together in limbo.*
> *Do you think of me?*
> *Of our relationship not yet begun?*
> *Can't you wait?*
> *I love you, follow you anywhere, and now this.*
> *Why Abdullah?*
> *Why hurt me like this?*

In pain but loving him still, I resolved to keep my commitment to my husband. Trying to bury my anguish, I numbly returned to the task before me, making the last preparations for our family's exodus from America.

Just before we left, Abdullah made one more short call to me. "Are you and the kids all set for your trip? I can't wait to see you!"

"Yes, we're all packed up and we've got a ride to the airport in New York," I said. "The kids are excited." I didn't mention my own conflicting emotions.

"Look, Amina left me. She wasn't comfortable with the situation, and we got a divorce," he explained quickly. "I'll be meeting you in Tunis."

"Oh, OK. We'll see you then." Surprised and suddenly relieved of the onerous burden I had shouldered, I hesitated. Then, regaining my equilibrium, I began to feel hope again. "It's been a long time, Habib."

Abdullah spelled out an address in Tunis that I might need, and I wrote it down on a scrap of paper, which I put in my wallet. He told me he loved me and ended the call.

It was a cold, dreary November day when I left the U.S.A. with an eight-month-old baby and two children, five and six years old. Our journey was beginning, and my heart was filled with anticipation. As the airplane lifted off, I knew that our lives were in the process of changing dramatically. What I didn't know was that a tumultuous and often dangerous passage lay ahead.

4

HOME FREE ALGERIA

1980-1983

"Since the world began has any man ever been able to know what would happen tomorrow? The world of men is today. I'm asking you to open your heart today. Tomorrow belongs to Allah..."

Paul Bowles[8]

If I had lost that scrap of paper, or if no taxi driver had known the way to that address, I would never have opened that unmarked door in the depths of the old medina of Tunis. But the children and I made it there safely. As I entered the stranger's house, I was keenly aware of the momentous step I was taking. That moment of trust was followed by weeks of anxiety as I waited for Abdullah to arrive, not knowing where he was or if he would find us. When he finally came for us, we tasted the air of freedom together, as a family, for the first time.

Since he was wanted as a fugitive in America, there were few countries where we could be safe from the reach of the U.S authorities. But Algeria — Jaza'ir in Arabic — was one of those havens. When we left Tunisia and entered Algeria in December 1980, we could not only taste but finally breathe freedom. We could stand upon the earth free together, hopeful of our future...

A refuge,
This land

---

[8] *The Spider's House*, Paul Bowles, 1955.

Welcomes us:
God's mercy
Brings us home,
Where a sea wind whispers
Under a vast sky.

Our first home together was in Boumerdes, a small city on the Mediterranean Sea east of Algiers. Entering the apartment, we were stunned by the clear, broad views of the rocky coastline and the whitecaps dotting the rough waters. I felt humbled by this blessing from the Creator. Abdullah put his arm around my shoulders as we stood at the open window, breathing in the fresh, salt air, "We're home Babe." We turned toward each other and embraced, feeling our love. Together, we would begin our new life.

Jamal and Yusuf had already staked a claim to one of the two bedrooms and were unpacking their toys. "Can we have this room?" Jamal asked.

"Sure," Abdullah replied, glancing at both bedrooms.

Looking around the sparsely furnished living room, Abdullah spoke first, "Let's take a look at what we've got here."

"Oops," I exclaimed as I sat down on the springy living room couch.

"Yeah, this furniture looks exactly like the furniture in my office," Abdullah said. He had already visited the English department at Institut Algérien du Pétrole — IAP — where he would be teaching. "I bet our neighbors here also have the same cheap furniture and black vinyl couches."

"I don't mind. At least it's something to sit on," I replied, "And the kitchen and bathroom are simple but just fine for us."

"You know," Abdullah continued, "I found out that IAP employees aren't the only ones to get free housing and utilities," Abdullah told me. "Everyone here has the right to free housing and free medical care."

"Wow. Socialism. So they don't have any homeless people?"

"Evidently not," Abdullah replied, "Frank, another teacher at IAP, told me he's never seen anyone sleeping on the streets here, and he's done a lot of traveling around the country."

"That's better than Philly or California, or most cities in the U.S." I was impressed. Algeria might not be fully developed, but it certainly outranked the U.S. in addressing the problem of homelessness.

Soon thereafter, I faced my first immersion into this foreign culture, shopping for food for my family. Abdullah had learned from his coworkers that the government-run department store — La Galleria — offered the best prices on food. When we went there, we found a large room with rows of low shelving. At the front of the store, a long line of women waited to pay for their purchases. I glanced at the items they were carrying — frozen fish, spaghetti, toilet paper, flour. The cashier looked both bored and harried.

Abdullah had started to roam the long rows of shelves. "Empty!" he exclaimed.

I joined him in the search for whatever groceries were available, "Two cans of tomatoes. Three boxes of what looks like detergent. Some bars of soap. Is that it?"

"Well, let's buy what they have," Abdullah replied. "I guess if we had arrived earlier, we might have gotten some fish and toilet paper."

"Abdullah, where will we get food for tonight?" I was worried. Our children were at home with the wife of one of Abdullah's colleagues, who offered to help us get settled.

"Don't worry," Abdullah reassured me. "I'm sure there is some other place that sells groceries. Let's get home so you can nurse Jubair while I find out where we can get food."

Shortages of government-subsidized goods was a downside to socialist Algeria. We learned that private grocery shops — often referred to as "the black market" — had nearly everything we needed, but at a high price. This was especially the case with meat, chicken, or fish, if available.

Since I was just learning to speak Arabic, I found it difficult to shop efficiently. If I didn't know the name of an item, I would identify it by sight and point it out to the shopkeeper. Some things were easy, such as the fresh bread in a basket on the front counter, and the boxes of eggs and half pint cartons of milk nearby. But all those mysterious boxes on the shelves of the shop remained unknowable to me.

Since we were on a very tight budget, I usually cooked vegetarian meals with rice, beans or lentils. On the rare occasion that I could afford a chicken, I tried to make it last several days by cooking it in broth and incorporating the broth and small chunks of meat into vegetable dishes to add flavor and protein.

One evening Abdullah invited his manager, Roy, to dinner. To make a good impression on the rather serious man, I tried to do my best vegetarian cooking, with rice, a stew of vegetables and beans, and a bit of chicken. I didn't feel the meal was particularly tasty, but Jamal and Yusuf chowed down with gusto. After dinner, the boys retreated to their room to play with their toy trucks and blocks. I put the dishes in the sink, put Jubair to sleep, and sat down to chat with Abdullah and his boss.

"I've noticed how eager the advanced students are to discuss current world events," Abdullah was saying to Roy.

"Well, be careful how far you go with that," replied Roy. "Discussions can easily get overheated here. Algerians are proud of their country and their independence, and they've learned the party line about so-called Western imperialism, especially with regards to America."

Though Abdullah agreed with his students on that score, he let his boss's comment pass. He didn't want Roy to get the idea he had any radical tendencies.

"Ummi!" Yusuf called loudly to me, interrupting the adult conversation. He wandered out of his bedroom and farted loudly. A foul smell followed him into the living room. "I've got gaaaassss. I've got gas reeeeal baaad!"

As the stench of Yusuf's digestive upset permeated the room, Abdullah groaned, and Roy looked nauseated. As I hurried Yusuf back toward the bathroom, I heard Abdullah opening windows and his boss taking his leave. As Roy exited through the front door, he called to me, "Thanks for dinner!"

The children were used to enjoying my baked goods — cookies, cakes, pies, biscuits, and breads — and Abdullah had a craving for them, too. But I was hampered by my inability to find baking powder or baking soda at the grocery store. I made some unsuccessful, hard cookies and experimented with unleavened, rubbery pancakes that the kids ate enthusiastically with more imagination than taste. I needed baking powder. My see-and-point technique of requesting an item at the store didn't work when I couldn't identify the product by sight. There were no familiar cans of baking powder and no boxes of baking soda. Although I tried to ask my neighbors in the apartment building, I couldn't make myself understood.

Finally, I encountered a neighbor woman who spoke a little English. I tried to explain what I needed a mixture of English, French, and Arabic. "I want to make gateau," I said. "I put zabdah, sucre, farine, baidh, and halib," I said, as I pantomimed mixing the ingredients in a bowl with a spoon. "Then, I put a little something to make gateau get big like this," I demonstrated the batter rising in the pan. "What makes the gateau get big?"

"Ah, you want levure chimique!" she exclaimed, using the French name for baking powder. She wrote the words on a piece of paper that I could show to the shopkeeper.

With the slip of paper in hand, I finally purchased this essential substance, discovering that it came in small, individually wrapped packets containing only a teaspoon portion each. The packets were kept in a box high on the shelf at the store, rather than in bulk boxes or cans.

The first homemade biscuits I made in Algeria were a tremendous hit with my family. "Wow, Habiba, these are delicious!" Abdullah was enthusiastic. "Can you make some more tomorrow?"

"Sure!" I was glad he was pleased. "Tomorrow I'll make chicken stew and vegetables with biscuits. Or dumplings if you like."

"Dumplings! Biscuits!" said Jamal, Yusuf, and Abdullah in unison. We all laughed. It was good to relax with the family around the table.

As I cleared the dishes away, I teased them, "I have a little surprise for you, but maybe I should save it for tomorrow…"

"Now! We want the surprise now!" begged the boys. They already knew what it was.

Abdullah looked at me with interest, "OK let's see this surprise."

I took the dishes into the kitchen and brought out a carrot cake, drizzled with icing. "All RIGHT!" Abdullah blurted out. "Please slice this sucker up!"

One day, I took the kids with me to buy groceries. Since we didn't have a car, the shops – a half mile away – were accessible only by narrow footpaths crossing rock-studded, bare ground. The lightweight, collapsible baby stroller that I had brought from the U.S. had already fallen apart under the rough conditions, so I carried Jubair in a backpack carrier while Jamal and Yusuf walked in front of me.

Returning from shopping, Jamal and Yusuf helped me carry the heavy groceries home. We were all tired, but the kids knew there was a reward for our arduous hike. "Do you want thé biscuit or glacée?" I asked them as we neared the sweet shop near our apartment.

"Glacée!" they responded. Tea cookies were fine, but Algerian ice cream was better. This frozen treat tasted like perfumed, flavored, and sweetened iced milk. It wasn't the same as the American ice cream we loved, but it was welcome on a hot day.

After unloading the groceries at home, I took Jamal and Yusuf outside to play soccer with the neighborhood children in the dusty street. Jubair, nestled in the baby carrier, watched his brothers with fascination.

Red earth creeps up walls,
Dirt puffs airborne,
Kids kicking,

Jamal shouts Arabic hey! pass ball! over here!
Yusuf joins raucous, friendly game.
Standing, I see blue sky pairing Mars-red Algerian earth,
Young bodies leaping from earth to sky and back.

As I watched, two women, shopping bags in hand, stopped to say hello and welcome me to the neighborhood, but all I could muster was the most basic greeting, "Salaamu alaikum." They spoke to me again, in Arabic and then French, but I didn't understand what they said. They smiled at me, nodded, and continued on their way. Sadly, I wondered how I could ever make friends here.

That evening, after I had put the children to bed, I asked Abdullah how he was doing with learning Arabic. In prison, he had studied more classical Arabic than me, so he had an advantage, but the Algerian dialect varied widely from the standard language.

"I don't use Arabic among the teachers at work," he said, "since they're mostly Americans and Brits. But my students are teaching me Arabic words. We have really interesting discussions, at least in the advanced English class. How are you doing?"

I paused, "Well, I'm learning a lot of words for shopping, fruit, vegetables, et cetera. But I can't really have a conversation with anyone. I mean, I can ask someone, 'How are you?' but I don't understand their answer. And then, they ask me a question, and I don't understand that either." I was discouraged.

"It takes time, Babe. You'll get there, just be patient." He gave me a hug. "Oh, and maybe you can help me with something. I'm supposed to be teaching the present perfect tense in class next week. Do you know how it's actually used? And how is it different from past perfect?"

I was adept with English grammar, and I was glad Abdullah had asked for my help. I was amazed that he had successfully plunged into English teaching without any formal preparation. After the first couple months, he had no need of my help.

To supplement my basic spoken Arabic, I relied on careful observation to interpret the people around me. I learned that the women I saw in the street had different styles of clothing that were a clue to their beliefs and culture. For example, a woman wearing a "haik" — a white, sheet-like overgarment draped over her head and wrapped around her body — was usually an older, more traditional person. A younger, religious woman would wear a modern style of Islamic attire — a long-sleeved, ankle-length, loose dress with a head scarf covering the hair. My own clothing was of this style. Women who were more secular wore relatively modest, Western style dresses as they went about shopping or going to work. Frequently, I would see three or four women walking home from the market together, chatting and laughing. Though each one might be dressed in a different style, they seemed unperturbed by their various lifestyle choices.

But visual cues were not enough for me when it came to social behavior. When I met someone, I didn't know whether I should shake her hand, as some women did, or hug and kiss her on both cheeks, as others preferred. And should I kiss her left cheek first or the right? Twice or three times? For me, just standing and talking with a North African woman was trying, even if she spoke English, since she obviously felt she had to be within an arm's length of me, as opposed to the six-foot distance that Americans require. All social interactions in this land made me feel awkward and stupid. It was exhausting.

I was beginning to worry about my relationship with Abdullah. His shifting moods kept me off balance. Some days he would be cheerful and glad to see me and the kids as he arrived home from work, while other times he was displeased with everything he encountered at home, from my housekeeping or the timing of dinner to the children's noise as they played. He also had a harsh approach to raising kids. As far as I knew, he had never had any experience in caring for and rearing children.

"You're too soft with these boys." Abdullah was angry that they had left toys on the floor of their room. He expected the entire apartment to be neat and spotless, so I knew he was blaming both the children and me.

"Abdullah, they are playing in their room! Let them play."

"They should be practicing their prayers, not playing. They know I'll get my belt out if they haven't learned Al Ikhlas!"

I knew that no matter how hard Jamal and Yusuf tried to learn the Arabic verses, they couldn't deliver a perfect performance with Abdullah looming over them with threats. "That's not the way to teach children. If you want them to love Allah, be merciful like Allah. Saying kind words to a child goes a lot farther than punishment."

"You gotta be tough with boys so they grow up to be men, not sissies!" his voice rose. "You don't know anything about raising boys. I do." He ended the exchange and left the apartment.

I was determined to support Abdullah through good times and bad. But I also needed to protect Jamal and Yusuf from their father's unrealistic expectations, I began to teach the boys their prayers when he wasn't home. With my help, I hoped that they would learn the verses well enough to please their father. I was sure he just needed time to learn how to relate to children. I took comfort in the words of Allah:

"And behold, with every hardship comes ease: verily, with every hardship come ease! Hence, when thou art freed [from distress], remain steadfast, and unto thy Sustainer turn with love." (Qur'an 94:5-8)

Meanwhile, Boumerdes was undergoing a severe water shortage, and household taps were only allowed to flow for an hour every week. During this short interval, I had to wash all the laundry by hand in the bathtub. Then, before the water was shut off, I filled the bathtub and several large jerry cans with enough water to last a week. Unfortunately, after we'd been there a couple months, the water ceased altogether. To obtain water, we stood in line to fill our five-gallon jerry cans with water from a truck that came once a week. Abdullah carried the heavy containers back to the apartment building and up the stairs.

With insufficient water to wash clothes, bathe, cook, and drink, we began to look for alternatives. Abdullah made inquiries and learned that there was a branch of IAP in the coastal city of Arzew, where there was sufficient running water. Fortunately, there was an open position for an English teacher there, so his transfer was approved. He bought a small, used Fiat, and in the spring of 1981, we packed up and moved to the western part of Algeria.

Standing on the hard clay street in front of our new apartment building in Arzew, I noted dirty red streaks bleeding up the exterior walls that may have been whitewashed at one time. Dirt rolled and blew into the stairwell of our building, but the entrance was clear of trash. Abdullah, the boys, and I began to unload the car. As we labored up the stairs with our belongings, we passed a smiling neighbor who was carefully sweeping each step, one after another.

Our second-floor apartment was clean and spacious, with tile floors, freshly painted walls, and high ceilings. There was a balcony off the small kitchen where I could hang clothes to dry. Looking out through the traditional privacy screen that encased the balcony, I could see a large expanse of packed scorched-red dirt where children played, men smoked and talked, and women walked to the market. About half a mile away, the port of Arzew sat on the edge of the Mediterranean, host to large ships that waited to receive shipments of natural gas, which was stored in numerous huge tanks clustered around the port.

Abdullah surveyed our new quarters, "Not bad. Three bedrooms. And look, there are two bathrooms, one with a toilet and sink, and the other for a shower. This set up will reduce traffic jams in the morning when the kids have to pee."

"Running water!" I was elated. "And hot showers!"

Abdullah turned on the kitchen faucet and cupped his hand under the flow. Tasting the water, he made a face, and spat it out, "Yeah, at the office they told me the water wasn't drinkable, but it was OK for washing and cooking. Tastes mineralized, salty."

"So where do we get drinking water?" I asked.

"People here buy cases of bottled water, so I guess I'll be hauling them upstairs. But it's better than hauling all the water we use."

"Are there water outages here?"

"Not like Boumerdes," Abdullah replied. "Only occasional, they say, for an hour or two."

"Great!" I was relieved.

The daily rhythms of my life now settled into a predictable, if monotonous, pattern. My day started early with nursing Jubair, bathing him, and changing his diaper. Then I got Jamal and Yusuf up and dressed. Next, I made breakfast to the family. Since there was no convenience food available, I cooked hot cereal — cornmeal mush or cracked barley cereal — and scrambled some eggs if we had them. After washing the dishes, I started Jamal and Yusuf on their lessons for the day while I put Jubair down for his nap. Periodically, I stepped away from lessons to get the laundry started. First, I rinsed the baby's dirty cloth diapers and soaked them in hot, soapy water in a large, plastic tub. Then I scrubbed them clean on a washboard and rinsed them thoroughly. I went through the same process with all the family laundry and then hung it to dry on the balcony.

By then it was time to heat up leftovers for lunch, but if Abdullah was coming home at noon, I would cook a meal. Afterwards, I let Jamal and Yusuf go out to play while I swept the floors clean of the endless sand that filtered under the door and through the window frames. Once a week, I mopped the floors as well, first cleaning with soapy water, then rinsing with clear water, and finally polishing the tiles with a dry cloth to make the floor shine. Then I started three hours of dinner preparation, serving, and cleanup. By evening, I was exhausted.

After work one day, Abdullah asked me if I'd like three of his female students to help me learn Arabic.

"If you want, they'd visit you once or twice a week," he said. "They could help you with Arabic, and you could help them improve their English."

"That would be great! Thanks, Abdullah." I appreciated his effort to help me.

"They're nice people. And smart. I think you'll like them."

I was fascinated to learn that these students were observant Muslim women studying a field that, in the U.S. in 1981, would be considered appropriate for men only — petrochemical engineering. I recalled my own struggles to pursue chemistry and physics in the U.S., and my father's outright disapproval of my entering the sciences or engineering. Thus, I was happy to see that in Algeria, social attitudes and Islamic values did not prevent these women from pursuing technical careers.

One day, my new friends and I decided to go to the grocery store for some ingredients for a recipe. Since Abdullah had left the car at home that day, I could drive to the shop. I told Jamal and Yusuf to stay in the apartment until I returned. I handed Jubair to one of the women to hold while I drove, but we hadn't gone far before the car got a flat tire. I sighed, unsurprised, for our Fiat was, as Abdullah called it, the "Fix It All the Time" car. The vehicle had already given him many headaches.

I pulled over, got out of the car, and looked at the totally deflated rear tire. "I can fix it," I spoke slowly in English to my friends. "Please get out of the car."

My passengers understood and stood on the side of the road. I got the jack and lug wrench out of the trunk and proceeded to jack up the car. But for some reason, two of the women thought that they needed to help by lifting the front corner of the car, rocking the jack as they did so.

"Oh no, don't do that," I said, startled. "Please stand there," I ordered, pointing to a spot four feet from the car on the dusty bank of the road.

"Stay there," I repeated, and watched to make sure they didn't move. Then I proceeded to change the tire.

Many cars passed us by, all driven by men. Not only did no one stop to help, but many drivers whizzed by hooting, honking their horns, laughing at us, and yelling insults. As one of the rare female drivers in Arzew, I was irritated but used to such men's ignorance, and I continued my task.

After I finished, my friends asked me how I learned to change a tire. When I told them my father had taught me, they were surprised that a man would teach his daughter such a thing. Similarly, I was surprised that an Algerian father wouldn't teach his daughter a basic safety skill. These young women weren't taught to drive or change a tire, but they were encouraged to become petrochemical engineers. Ironically, in my American family of the 1960s, the situation was the reverse.

From my friends, I learned the art of making bread Algerian style, which resulted in a chewier, more satisfying bread than the American loaf bread that I was used to making. They also taught me how to make the famous North African dish of savory meat and vegetables served over hot, steamed couscous. Though I appreciated my friends' visits and cooking lessons, I felt unable to develop a true friendship with them.

In retrospect, my inability to connect with others sprang from the childhood I spent as a loner, safe in my aloneness from hurt caused by others. Thus, I wasn't entirely comfortable in American culture let alone a foreign culture. In Algeria, although my Arabic was improving under my friends' guidance, I didn't have the facility to talk about meaningful subjects. But even when I was among English speakers, I found it difficult to broach topics that might somehow get out of my control and lead too closely to my own raw feelings.

Whenever my friends visited me, I also experienced an underlying tension that made me uneasy; because of their visit, I wouldn't be able to finish the day's housework. When Abdullah arrived home, he would undoubtedly notice this and express his disapproval. Even on a day when I managed to keep the children quiet and the house neat and pristine for the moment he walked in the door, he might be silent and cold. When I asked him what was wrong, he rebuffed me and refused to speak at all. At these times, I felt desperate to communicate with the one human being whom I counted on to be my love and partner.

At other times, he was upbeat and relaxed, particularly on weekends. For me, it was as if our relationship had completely turned around and was now headed in the right direction.

"Hey, Habiba, how about a ride out toward Mostaganem? Let's see what the coast looks like. Maybe we could find a place near the sea where we could have a picnic."

My cares were suddenly lifted as he spoke. "I'm making lunch to go, right now!"

The kids were excited, too. Jamal asked, "Can we swim?"

"No, it's still too cold," Abdullah replied. "But bring that kite you made, and we'll see if we can fly it."

We were all happier when we were able to travel someplace new, if only for a day. Abdullah didn't have to think about work, I'd escape from the drudgery at home, and the whole family enjoyed visiting new places.

The coastal area along the Mediterranean was a fertile land of farming villages and vineyards, and it included most of the major cities, including Algiers and Oran. On a weekend excursion, we drove two hours west along the coast to visit one of Abdullah's students at his family's home. We arrived at a tidy, quiet villa surrounded by a perfectly whitewashed wall covered with fragrant flowering vines. Palm trees rose from behind the wall, their branches waving gently in the cool sea breeze.

Ahmad opened the heavy wooden door in the wall, welcoming us with the traditional greeting, "Ahlan wa sahlan!"

"Ahlan bik!" Abdullah responded, as Ahmad showed us into the courtyard, which was filled with lush flowering bushes, tall palm trees, aromatic rosemary shrubs, and a gurgling fountain at the center. I felt I had suddenly entered another world, far from the dusty streets of Arzew.

Ahmad showed us into a front room of the house, which was sparsely furnished with a couch, a handmade Algerian carpet, a small table, and his musical equipment. Talking and drinking hot green tea together, we learned that Ahmad's parents were both traveling in France at that time. He had stayed home to continue his technical training and English classes at IAP. Picking up his guitar, he played selections of popular French music for us. Jamal was impressed with the speed and dexterity of Ahmad's fingers as they danced over the strings, and he was pleased when the young man showed him how to strum a cord on the instrument.

On the drive home, the kids slept while Abdullah and I talked. He told me that Ahmad's father had an important position at Sonatrach, the

Algerian oil company, which is one of the largest oil consortiums in the world.

"That's how they can afford that beautiful villa," Abdullah said.

"It felt like an oasis to me, a retreat from the world outside," I replied. "But Ahmad's room was so bare of furnishings. I expected more, after seeing that garden."

"Algerians with money try not to flaunt it," Abdullah explained. "They prefer to live simply, at least when they're in Algeria."

"It's a big contrast, though, to the way the majority of Algerians live."

"Well, my students joke that here in Algeria, there is socialism. Socialism for the poor. And then for the rich, there is capitalism."

I knew that well-to-do Algerians went to France for medical treatment, vacations, and shopping for quality goods not available in Algeria. If you weren't among the small number of affluent people, you made do with whatever socialist Algeria provided. Still, I felt that the right of all Algerians to decent housing, medical care, and education — paid for by the country's oil and natural gas wealth — was an achievement worth celebrating.

As it turned out, the children and I, like some Algerians, would travel abroad in the summer of 1981, but it wasn't for vacation or shopping. I had received word from my family that my father was seriously ill with cancer and not expected to live much longer. Four months pregnant, I flew to the U.S. with Jamal, Yusuf, and Jubair, using airline tickets that were one of the benefits of Abdullah's job. Of course, Abdullah couldn't return with us, so he took some vacation time with friends in Algeria.

My father, though emaciated and bedridden, was able to talk when I first arrived. We spent precious moments sharing insights about our separate experiences in North Africa. Dad had been in the U.S. Navy during World War II, and during that time he had the opportunity to visit the Algerian ports of Oran and Algiers. This was after the Allies defeated the Vichy French in the effort to control the Mediterranean and its ports. My father sent home to his mother a small, hand carved alabaster sculpture of macaques and bats, two creatures that are celebrated in North Africa. My grandmother, in turn, gifted this souvenir to me before she passed away. I cherished it as a poignant reminder of my father. As an American sailor during the war, he would never have imagined that one day his oldest daughter would travel and live in that part of the world.

Our conversation wandered from fond remembrances to family ties, as my father mentioned small gifts he had set aside for Jamal and Yusuf. But this moment of tenderness turned to severity when he told me he did not consider Jubair or any future children I might have by Abdullah as his grandchildren. I was not surprised, for I knew my father's long-held racist beliefs. But I was dismayed that on his death bed he persisted in those beliefs instead of taking the path of kindness, especially since little Jubair was just as much his grandson by blood as Jamal and Yusuf. And the same would be true for Jubair's younger sibling, who was nestled in my womb…

Why reject this child?
Innocent, he would love you
As his brothers do.
Yet you hold hate:
More deadly than cancer,
Worse than dying,
Crippling your soul.
I grieve for you
And your last, lost chance
To love.

Shortly after this exchange, my father lapsed into a coma. Even if we had had more time to talk, I know he would not have budged from his position. He died refusing this final healing.

When the children and I arrived at the airport in Algeria, Abdullah greeted us enthusiastically with hugs for the boys and a big kiss for me, "I missed you guys!"

"And we missed you, Habib," I smiled. "Reagan-stan wasn't the same without you. I'm so glad to be back, away from the craziness in the U.S."

"How are your family?"

"Everyone is fine. It was good seeing them. But American culture is… I don't know… Everything is shiny and new and clean. But so shallow? I've been gone less than a year, but it felt strange being there."

"And your father?"

"He died with little pain, since he was on heavy painkillers," I replied. "I got a chance to talk with him, but he hadn't changed his attitudes."

"About me, you mean," Abdullah stated.

"Yeah, about you. About anyone who isn't white."

"Welcome home, Habiba." Abdullah embraced me again, lingering. I melted into his arms and felt so glad to be back. Any worry I had about the state of our relationship faded in the warmth of his welcome…

Home at last, home
With my love:
Oh Allah thank you
For caring husband,
Sweet children,
The path of light,
Algerian sunsets,
Red earth,
And living seas.
I pray:
Let us always
Cling to You.

Jamal and Yusuf picked up their activities in the neighborhood as if they had never left. With their Arabic improving steadily, they could run errands to buy milk, eggs, cilantro or parsley, or other groceries. I also allowed them to play outside by themselves within sight of the apartment building for short periods of time.

One day they came home very pleased with themselves. "Ummi, look what we found!" Jamal held out a rusty tin can, filled with murky water. Peering into the can I saw a large frog wiggling and trying to hop out of the container.

"Ummi, come see the pond!" begged Yusuf. "There are lots of frogs!"

"Sure, just let me put Jubair in the baby carrier." I slung the baby onto my back. "OK let's go!"

"I counted seven frogs," said Jamal proudly. "There might be more."

Yusuf ran ahead to a pipe exiting the side of a slope, with stinking, black water trickling down a gully filled with trash, "We caught the frog here!" he yelled excitedly.

"Uh oh, boys, this water comes from everyone's toilets," I said, trying to control my nausea. "See the pipe it comes out of? That pipe goes all the way up to our building. The water from all the toilets comes down the pipe and empties here, where you've found the frogs."

Yusuf looked uncertain, "You mean the frogs swim in poopy?"

"Yup. And if you play near this water, you'll get very sick."

"Eeeew," Jamal understood now, but he was disappointed.

"You have to let the frog go. Don't catch any more frogs. And you must not play here again," I hoped my language and tone of voice was strong enough to keep them away from this place.

In September, Abdullah and I discussed what to do about school for our older boys. There was a small school for the children of English-speaking employees of American oil and gas companies in Arzew. However, since Abdullah worked for an Algerian organization, our children were not eligible for the program. We decided Jamal and Yusuf should learn to speak Arabic fluently and read and write it, while continuing their studies in English reading and writing at home under my guidance. We would enroll them in a public school within walking distance of our apartment.

Although Jamal had completed first grade already, the principal of the school told me both boys would go into first grade since they didn't speak fluent Arabic. Here, there were no Arabic language classes for kids who weren't native speakers. When we were shown into the first grade classroom, I counted at least sixty children, many of them standing for lack of enough desks and chairs. The kids who were lucky enough to have a seat were sitting two or three to a small desk meant for one student. At the front of the classroom, there was a single teacher. Seeing me, he was kind enough to find desks Jamal and Yusuf could squeeze into with other students.

Both boys seemed to be making progress in learning the Arabic alphabet and reading simple words. But after a few weeks, they complained that they couldn't hear the teacher because of the noisy children. Some days they couldn't get a seat in class and had to stand. Often, kids would steal their pencils.

Eventually, the beleaguered teacher began to crack down on the unruly students to gain control of the class.

"The teacher has a stick for the boys!" Jamal reported. "To hit them if they're bad."

"Or if they don't know the lesson," Yusuf added.

"And a whip for the girls!" Jamal continued. "I hope I don't get hit."

I couldn't see how any children were going to learn well in that chaotic environment. On top of that, my kids had a disadvantage in not being fluent in Arabic. I decided to pull them out of public school and return to home-schooling them in English.

Meanwhile, Jubair followed the older boys around at home, trying to play with their toys. Skipping the crawling stage, he quickly learned to stand and then run to keep his balance as he chased his big brothers. He had frequent falls on the hard tile floors, but he would cry only briefly as he hauled himself up and started running again. His brothers, in turn, complained that he wrecked their carefully constructed Lego projects. Abdullah bought Jubair a plastic tricycle, which he loved trying to ride, sometimes with a push from Yusuf or Jamal. Cheaply made, it broke within a couple weeks.

Most children we met in North Africa had only the toys they made themselves. Boys often created balls out of strips of bicycle inner tube tied together in a bundle. A small "ball" of this type was used in a collaborative game in which boys stood in a circle and kicked or kneed the ball to each other, with the goal of not using the hands and not letting the ball touch the ground.[9] Bigger balls were often wrapped with additional strips of rubber tube to make a smoother surface for a soccer ball, and these were favored over the plastic or rubber balls that would be destroyed in a single game of soccer in the rough terrain.

Though girls were usually busy with cooking, cleaning, and caring for their younger siblings at home, I occasionally saw them from my balcony. They sang and played circle games or jump rope on the hard packed dirt field behind our apartment...

> *Below, I hear young voices,*
> *Girls sing singing*
> *Like my own voice long ago:*
> *A sailor went to sea sea sea*
> *To see what he could see see see.*
> *But they have circled*
> *To sing their own songs,*
> *One calls out*
> *Others reply*
> *In one voice,*
> *One sweet voice.*

---

[9] I later learned that kids in the U.S. were doing the same thing with commercially made "hacky sacks."

Late autumn brought cold rains to the Algerian coast, and the dirt streets and paths of Arzew became seas of mud. It was getting much harder for me to carry Jubair, as I was now heavily pregnant. In preparation for the birth, Abdullah and I visited the maternity ward of the hospital in Oran, twenty miles west of Arzew, and were appalled at the filthy conditions. I would not endanger my health nor the well-being of my baby there.

I had Abdullah inquire of his married Algerian coworkers about reliable, expert midwives in the area, and he learned of a birthing center in nearby Oran. We visited the clinic, which consisted of two small, well-scrubbed but otherwise unadorned rooms staffed by a midwife who lived in a second floor apartment. I made sure that the midwife had no objection to Abdullah being with me at the birth or to me using my own technique for getting through labor. I was pleased to find the midwife accommodating and professional. Her fee was the equivalent of two hundred dollars. All that remained was to wait for the big day and practice strengthening exercises and childbirth breathing.

On a cold, rainy winter morning in 1982, the Mediterranean skies were stormy and gray, but I paid no attention to the weather. I rose quickly from bed, let Abdullah know that the baby was on its way, and began to prepare for our big day. I had been awakened by contractions, which now were getting stronger. But I had a terrific back ache, and I knew that the back of the baby's head was rubbing along my spine. I did periodic pelvic rocking exercises, hoping to turn the baby into a better position for birth. My efforts were successful, and my back ache disappeared. When the contractions began to come faster, I told Abdullah it was time to make the forty-five-minute drive to the midwife's clinic.

For the births of my three other children, labor had taken place in slow motion. But not this time. Before we reached Oran, I was doing the intense breathing of the transition stage. By the time we reached the midwife's clinic, I knew the baby was ready to be born. I climbed onto the delivery table, and the midwife confirmed my assessment. I began pushing as hard as I could, while the midwife guided a beautiful baby boy into this world. She placed this precious little one on my chest

"Abdullah, look! Another little boy!" The baby's pure eyes were gazing into mine, and I was overwhelmed with love.

"What's wrong with his legs? And he looks so wrinkled!" Abdullah looked worried. He had never seen a newborn infant.

"Blessings!" said the midwife in Arabic. "Your child is healthy and strong, alhamdulillah."

"Shukran, thank you," I said to her. She had been just as professional as the American midwives who had delivered Jamal, Yusuf, and Jubair.

"Habib," I reassured my husband, "His legs are fine. Those long legs and big feet mean he's going to be a tall boy! And newborns are always wrinkled." I put the baby, whom we named Taha, to my breast and he nursed eagerly.

The midwife moved me from the delivery room to the adjacent recovery room, where I slept for several hours with the baby at my side. When I awoke I had a ravenous appetite. Anticipating that, the midwife had made me hot, home-cooked couscous with fresh chicken and vegetables. Certainly, it was the most delicious food I have ever eaten, before or since! When Abdullah returned several hours later, the midwife cleared me and the baby to go home.

Jamal, Yusuf, and Jubair were awaiting my arrival anxiously. I gave each of them a big hug. letting them know how proud I was of them. After they made sure that their mother was happy and in good health, they turned their attention to their new little brother. I let Jamal hold him.

"What's his name?" asked Jamal, touching the baby's cheek. "He's so small!"

"Baby baby baby!" said Jubair reaching out to grab him like a doll.

"Ooops," Abdullah caught Jubair and sat him in his lap, "He's too little to play now. You can touch his hand very softly, like this."

Yusuf had been waiting for his turn. "Can I hold him now?"

"You sure can," I said, lifting Taha from Jamal's arms and then putting him in Yusuf's lap.

There was a moment of quiet as Taha's family gazed upon his little form with awe and love. I felt my connection to him strengthen...

> *Child, we meet on our outside,*
> *Knowing each other.*
> *Child of my heart, my blood.*
> *Welcome,*
> *I give you food, comfort, shelter.*
> *Rest in my arms, little one,*
> *My sweet love.*

The Fiat was falling apart faster than we could repair it, so we would have to find another car. Abdullah asked around among his coworkers and found that a used car was for sale by an expatriate worker. It was a Mercedes, but not the luxury vehicle one might see in Europe or the U.S. In North Africa, well-used vehicles were used for commercial transport. The car was sound, so Abdullah agreed to buy it, promising the first payment with his next paycheck. After showing it to me and the kids, he drove it to the motor vehicle bureau to register it.

After hours at the motor vehicle bureau, he returned in a foul mood. "They told me the there was something wrong with the registration or title," he said. "I couldn't register it."

"What are you going to do?"

"I went back to the guy that sold me the car, but he denied there was anything wrong with the papers. I asked him to go with me to the motor vehicle office, but he refused."

"So, you'll return the car?" I asked.

"No, I'll try another motor vehicle branch and see if they'll issue a registration."

After a couple months of fruitlessly navigating the Algerian bureaucracy, Abdullah announced that he had registered the Mercedes by paying baksheesh – a bribe – to someone in the motor vehicle bureau. He never did pay the previous owner for it, claiming the man knew it couldn't be registered. I argued that this was stealing, regardless of the seller's intentions. But Abdullah was adamant.

One dark and rainy spring day our family was seated in the dining room, and I had just brought lunch to the table. After Abdullah said grace, I served the macaroni and cheese, and the kids dug in enthusiastically. I had just sat down to eat when an unbelievably loud roar of sound engulfed us. In the next instant, many things happened at once – I saw the walls and windows of the room swaying back and forth, I felt the floor trembling beneath my feet, and the lights went out. My first thought was that the natural gas storage tanks had blown up. But the roaring sound continued, and I then knew…it was an earthquake! Abdullah and I jumped up. In the pitch dark

of the apartment, we grabbed the kids and scrambled at breakneck speed
down the three flights of stairs into the street…

> *Hundreds of people crying, screaming, praying,*
> *Allah save us Allah have mercy!*
> *Jamal beside me. Jubair firmly in hand. Taha clasped to my chest.*
> *Suddenly together Abdullah and I yell, WHERE'S YUSUF?*
> *Abdullah bounds leaps stairs frantic, every second precious.*
> *I'm praying: Allah protect save Yusuf save my husband save us*
>   *all.*
> *Building swaying, oh no don't collapse. Please!*
> *I'm crying, Jamal and Jubair crying, Taha whimpers in my arms.*
> *Where. Are. They. Abdullah!*
> *He rushes out breathless, Yusuf in his arms. Safe. Both safe.*
> *Oh thank God thank God Alhamdulillah.*

Abdullah told me that he had burst into the dark, quivering apartment,
found his way to the dining room table, and detected movement there.
Yusuf was calmly eating his favorite meal, macaroni and cheese, in the dark.
He was oblivious to the earth roaring, the building shaking, and the chaos
of his family's flight from the apartment. Again, I thanked God for
protecting him and the whole family.

Nervous about re-entering our apartment, we drove off to visit a friend
in Oran for the rest of the day. When we returned, we found long cracks
in the living room wall. Worse, there were still aftershocks which kept me
unsettled. Neither Abdullah nor I had realized that coastal Algeria was an
active earthquake zone. We learned that Algerians were particularly fearful
of a "zalzaal" because just over a year earlier El Asnam (now called Chelif)
had been decimated by a massive 7.1 magnitude earthquake which killed at
least 2,600 people, injured over 8,000, and left 300,000 homeless.[10] In
2003, long after we had left Algeria, an earthquake of similar magnitude
devastated our former home of Boumerdes, killing an estimated 2,300
people. It was said that inferior building materials were used in the
construction of the concrete apartment buildings — such as the one where
we used to live — resulting in greater damage than might otherwise have

---

[10] https://en.wikipedia.org/wiki/1980_El_Asnam_earthquake

been the case.[11] The bone-rattling quake we experienced in Arzew was minor in comparison.

Within a few weeks, the family had settled back into our routine. Not long afterward, my mother wrote me that she and my sister Karen would like to visit us. They were eager to see Jamal, Yusuf, Jubair and me again, and they wanted to get to know Abdullah and meet baby Taha. They hoped to see a bit of Algeria, too.

In preparation, Abdullah and I discussed several possible sightseeing trips. Together, we gave the apartment a thorough cleaning, and he purchased extra beds and arranged the spare room for our guests. I planned meals and purchased extra groceries. Finally, the day of their arrival became reality.

On his return from the airport, Abdullah honked the car horn as he pulled up below our apartment. The kids and I flew down the stairs.

"Oh, it's so good to see you!" I gave Mom and Karen hugs. "How was your trip?"

"Looooong!" they both said, laughing.

Abdullah began unloading their luggage and carrying it upstairs, while the kids and I showed them into our apartment.

"Nana! Karen!" Jamal, Yusuf, and Jubair ran up to them. "Come see our room!"

"Wait boys, give them a chance to rest a bit," I admonished.

"No, it's OK," said Karen, turning to the kids, "Show me your room!"

"Room!" exclaimed Jubair, as they disappeared into their bedroom with Karen.

"Oh, look at this chubby little baby!" my mother exclaimed. She smiled and stroked Taha's cheek.

The baby started to work his mouth and turn his head, looking for milk, so I sat down to nurse him. My mother moved toward the window to gaze out on the packed clay field below, and beyond that, the propane refinery and tanks by the port. Standing next to her, I pointed out the huge tanker ships moored at long docks located out in deep water, far from the shore. We both were thinking of my late father and his love of the sea and sailing.

---

[11] https://eeri.org/site/images/lfe/pdf/algeria_20030521.pdf

As I heated up the pot of soup I had made earlier, I reflected that this was the first time my mother had visited me in my own home. While my father was alive, she undoubtedly didn't want to anger him with a visit to me in my African American community in Philadelphia or North Carolina, or even in New Jersey, just miles away from my parents' home. Neither of us spoke of him now…

> *Mom seems the same,*
> *Her smile pleasant, not warm,*
> *Happy with grandkids.*
> *But no big hugs.*
> *I've changed:*
> *Like her I can be stoic, disciplined,*
> *But I laugh, hug, play,*
> *Often weep desperately,*
> *Feel awe of sunrise.*
> *Can she and I begin anew?*

After a good night's sleep, Karen and Mom were refreshed and eager to see some of Algeria. Karen and I packed a picnic lunch for a day trip while Abdullah and the boys washed and shined the car until it gleamed. Somehow, we managed to cram four adults, three kids, and a baby into the Mercedes, and off we went for a drive west along the Mediterranean.

As the deep, earthy reds of Arzew receded behind us, the Mediterranean horizon spread its arms wide to welcome us to deep teal waters dotted with whitecaps. Opening the windows of the car, we breathed the salt air and felt the stiff breeze that was whipping up the sea. We now were treated to an ever-shifting array of sea shades, from distant azure to the turquoise rimmed shoreline. As always, the sea embraced and nurtured me. Glancing at my mother and sister, I could see that they were moved, too.

Driving along the coast, we first stopped to look at Mers El Kebir, the busy commercial port and naval base. The "Great Port" had been used for centuries, as evidenced by an ancient fort overlooking the harbor as well as modern facilities built for large ships.

"It's amazing to think of this port being in continuous use for two thousand years, from Roman times until now," I said. The port had been occupied by successive rulers — Romans, Berbers, Ottomans, Spanish, Portuguese, and French.

"During the War, your father's ship would have been docked there." My mother pointed to an obviously military area that housed the Algerian navy.

Abdullah guessed my mother's wish. "It's too bad we can't get closer, but the port is restricted. But we'll be getting a chance to get close to the Mediterranean up ahead."

As we drove further, scrubby brush dotted the roadside and the coastal view broadened. When we began to smell the sea, the boys became restless.

"Where's the beach?" asked Yusuf. "Aren't we going to the beach?"

"Yes, we're almost there," replied Abdullah. "Look, here we are. Ain El Turk."

"What does Ain El Turk mean?" asked Karen.

"Spring or water source of the Turk," I translated. "But I don't know who the Turk was."

Abdullah pulled the car off the road. "OK boys," he announced, "Find a smooth spot to put the blankets down for our picnic."

Jamal and Yusuf grabbed the blankets and ran off on their mission while Karen and Mom took Jubair for a walk along the beach. Abdullah carried the food, bottled water, plates, and utensils to the spot the boys had chosen.

After nursing Taha and putting him to sleep on a corner of the picnic blanket, I stood up. I called, "Lunch is ready!" Jamal and Yusuf had taken off their shoes and were wading in the shallow water, looking for shells and sea life. "Hey! Boys!" I yelled. "Time to eat!"

This time, they heard me and came running. When the family was seated in a circle around the food, I served and passed the plates, and Abdullah uttered the blessing. The sea gently lapped the shore as the spring sun beamed heat onto the sand. Everyone fell silent in this peaceful moment. Perhaps, like me, they felt grateful and content as we shared food and family ties by the peaceful Mediterranean.

Abdullah spoke to Mom and Karen. "I've been thinking we might make a longer trip, if you'd like," he said, nodding to them. "A trip to the desert."

"Wow that'd be great!" exclaimed Karen. "You mean the Sahara?"

"Yes, the Sahara."

"That would be a real treat, Abdullah," my mother said. "I'd like that."

"It's about a ten-hour drive from Arzew, so we won't all be able to fit in the car. But Elaine," he spoke to my mother. "Perhaps you, Aisha, and

Taha can fly. There's an airport in Bechar, and a hotel. I'll drive the car with Karen, Jamal, Yusuf, and Jubair. What do you think?"

"Yay!" Jamal and Yusuf erupted, joined by Jubair, who agreed with whatever his big brothers said. "Yayooo!"

My mother smiled, "Sounds good. That should work out nicely."

I don't know what I expected, but when I saw the airplane we'd be flying in, I was concerned. The small, 1930s era, two-engine airplane had a bare metal floor, and the walls revealed the bolts and framework that held the aircraft together. The pilot and copilot were visible in their doorless cockpit, and in the main body of the plane sixteen wooden chairs had been bolted to the floor for passengers. The rest of the interior was filled with barrels, boxes, canvas mail bags, and crates of live chickens. The sounds and smells of the birds and sweaty humans were overwhelming. There were no seat belts, trays, or magazines, and no food served. If there was a toilet, I was sure that I didn't want to use it. When the engines started up, the noise was deafening. All my senses were under total assault.

Any conversation was impossible, so I turned to my mother and gestured to my ears. Yes, she agreed, nodding wordlessly. The pilot turned the plane onto the runway and drove it at increasing speed. The aircraft wobbled and bounced alarmingly but finally jerked up into the sky. Beneath us now lay Algeria, the green coastal area falling quickly behind, to be replaced by huge, dry, rocky mountains, whose history lay recorded and exposed in multiple layers of rock. Barren, massive, and beautiful! Glancing at the other passengers to see how they reacted to this grand view, I flinched. Everyone, it seemed, was frantically praying, murmuring pleas for safe passage for this metal box flying unnaturally through open sky.

Then we hit turbulence. "Allah! Allah! Allah!" several traditional women on board cried out loudly. My mother and I looked at each other, worried. As the plane was pummeled and tossed about like an insect, my stomach lurched. The airplane suddenly lost altitude and plunged toward the earth below. My body went airborne, and I grabbed for the seat-back in front of me, holding Taha tightly with my other hand. He was sleeping through it all, but the other passengers were crying, screaming, praying as hard as a human being can pray. I glanced at my mother, and her usually inscrutable face betrayed sheer panic. I'm sure my face showed the terror that had possessed me...

Looking out the window I note
Two engines:
If one fails, we're screwed.
Down below I ascertain
Massive fire-red-orange dunes
As far as I can see,
Hostile to life.
God save us!
Sinuous, sculpted ridges and valleys,
Crimson and blood,
A hellish, gorgeous landscape:
The Sahara,
The most terrible terrain, most awesome.
A crashed plane
Would never be found.

The airplane suddenly gained altitude and leveled off. Perhaps we weren't going to crash, at least not yet. But the other passengers had come this way before, and they continued to pray fervently. Though the plane was experiencing only occasional jumps and bumps, I knew that our luck could change at any moment. The dread wouldn't leave me. I waited for the crash. It wasn't until we finally landed in Bechar that I was able to take a deep breath, though my heart was still racing. My legs wobbled when I took my first steps back on firm earth. Alhamdullillah rabbil alameen. Thank you, merciful Lord of the worlds.

In 1982, Bechar was a dusty, unimpressive Algerian town on the edge of the Sahara, near the western border with Morocco. But it did have a hotel. Walking toward the building, which was undergoing construction of a new wing, we noticed that something odd. The new wing didn't line up with the old wing, and there was a gap of a foot between the bricks of the two wings. Evidently the builders had stopped working when they realized that the two wings had different depths and heights. The new wing was left disconnected and empty.

Our rooms in the old wing were bare, undecorated, and dark. While Abdullah and I and the kids had a room with a lamp, Karen and Mom had no lamp in their room, and no electrical outlet either. While they had a working toilet, our toilet was foul and inoperable. For the entire hotel, there was no water except for a few hours in the evening. Some male staff kept propositioning my sister, so I tried to stay with her to fend them off. The waiter at the restaurant didn't know what items were on the menu. In fact, it turned out there was almost nothing to eat there, so we purchased fixings for our meals at the small, local market.

The next morning, we got up early, stopped by a grocery store, and then sat in the shade of the store's awning to eat a breakfast of hard-boiled eggs, fresh bread, dates, and oranges. We also purchased food and water for a day trip to Taghit, an oasis that lay at the edge of the Grand Erg Occidental, a sea of sand dunes covering thirty thousand square miles, with no vegetation, no roads or settlements, and virtually no rain.

Driving southeast on a two-lane, paved highway from Bechar, we passed through miles of flat, rocky desert which featured wind-carved plateaus and outcroppings that resembled ancient, abandoned buildings. But there were no actual buildings, nor was there any sign of human life.

"Ummi, I gotta pee," piped Yusuf.

"I pee!" exclaimed Jubair.

"OK, boys, let's make it quick," said Abdullah, who pulled over to the side of the road. We extracted ourselves from the car and stretched our legs.

"Look!" cried Karen. "Camels! Oh, and there's a white camel!"

My mother got her camera out and started to take pictures. The small group of perhaps four or five camels were over a quarter mile away. The white one was young and stayed close to its mother.

"Do you think they're wild? Or are their owners nearby?" I asked Abdullah.

"Probably wild. We haven't seen any signs of people for nearly an hour."

"Abu, can we go see the camels?" asked Jamal.

"No, they'll just run away if we approach them."

Disappointed, Jamal went off to see what Karen was doing. She was taking pictures of Yusuf, who was hopping around like a jumping spider trying to catch its prey. He had spied something moving among a few scraggly, grey-green plants on the hard desert floor.

"He caught it!" Karen called out. "A lizard!"

The creature struggled to escape from Yusuf's expert grip. He knew how to catch one of these fast little reptiles while not getting bitten. He thrust the lizard toward Jamal to scare him, but his brother knew this was coming and jumped backwards.

"All right, let's get moving. We're almost to the oasis," said Abdullah. "Let the lizard go, Yusuf."

The rocky desert seemed interminable, and we were hot in the crowded car. Temperatures in April in the Sahara could rise to 85 or 90 degrees (F) as the sun beat down on the dry terrain. The landscape that had initially seemed exotic and new now seemed monotonous. It was just endless expanses of hard-packed earth and rocks. We passed a large, cliff-like outcropping, and the road rose and curved around it. Suddenly, Abdullah brought the car to a halt as we gaped. Below, a lush, green valley sprang from the sere, sandstone desert. Palm trees towered over wild thickets of plant life that seemed impossible in such an arid land. Breathtaking life erupted from death. This was the oasis of Taghit!

Driving slowly in the narrow alleys of the oasis, we fell silent with awe. Narrow canals, pools, and fountains brought water to the village, where thousands of small miracles of life thrived under tall date palms. The people of the village grew vegetables, fruit, greens, and fragrant herbs in every available square inch of soil. And the air, dense with humidity, was alive with bees, insects, and birds flitting among thickets and flowering bushes. Oh God, the Living!

Within the sublime oasis, mud brick homes nestled together, connected by common walls and narrow alleys. Each home was topped with a flat roof that was walled so that family members could gather to sleep in the open air on hot nights. During the day, freshly washed laundry fluttered from the roofs. The front door of each home opened onto one of the many dirt pathways that wound their way through the settlement, leading to a mosque, a school, shops, and family garden plots.

Taghit was bordered on the west by Oued Zousfana, a desert river that provided water at least part of the year. On the east lay the expansive, huge dunes of the erg. It was there that Abdullah led us. Just a stone's throw to oasis garden plots and date palms, a towering, six-hundred-foot sand dune rose up. Abdullah, Jamal, Yusuf, and Karen proceeded to climb the dune, followed by Jubair, who insisted on being part of the hike. Mom and I watched from the shade of a palm tree as the family slowly made their way up the steep, sliding sands. Two-year-old Jubair struggled but didn't give up his stubborn effort to follow his brothers up the sand mountain. I saw that it would be a while before they completed their ascent. With Taha strapped to my back, I wandered with my mother through gardens fed by irrigation canals. We were enchanted by the gurgling sound of running water and the sweet songs of birds roosting in shrubs and fruit trees.

She told me news of my brother Gerry, my sister Judy, and their families, and of aunts, uncles, and cousins. She described her own community projects, artwork, and gardening. I talked about my home schooling of the boys and asked her advice on Taha's cholic. But in this precious time, without the distraction of the children, we couldn't talk about what was important to us. I didn't tell her — and she didn't ask — about Abdullah's and my troubled relationship, or the isolation I was feeling because of my poor command of Arabic and the burdens of constant childcare. She didn't tell me how she felt about the absence of her lifelong partner, my father, and we didn't discuss the possibility of building a new relationship together now that Dad was gone. I felt a nagging dissatisfaction with our shallow conversation, but I didn't know how to remedy it. Perhaps she didn't either.

An hour and a half later, my weary family returned from their trek up the dune. Abdullah, sweating, was carrying an exhausted Jubair. Karen looked hot and tired, and her feet seemed to hurt. But Jamal and Yusuf had enough energy to climb another dune. They ran to tell me all about their excursion.

"We kept sliding down when we went up!" said Yusuf.

"And sliding down when we came down," added Jamal.

Jubair had woken up, and Abdullah set him down. "This boy's heavy!"

"What did you see from the top of the dune?" I wanted to know.

"Dunes," Karen said with awe. "Dunes, endless dunes as far as we could see, all of them just as big as this one, row upon row of dunes. Nothing but beautiful dunes."

We returned to the hotel at Bechar for the night. The next day, we rose early to prepare for our return to Arzew. I was not looking forward to the flight, but I told myself that the plane had made it to Bechar without falling out of the sky, so it probably would arrive home safely. In the morning, Abdullah got the car ready for the journey, checking over the engine, adding oil, topping off the radiator, and filling the gas tank as well as an extra gas can. My mother watched Taha and the kids so that Karen and I could go for a last walk in the desert outside the city.

"You seem content here in Algeria," said Karen. "It's so different in so many ways from the U.S."

"I'm beginning to feel comfortable here," I replied. "Life is difficult, it's true. But I love the beauty of the Sahara, the mountains, and the Mediterranean. People have been kind and helpful to us. And the kids and I can be with Abdullah."

"I'm happy for you Aisha," Karen smiled.

Walking uphill, we topped a small mound of sand and then stopped, surprised to be face-to-face with a small, old woman who was dressed in a long, tattered, black dress. It was impossible to tell how old she was from her weathered, leathery face, but her black eyes were friendly. A worn but colorful scarf was wrapped around her head. Behind her was a tiny one-room shack, half-buried in the sand.

"Salaamu alaikum," she said, smiling at us.

I responded with the same greeting, and made to turn away, but she spoke again, inviting us to come visit with her. She gestured to a woven rug in the sand, shaded by a ragged tarp attached to her house. "Please, sit with me! Drink tea!" she insisted in Arabic.

Although I would have preferred to decline graciously, my Arabic wasn't up to that delicate task, and I didn't want to offend her by refusing her hospitality. I gave Karen a look, and she nodded. With smiles, we sat down at the rug. The woman ducked into the house, put the kettle on for tea, and then sat down to chat with us. My Arabic was sufficient to manage most of the conversation.

"Where are you from?" she asked.

"My sister is from America," I replied. "My husband and I and our children live here in Algeria."

"Welcome! Welcome to our country!" she exclaimed. She turned to enter the dark, unlit interior of the shack to fetch the tea.

I took that moment to tell Karen, "Don't drink the tea. Pretend, if you have to, but don't drink it. She has no running water, and…"

The lady returned and handed each of us small tea glasses of the hot tea. She noted Karen's camera. "Could you take a picture of me? I want to send it to my son. He lives in France."

When I explained the request, Karen happily agreed and took a picture. But when the woman realized the photo wouldn't be available instantly, she was disappointed.

"Aisha, tell her I'll mail it to her son when I return to the U.S." Karen said. I translated this offer, and the woman grinned, hopping up to go into the house again.

"Dump the tea in the sand," I ordered Karen. "Quick before she returns."

We had just set our empty tea glasses on the rug when the lady returned. She had written her son's name and address on a slip of paper, which she handed to Karen, "Thank you! God bless you!"

"Thank you and God bless you too," I replied as we stood to leave.

"Go in peace," she said as we went on our way.

"The tea was hot enough to kill any germs, wasn't it?" Karen asked on our walk back to the hotel.

"Perhaps," I replied. But the tea glasses might not be too clean. She's a sweet lady and I hated to dump her tea like that, but there are lots of serious germs here in Algeria, like typhoid, dysentery, and hepatitis. One can't be too careful."

The visit of my mother and sister to Algeria ended sooner than I wished, but I saw that Mom was tired, and even Karen seemed a bit under the weather. On the day of their departure, we didn't have much to say. What could be said about an absence that might last months, years, or even decades?

> *In a world far from her home,*
> *Mom meets a daughter she never knew.*
> *I meet the mother still closed to me,*
> *But I feel a glimmer of light.*
> *My sister opens her heart,*
> *Accepts me and my world:*
> *We could one day be*
> *Real sisters.*

Our family had never been affectionate with each other, but before Mom and Karen departed, I hugged them and told them I loved them, something I had never done before. I watched them leave with sadness in my heart, but I had no regrets at living so far away from them in the world I had chosen, with the man I had chosen. This was where I belonged. I was now trying to live my own spiritual life, my own family life. It felt right to me. I knew I would have difficulties in becoming acculturated into Algerian society and turning my relationship with Abdullah into a successful marriage. But God willing, I would rise to the challenges.

Now that we had a reliable car, Abdullah began making trips to Oujda, the Moroccan border town one-hundred-fifty miles west of Arzew. There, he bought goods unavailable to us in Algeria – a short-wave radio for listening to BBC English broadcasts, sturdy blue jeans for the kids, and cheap Cassio watches for him and me. After one such excursion, the kids and I met him at the door to welcome him home.

"Guess what I've brought you from Morocco!" Abdullah teased me.

"Uh, I don't know…"

"Wait here," he said. Returning to the car, he pulled something out of the trunk and hauled it upstairs.

When he got to the apartment door I stared at the object, puzzled. "What is it?"

The blue plastic, two-foot-high cylinder was mounted on wheels and had a lid on top, with an electric cord trailing. He didn't answer my question but smiled broadly. "Let me show you," he said, rolling the device into one of the bathrooms and plugging it in. Then removing the lid, he showed me the inside of the cylinder, which had a kind of propeller at the bottom. He pressed a button, and the propeller started to whir. It was a simple washing machine!

> *Oh Babe you're the best!*
> *So thoughtful.*
> *I didn't know you noticed*
> *My hands red, wrinkled, cracked,*
> *My back aching bent over tub.*
> *Thank. You. Habib.*
> *You're so good to me.*

Testing my new washing machine, I put water and detergent in it, added clothes, pressed the button, and put the lid on. It agitated the clothes, swishing them around in the soapy water. When I thought the clothes must be clean, I removed them, drained the water, and then put them back in the machine to rinse in fresh water. Afterward, I would wring the clothes out and hang them to dry. After nearly two years washing all our clothes laboriously by hand, this tiny machine was a miracle.

Unfortunately, buying Western goods was not the only reason he was making trips to Morocco. I learned he was buying hashish and marijuana there, too.

"But hash and grass are intoxicants, Abdullah," I objected. "Forbidden, just like alcohol."

"There are scholars who have ruled it permissible," he replied.

"But most say it's haram, Abdullah."

"Well, I'm following the scholars who allow it."

I disagreed but kept silent, since there was no persuading him. However, I felt uneasy, as I was pretty sure grass and hash were illegal in Algeria. We didn't need any trouble.

The trips to Morocco stopped abruptly when Abdullah became very ill. The whites of his eyes were tinged with yellow, and he was nauseous, sick to his stomach, and utterly exhausted. The doctor at the clinic in the American compound

diagnosed him with hepatitis and ordered him to stay home until he recovered. I was advised to feed him apart from the family and keep his dishes, utensils, towels, and washcloths separate from the rest of the family. Everyone in the English department at IAP received gamma globulin shots to increase their immunity against hepatitis, but the doctor told me that our family didn't need this injection as we would already have developed an immunity to hepatitis from our exposure to Abdullah. I later found out this was not true, but Abdullah was the only one in the family to become ill, thank God. Abdullah believed he got the disease from drinking tea at a roadside tea shop outside Oujda. He was sick for about four weeks, but his full recovery took longer than that.

After he was better, Abdullah resumed his social life with the Americans who worked at IAP and Sonatrach. At his invitation, a group of his colleagues met weekly for lunch at our apartment. Abdullah told me he hoped this would help me feel less isolated. But though I craved adult conversation, I found I had little in common with them. They talked about their work and gossiped about the students and supervisors. I didn't know how to insert myself into a discussion and steer it to topics that interested me. And I was invisible to them.

One day after the Americans had left to return to work, Abdullah said, "Do you know what Betty and Anne told me?"

"What?"

"They wondered why I married you. They said, 'Aisha ain't got no aish.'"

They meant I had no life, no liveliness, and the way Abdullah said it gave the expression sexual overtones. I was outraged, "Why are they talking to you like that? About me? Implying I'm not good enough for you. Do you know how hard I work to put on these lunches for your friends? And they insult me in front of you? And what did you say to them?"

"Calm down," Abdullah tried to backtrack. "You're getting upset over nothing."

"You can tell your friends," I shouted, "there will be no more lunches here."

"OK your choice," he replied in a harsh voice, slamming the door as he left the apartment.

Where was the kind, religious man I had gotten to know in the years he was in prison? I was deeply hurt by Abdullah's words and furious that he was discussing our relationship with these women. He had told me that Anne was "just a friend," but now I wondered about that.

However, I needed to believe that whatever faults I found in him and whatever ways he hurt me, he would return to being the good person I knew him to be. And it was true that I had little energy left at the end of each day of grinding housework, cooking, and childcare. I would try to remedy that, somehow. And perhaps, I thought, we could strengthen our relationship on the weekends. We had always enjoyed traveling, so I suggested we get out and see more of Algeria.

Nearly every weekend thereafter, we took the children for long drives into outlying rural areas or along the scenic coast. During these excursions, he and I felt more relaxed, and the children were happy to run free on hills, fields, or beaches. In the wide open, natural spaces, I could put aside my worries and feel some hope for our future together.

Roughly the size of the U.S. east of the Mississippi River, most of Algeria is desert. In our travels, we experienced only a tiny fraction of the diverse landscapes, but what I saw inspired feelings of awe, especially at sunset...

Mountainside dusky gold-bronze
Earth layers tilt steeply down,
Arrows into earth.
Burgundy shadows grow deeper, longer.

Then. Suddenly!
Brilliant solar disk drops
Over the edge,
Casting wild sun streams, a hundred hues,
Outward, mellowing
Into endless sky.

Our time in Algeria was drawing to a close. Abdullah had been corresponding with an Iranian friend we had met in the States. Hossein, who had returned to his country after the Iranian Revolution of 1979, now held a post in the government of the new Islamic Republic of Iran. He invited Abdullah and me to come to Tehran to teach English to employees of his department. Abdullah was passionate about the prospect of living in a truly Islamic society that was being built from the ground up after the success of the revolution. The U.S. would not be able to extradite him, and he would have a steady job that would provide our family with the stability we needed.

I had mixed feelings about moving. I was beginning to feel more confident in my use of Arabic to communicate, and the beauty and stark contrasts of Algeria moved me. I wanted to learn more about the people I met, their lives, and their families. I wanted to plunge into the culture of North Africa and learn to navigate that world.

On the other hand, I was excited about the opportunity to move to Iran, where I believed a modern Islamic way of life was being established. This new republic was replacing the brutal, corrupt, and authoritarian monarchy of Shah Mohammad Reza Pahlavi, who had tried to remake society in the mold of Western countries.

A major influence on my thinking was a book by Ali Shariati, a leading Iranian proponent of social justice, a classless society, and the enhancement of human potential through the revolutionary foundations of Shia' Islam. He was a strong opponent of both Western influence in the internal affairs of Iran and the ultraconservative Iranian clerics, whom he considered capitalist and regressive. Shariati was popular among a broad spectrum of Iranians who wanted both freedom and respect for their culture and religion. His ideas resonated with my own political views.

Abdullah and I were energized by the opportunity of living and breathing the Islamic revolution in Iran. We would have to uproot the family again, adjust to a new culture, and learn a new language, Farsi. But together, we made the decision to go, for this was the chance of a lifetime.

In the three years since Abdullah's escape from prison, we assumed that the U.S. authorities had been looking for him. They would have notified other countries and Interpol — the international police organization — about the fugitive Rick Briar, also known as Abdullah Khalid. We knew that for his security, we would have to avoid airports and border crossings in Europe, which most likely had computer systems in place.

To travel to Iran, the safest route would be through the Middle East, where computers were only rarely available, and telephone coverage was spotty. Although we were concerned about our lack of current information about unstable areas, we decided to risk driving east through Tunisia, Libya, and Egypt, and then north through Israel, and Syria. In Türkeye, we would turn east into Iran.

Unfortunately, when Abdullah attempted to obtain visas for our travels at the relevant consulates in Algiers, he learned that the border of Egypt with Israel was closed. Furthermore, he was told that if we had an Israeli visa in our passports, many Muslim countries, including Algeria and Iran, would prohibit us from crossing their borders. Thus, the route we had planned was out of the question, and our choices were now narrowed to two options. We could stay in Algeria, or we could take a ferry from Tunis to Italy and drive across Europe and Türkeye to Iran. After some thought, we decided to chance the latter.

In the early spring of 1983, we made one last trip to the Algerian desert during Abdullah's spring vacation. One purpose of this trip was to determine how well the car pulled the small, used camper trailer Abdullah had bought. We would also practice setting up and breaking down camp, including the new family-sized tent I had bought in the U.S. Most of all, it was a trip to say goodbye to the Sahara.

When the day of our trip to the desert came, we loaded up our camping gear and traveled south, following the same roads Abdullah had taken when he drove Karen and the kids to Bechar. We passed quickly from the populated cities and towns of northern Algeria into semi-arid mountains and hills, where row upon row of evergreen trees had been planted to hold back the desert. Finally, the terrain became dry and barren, with endless expanses of hard-packed, red earth interspersed with strange rock formations blasted by the wind and sand. Six hundred miles south of Arzew, we stopped and climbed out of the car, our legs stiff and our bodies tired.

Embracing the harsh beauty of the rocky desert, I took deep breaths of the clean air, reached my arms toward infinity. I whirled around to see a 360-degree view of desert wilderness under a huge, cloudless, blue sky. The kids joined me, spinning, laughing, and waving their arms and legs in a wild dance...

Desert home soothes spirit, empties mind,
Holds me, touches my heart:
Where humans are small,
Where nature is great,
This is where I feel joy.

Arriving at Bechar, we put more gas in the car, bought supplies, and continued another fifty miles to the oasis of Taghit. Although we had been there recently, the towering crimson and ginger sand dunes again awed us to silence. They stood as a testament to the power of ancient geologic forces that formed the 3.6 million square mile Sahara, covering a swath of Africa nearly the size of the United States.

At the edge of the oasis, next to the date grove, we set up camp. Our trailer, with its tiny propane stove and sink, was to be my kitchen. We would eat meals at the small table with a bench on either side; this arrangement would fold down to make a bed. Our new tent provided the family with shelter from the sun and mosquitos and a bedroom for the kids.

The kids' days were full of running and playing in the sand and exploring the oasis. For all of us, the nights in the desert were glorious...

Night sky bursts with starlight, a billion, billion glittering suns.
Shadows of date palms shade young hiders from seekers,
Father and sons playing in the dark,
The smiling moon watching over:
Peace to us all.

Scouting the oasis, Abdullah found a butcher shop and returned to camp with a couple pounds of inexpensive meat. I cooked up a pot roast, and the family appreciatively chowed down on the first red meat we had eaten in nearly a year. It didn't taste like beef, mutton, or goat, and we wondered what it could be. The next day, at Abdullah's request, I walked to the market to buy more of it for our family. On the ground in front of the butcher shop, I saw the source of our enjoyment, a large camel's head. The kids and I were enthusiastic about a second meat dinner, but Abdullah less so.

Our short vacation was over too soon, and with sadness we prepared to return to Arzew.

"Ummi, why can't we live here?" asked Jamal.

"Yeah, you and Abu could get jobs here," suggested Yusuf. "And we could play in the dunes." The children echoed my own feelings, though I knew that our decision to go to Iran had already been made.

As we drove away from our camping spot, we saw two foreigners driving down a dirt road away from the oasis into the flat, rocky desert. Curious, we followed. The road soon came to an end, and the other car turned around to leave. Although we didn't see anything special there, we parked and told the kids to go pee and run off their energy.

Jamal and Yusuf raced out into the desert laughing, but within a few minutes, they ran back to me, out of breath. "Come see, Ummi! Come see – pictures on the rocks!" They turned and ran back toward a cluster of rocks a hundred yards away.

When Jubair, Taha, and I arrived at the rocks, I was stunned to see pictures of lions carved into the rocks. "Lions! Wow!" I exclaimed. "Boys, that means this area wasn't always a desert. It used to be home to lions, and probably other animals, too. And home to people who carved pictures on rocks."

Yusuf was kneeling under an overhanging slab of rock that was blackened, evidently from smoke stain. He pointed to the ceiling of the overhang, which was marked by a series of short, vertical red lines, perhaps a counting device.

Much later, I discovered that this site was one of many places near Taghit where Neolithic-era petroglyphs could be found, evidence of New Stone Age human settlements from seven thousand years ago. But the history of the human occupants of Algeria went back even further. Excavations in 1992 in the northeastern part of the country unearthed stone tools made by humans 1.8 million years ago.[12]

---

[12] https://en.wikipedia.org/wiki/History_of_Algeria#Prehistory

The thought of leaving the Algerian landscapes that inspired such strong emotions saddened me. I was beset with an uncurable thirst ...

> *Oh Jaza'ir, what mysteries you hold –*
> *Your ancient lands and peoples and stories,*
> *The moody sea,*
> *A vast Sahara,*
> *Earth cracking open,*
> *Gathering me into its heart.*
> *I will miss all of these,*
> *But most of all*
> *Your sunsets blooming intensely before night falls,*
> *Deepest black.*

5

THE ISLAMIC REPUBLIC OF IRAN
1983

God says: "I am with those whose hearts are broken."
Hadith Qudsi

We had long since left the rocky shore of Algeria and the sparkling Mediterranean, though I still held that memory in my heart. Our drive through Europe was quick and tedious, and the only mishap we encountered was a flat tire on the camper. Fortunately, we had experienced no trouble at any European borders. Now leaving Türkeye, we were on the brink of our new life in the Islamic Republic of Iran. The Iranian border guards motioned to Abdullah to park the vehicle and bring the family's passports to the one-story, concrete border and customs building.

"Stay in the car," he ordered the children. Nodding to me, he turned and followed a guard inside.

The children were restless. Jamal asked, "Is this Iran?"

"Are we going to live here?" asked Yusuf, gazing hopefully at the high mountains surrounding us.

"I gotta pee!" proclaimed Jubair.

"Oh Jubair, can you wait until Abu comes back?" I turned to face the kids in the back seat. "Yes, this is the border of Iran, and no, we won't live around here. We still have a long drive to our new home."

Abdullah had been in the border post a long time, too long. Anxiously, I looked at my watch. Almost an hour. Was there a problem? Finally, I saw him step out of the doorway, accompanied by two border guards, who asked us to get out of the vehicle while they inspected the contents of the car and camper.

Abdullah gave me a glance that said, "Just stay cool."

Holding Taha on my hip, I helped Jubair pee at a pile of stones by the side of the road and then held his hand firmly so he wouldn't wander off. Jamal and Yusuf knew to stay close to me. When the guards had completed their inspection, Abdullah went with them back into the post. The children and I got into the car and continued to wait for another half hour or more. I had seen no indication that we would be allowed into Iran, and I struggled to keep my nerve.

When I saw Abdullah walking toward the car, I couldn't tell from his serious expression whether we were being allowed to enter Iran or not. Before I could ask him, he said quietly, "Let's go through, now. We'll talk later." He started the car and forced a smile for a guard who waved a friendly welcome to us.

Suddenly, a scruffy man in a uniform came running up and commanded us to stop. He showed Abdullah his official badge and in broken English ordered us to drive him to a city on the road to Tehran.

"We don't have room!" I objected. The back seat was filled with four kids, travel bags, extra clothes, and blankets. Their father and I sat in the front, in two bucket seats on either side of the central gear shift, with my purse, diaper bag, and bags of snacks packed into the limited space.

Abdullah turned to me, "I don't think we have a choice…" He hadn't finished his sentence before the guard yanked open the back door and jumped into the seat, landing squarely on Jubair, who screeched and began to cry loudly.

"Just see if the kids can make room for this guy," Abdullah said. "Maybe his city isn't too far."

I took 16-month-old Taha into the front passenger seat with me, while the older children grumbled. Jubair kept crying. The stranger in the back seemed oblivious to the discomfort he was causing the family. In the tight quarters of the back seat now, he took a position leaning forward toward the front passenger seat. I asked Jamal to distribute cookies to his brothers and prayed our unwelcome passenger would leave us soon.

We began the long drive to Tehran. A couple hours passed and Taha woke up hungry. As I nursed him discretely under my hip-length overblouse and waist-long head scarf, he eventually fell back asleep. It was then that I felt a hand stroking my right breast. I looked down at Taha, who was sound asleep in my arms with his little hands tangled in my scarf. I felt the stroking again.

With sudden, horrified realization, I lurched forward, recoiling from the stranger behind me, screaming loudly, "Get your hands OFF ME!" Leaning on the back of my seat, the filthy man had reached around with his right hand to surreptitiously stroke my breast as I nursed. My horror was amplified by a sudden realization: since I hadn't responded earlier, thinking it was the baby at my breast, the predator in the back seat thought I enjoyed it.

"OFF!" I screamed again. Poor Taha woke up wailing. At the same time, my eyes beseeched Abdullah's help.

Abdullah understood my message perfectly. Glancing at me with wide eyes, he slammed on the brakes and turned, thundering at the man, "YOU!"

I was terrified now for whatever was coming next, for my husband was in an uncontrollable rage. Simultaneously and with extraordinary speed Abdullah grabbed the long, dangerous diving knife he kept under the driver seat, leaped from the car, and ran around to yank open the back door. His face was contorted with fury as he leaned over the man, holding the knife against his throat, screaming "I'm gonna KILL YOU!"

Jubair, Yusuf, and Jamal all started wailing, their eyes wide with terror at Abdullah's volcanic wrath and the sight of the deadly knife he wielded. The man tried to back away, sprawling over the kids in the back seat and babbling in Farsi, begging for his life. Abdullah responded by jerking him out of the car, slamming him against the trunk, and then dragging him away without lowering the knife at the man's throat. He hesitated briefly, and then opened the door to the camper, threw the man in, and locked the door behind him.

Tears streamed down my face. I felt violated. With my husband at my side. With my children in the back seat. Modestly covered as a Muslim woman. In a Muslim country. Defiled. Angry. How many showers would it take to remove the grime of that stroking? How many years to forget?

"Are you alright?" Abdullah spoke to me softly. "What happened? What did he do?"

"He had his hand under my blouse and was stroking my breast." I sobbed. "At first I thought it was Taha touching me as he nursed. But when he fell asleep, I felt it again and I looked down at Taha. It wasn't the baby touching me but that man. Touching my breast." My tears were a deluge of loathing and hatred.

Jamal, Yusuf, and Jubair were weeping hysterically, and I turned to them, wiping tears from my face. "It's all right, now. Don't be afraid. It's OK. I'm OK. We're all right now."

But it wasn't all right...

> *Uncomprehending terror carved on kids' faces.*
> *Seeing Abu crazed, eyes bulging*
> *Shark-killing knife*
> *Razor edge pressed*
> *On stranger's neck,*
> *Inches from their own eyes:*
> *They fear he'll kill them too.*
> *Oh my loves.*
> *I fear I can't protect you,*
> *Nor erase*
> *This from your hearts.*

I slowed my breathing. The children needed me. I started to get out of the car so I could comfort them.

"Wait," Abdullah stopped me. "He's trying to break out of the trailer. Get back in the car."

We heard the man banging something heavy on the inner walls of the camper, trying to break a hole to escape. Abdullah put the car in gear and drove on at a furious pace, swerving the car frequently and careening around mountain curves. He tried to give the man in the camper as rough a ride as possible.

"What are we going to do with him?" I asked.

"I would have killed him," Abdullah said grimly.

I was silent, unable to respond. My heart was broken. I was numb. I was on fire. My grief was a deep, burning anguish, punctuated alternately by fury and abhorrence. I couldn't sort anything out.

He continued, "But that would have caused a world of trouble for us. We'll take him to the nearest police station and turn him over to them."

Eventually, we came to a small city where the local headquarters of the Islamic Revolutionary Guard Corp was based. After they found a translator who spoke English, Abdullah was able to explain to them what had happened to us. The border guard was taken into custody, and then a committee of five or six Pasdaran, or Guardians, interviewed Abdullah and me to determine the facts. They took the case seriously because they had telephoned our sponsor in Tehran and learned that we were guests of the Islamic government. Finally, the Pasdaran informed us that they had the information needed to bring charges against the border guard. We were free to resume our journey to Tehran.

As Abdullah drove, the scenery of the countryside unfolded before us, but I didn't see any of it. I couldn't stop reliving the psychological and spiritual disaster that our introduction to Iran had laid upon me. My heart was still pounding, and I felt a wild array of emotions, from anxiety to outrage, from disgust to dismay. Hijab was supposed to protect Muslim women, and I had found that in Algeria, Tunisia, and even the U.S., men respected it. But here in the Islamic Republic of Iran, this was evidently not the case. In fact, I had been sexually molested by a government official. My dream of living in an Islamic society was shattered on our first day in Iran. I knew I should pray for help and healing, but I felt unable to do so. My faith was plummeting to depths I had not experienced since I became Muslim.

Relieved to finally arrive in Tehran, I was gratified by the warm welcome Hossein gave us. It had been a few years since we last saw him in the U.S., and I looked forward to catching up on news with him and his family. But first, he showed us to our home, a spacious, two-bedroom apartment on the 24th floor of a modern skyscraper in the Shahrak-e Gharb area of northern Tehran. I was stunned at the pristine, wall-to-wall carpets and the modern kitchen appliances of this luxurious accommodation.

"I'm sorry," Hossein was apologizing to Abdullah. "I wanted to find a place for you among the real Muslims in South Tehran. We'll find an apartment there for you, don't worry."

"This is fine for the time being, Hossein," said Abdullah. "I appreciate your efforts to help us."

"I'll give you a couple days to get settled. Ask my assistant, Mehdi, if you need anything. On Saturday, the beginning of the work week, I'll send a car to bring you to the office. We desperately need your help teaching English to our lawyers."

"We're looking forward to it."

South Tehran, we later learned, was a crowded, grimy, urban area populated by poor, devout people who fervently supported the Revolution and Imam Khomeini. Our residential building, on the other hand, was one of a cluster of tall, modern skyscrapers built by American companies before the revolution. Though I could see there might be a political advantage to living in South Tehran, Abdullah and I hoped we could stay in North Tehran, where we had a modern kitchen with appliances and there was no shortage of hot and cold running water, serviceable bathroom facilities, and reliable electricity. A definite bonus was the balcony view of the surrounding mountains, tens of thousands of feet high...

> *Buildings like stalks reach into the sky,*
> *Proud mountains soaring even higher,*
> *An army of colossi.*
> *Distant Damavand, the behemoth,*
> *Spills power into a crystal sky,*
> *While in the city below*
> *Channeled beside city streets,*
> *Cold mountain streams*
> *Urge the thirsty to rejoice.*

The beauty of the mountains was unfortunately offset by city air quality so bad that the authorities had limited the number of automobiles. There were horrendous blockages that caused all traffic to stop for hours. Later, I learned that this problem was sometimes intentionally caused by drivers who were passively protesting government policies. Frustrated drivers would turn off the ignition of their cars, leave them in the traffic jam, and walk to nearby cafes or shops, ensuring continued gridlock.

At our first opportunity, Abdullah and I went to Friday prayer, which was held at Tehran University. Having parked our car, we joined throngs of people walking in a boulevard leading to the event.

"I hope the kids are being good with Ferideh," I said. A neighbor one floor down from us had offered to babysit the kids for me.

"Oh, they'll be fine," replied Abdullah. "Look at all these people! Shia Muslims have Friday prayers in one location per city. Not like the Sunni neighborhood mosques in North Africa."

"It seems to be getting really crowded," I commented.

"Yeah, I think the plaza at the university is full," Abdullah replied. "Look Habiba, the women are forming their lines here. I'll go up and join the men's lines. Afterward, stay right here. I'll be back to get you."

I joined the chador-clad women sitting on prayer rugs. One of the leading mullahs was speaking, his emphatic words broadcast by huge loud-speakers. Though I didn't understand the gist of the speech, I gathered it was political, as it was punctuated by emotional cries and angry shouts from the congregation. When the sermon finally came to an end, the mullah's exhortations were echoed by the people. With my rudimentary Farsi, I knew they were chanting, "Death to America! Death to Israel! Death to Soviet Union! Death to the enemies of the Islamic Republic!"

I shivered, suddenly wondering how the religion of peace had morphed into a political movement wishing death on others and on the land where I was born. I had come to pray in solidarity with the Muslim community, and instead I felt alienated and sad. Standing in line with the women around me, I prayed for peace, not death, and surrendered to the love of the One. Among the women around me, I sensed the sweet vibration of other prayers for peace. Perhaps there was hope, then, in this strange land.

Present-day Iran's culture is the result of a long, complex history and the contributions of numerous ethnic and linguistic groups. The known history of Persia — now called Iran — arose about six thousand years ago in Bronze Age civilizations. As new technologies developed, including written language, there arose a long succession of ancient empires, including the Assyrians, Medians, Achaemenids, Parthians, and Sasanians. Then, around 654 CE, Islam was introduced to Persia, which became a center for Islamic culture, literature, and architecture. By the 1500s, Iran had become a unified Shia Muslim country. After tumultuous centuries of conflict with the Ottoman Empire and then with Russia, Iran lost control over outlying territory, reducing its borders to what we see on today's maps. Finally, in 1979, the Shah of Iran, Mohammad Reza Pahlavi, was deposed during the Iranian Revolution.

Leading up to the Revolution, the United States, Britain, and the wealthy minority of Iranians had supported the Shah, while the majority of Iranians opposed him for his corruption, scandalous waste of resources, and brutality toward opponents of his dictatorial regime. His strong depen-dence on Western governments and his emphasis on emulating Western culture offended proud, nationalist Iranians. Muslim fundamentalists and political liberals alike opposed the Shah. Socialists, student activists, and non-political Iranians joined in the demonstrations that eventually brought about the downfall of the monarch.

However, the key component of the successful revolution, and the government that followed, was the centralized authority of the mullahs under the leadership of Ayatollah Khomeini. Their powerful network of influence spread to all corners of Iran. Because the clerics were well-organized, they quickly took control of the people's revolution. Khomeini was propelled to the status of Supreme Leader, and eventually to Imam – the supposedly infallible, divinely inspired religious leader. The relatively rapid shift from the people's revolution to an Islamic revolution of the most conservative type left many people dismayed and without political voice.

I had expected a revolution such as the vision proposed by Ali Shariati, the popular Iranian sociologist. Although his teachings were fundamental to the explosive revolutionary agitation against the Shah, they were not incorporated into the newly born Islamic Republic. Any opposition to the clerics became increasingly dangerous as the new government cracked down violently, often murderously, on any opposition. When Abdullah and I arrived, even ordinary citizens were subjected to authoritarian brutality. In the streets of Tehran, I was shocked to find young, aggressive Revolutionary Guards patrolling with machine guns. They looked for any kind of religious, social, or political infraction – real or imagined – that would warrant the summary arrest and imprisonment of an unfortunate citizen who crossed paths with them.

Our apartment building was primarily populated by wealthy Iranians who for some reason hadn't fled Iran after the revolution. Many of them shunned us because of our ties to the government. However, we did meet others who welcomed us and invited us into their homes. Yazmeen, for example, was the mother of a young daughter and wife of a husband who traveled frequently on business. She was happy to watch my kids when I taught a class at the office, and I babysat her daughter when she went out shopping.

Another neighbor stopped by one day to welcome us to Iran. In excellent English he introduced himself, "Hi, I'm Kamran Shirazi and I live on the fourteenth floor. I thought I'd welcome you to the building."

"Come on in," Abdullah smiled at the middle-aged man with smooth skin, jet black hair, and a trim beard. "This is my wife, Aisha. And our children."

I shook his hand, "Nice to meet you, Kamran." Abdullah glanced at me, and I realized my error. Women and men were forbidden to shake hands in conservative Iran.

"Come have a seat," Abdullah said, motioning to one of the three chairs we had in the living room. "Sorry, we haven't furnished the place yet."

"When I heard Americans had moved into the building, I had to see for myself," Kamran chuckled. "Americans built this apartment complex, you know. We haven't seen anyone from the U.S. since they left in 1979." Kamran's American accent was almost perfect.

"Where did you learn English"? I asked.

"First, Iran and then, New York," he replied. "I did a degree in economics at NYU. I loved the City! But I came back here after graduation to help my father with his business."

I went into the kitchen to make tea. As I brought it into the living room, Abdullah was replying to a question from our guest, "We came to Iran to become part of the new Islamic Republic. Before this, we lived in Algeria, where I taught English."

"I hope you aren't too put off by all the chanting of 'Death to America,'" said Kamran. "Most people don't really mean that personally. They are opposed to the U.S. government, not the American people."

"Thanks," replied Abdullah. "Yeah, at first it seemed strange. But we're Muslim, so we don't feel they mean us."

Kamran became thoughtful. "I'm Muslim, of course. I used to pray every day. Even in the U.S. I often went to the mosque for prayer. It was so peaceful. But with the regime, everything has changed. The mullahs force their version of Islam on everyone. No other ways are accepted. They've ruined Islam for us!" Our guest was agitated. "Living here in my own country since the revolution has changed me. I can no longer bear to go to the mosque. I can't even pray anymore." The poor man's deeply felt sorrow affected me…

He's lost so much:
Prayer, faith, and meaning,
Listening, my own faith quivers,
But I pray:
Merciful One, let him feel your mercy,

He was not the only Iranian to tell me of spiritual heartbreak and loss of faith. Any deviation from the norms prescribed by the mullahs was punished severely, through public humiliation, imprisonment, execution, or extrajudicial "disappearing." As a result, people made public displays of devotion to Khomeini and the Islamic Republic in order to survive. But in their hearts, many had lost the most precious gem, the peace of Islam.

Even this early in our stay in Iran, I knew that some things were not right in this land. Forcing anyone to conform to a specific view or practice of Islam or forcing anyone to become Muslim was forbidden by the ultimate authority in Islam, the Qur'an:

"There is no compulsion where religion is concerned." 2:256

I wondered what Hossein, a government official, thought about this ultra-conservative version of Islam. In my conversations with him and his wife in the U.S, they had presented a modern, balanced view of Islam. Now, visiting them at their home in Tehran, I hoped to ask about this issue.

"Welcome! Welcome! Come in and sit with us." Hossein, a stocky, handsome man with the appearance of a professor greeted us at the door of his home. His petite wife, Zainab, smiled in her quiet, intelligent manner. She showed us into their living room, which consisted of a gorgeous, handmade Persian carpet surrounded by large pillows to sit on.

"Are you finding your way around Tehran all right?" asked Zainab.

"Yes, we've learned where the local grocery stores are, and how to use coupons to buy milk, rice, and eggs," I replied.

"And gasoline," added Abdullah, wryly.

Hossein laughed, "Yes, it's hard to believe that in our oil-rich country we have to wait in line to buy small quantities of expensive gas with coupons. No coupon, no gas!" He softened what might be perceived as a complaint with an explanation of the government's position, "But of course, as we know, the war with Iraq is requiring many resources such as gasoline. Our sacrifice is little compared to that of our soldiers who are fighting in the way of Allah."

"And how have you been, Zainab?" I asked. "It's been so long since we've seen each other!" The last time I had visited her and her family was in the mid-1970s in North Carolina.

"Fine, fine," she said. Something in her voice told me she wasn't well, but I could see she didn't want to talk about it.

Hossein explained briefly, "She was in the wrong place at the wrong time. She was injured by a bomb intended for me. She's still recovering."

Before I could express my concern for her, and for him as the target of a bomber, he abruptly changed the subject, "But Abdullah, meet my son Jawed."

"Salaamu alaikum," Abdullah smiled. He had met Hossein previously but not his family.

"You've grown up, Jawed!" The last time I saw him in the U.S. he was a young boy. He flushed and I realized I should have spoken more circumspectly to this quiet, serious young man.

"And this is my daughter, Nasrin," Hossein continued. "You remember her, Aisha. She has just graduated with honors from one of our best secondary schools."

"Congratulations, Nasrin!" I was proud of her. "Will you be going to college?

Nasrin, whom I had met when she was a child, had now become a bright, confident young woman, but I could see she was troubled. "Well, I'm not sure," she replied. "I want to go to the University of Tehran, but..." she hesitated.

"You're not sure what you want to major in?"

"Oh, I know what I want to major in. I want to become a doctor. I don't know if you've heard about this, but Imam Khomeini has issued a statement about women's education."

I hadn't heard about this. "What did he say?"

Nasrin glanced at her father, who looked at the floor quietly. She replied, "He said that women don't need advanced education, since their job is to stay home, get married, and raise children. If a woman must work outside of the home, she has the choice of four careers — nurse, midwife, secretary, or teacher of girls. I don't want to be any of those things. I want to be a doctor! I've always wanted to be a doctor."

Uncomfortable silence descended on the room. Nasrin, a devout young Muslim, was conflicted. She respected the decisions of the Imam, but she strongly disagreed with him on this. Her lifelong dream was now forbidden to her, not due to merit but to her gender. She bit her lip and remained silent. She knew she couldn't win this battle. Furthermore, as the daughter of an official of the Islamic Republic, she knew her father's career would be negatively impacted if she let her frustration be known to anyone outside the family.

There was nothing I could say to her that would make her feel better. She was absolutely right to be angry. There was nothing Islamic about restricting a woman's education and career choices. The Qur'an does not put any restrictions on women's employment, and in fact, mentions women working (28:23). The Prophet's wife, Khadija, was a successful business-woman before and after her marriage and her conversion to Islam. His wife, Aisha, was a highly educated woman whose advice was sought by women and men.

Not only did Khomeini's policy contradict the Qur'an and the example of the Prophet, but it was also a denial of women's human rights and a terrible waste of human potential. Surely, I thought, Iran needed all its citizens, not just men, to rebuild a new, just society.

The government of the Islamic Republic closely controlled what women could wear in public. When I came to Iran, I had expected that most Muslim women would observe hijab, covering their bodies except for face, hands, and feet. But I didn't expect that all women, even non-Muslims and foreign women, would be forced to do so. Nothing in the Qur'an or the hadith justified this, especially since it involved coercion.

Neither did I expect the strong social pressure for women to wear a specific style of hijab. Traditionally, women in different countries observed styles of hijab that varied with local and cultural traditions, and within those traditions there was often room for personal taste in styles, colors, and fabric. In Iran, there was strong pressure to wear the black chador in public, since it was considered symbolic of the Iranian Revolution and the Islamic Republic of Iran. Thus, it became a uniform for female supporters of the regime, who would wear the chador over a long, dark dress, pants, and headscarf. Older, traditional women wore a light colored, flowered chador, which I thought looked much nicer than the black one.

On one occasion, Zainab took me aside. "I've been wanting to talk to you, Asiya."[13]

I turned toward my friend, expectantly.

"You know," Zainab said, "You really ought to have a black chador to wear out in public. It will show you are a supporter of the Revolution."

My heart fell. "But it's too expensive!" I replied. I had already inquired, and I had learned the price of a single, ordinary chador was about $200 (valued about $500 in today's money). There was no way we could afford that, even if I wanted to wear one.

"I can loan you a chador until you can buy your own," Zainab offered.

"Thank you," I replied politely, but I didn't pursue the matter.

The truth was that despite pressure from conservative friends, I didn't want to wear a chador. It was an impractical garment that hampered a woman's free movement since it required one hand to hold it closed at all times. When I went grocery shopping, usually with a couple small children in tow, I needed both hands free. And I didn't need the flowing black fabric pooling around my feet, threatening to trip me up. My scarf, loose trousers, and long tunic – "manteau" in Farsi – was comfortable and fulfilled the requirements of hijab, in my opinion. I understood that my style of hijab was also worn by the so-called "westernized" Iranian women, so my embrace of this fashion might not be appropriate for a guest of the Islamic Republic. But I stubbornly resisted this politically correct but impractical fashion.

Clothing was not the only aspect of a woman's life that was prescribed by the mullahs and enforced by the Basij, a branch of the Revolutionary Guard tasked with controlling the populace of the country. In Tehran in 1983, a woman who wore makeup or allowed a few strands of hair to escape from her headscarf could be stopped by a female Basiji and berated, harassed, or arrested. It was rumored that the Basij also targeted and questioned any man and woman walking down the street together, often requiring them to present their marriage certificate on the spot or be imprisoned for adultery.

---

[13] While in Iran, I called myself Asiya because it was more acceptable than the name Aisha. The latter was the name of the Prophet's wife, who is disfavored by Shia Muslims for historical reasons.

One day, eager for some exercise, Abdullah and I borrowed tennis rackets and balls and walked to a public tennis court in our neighborhood. As mere beginners, we began by trying to lob the ball back and forth across the net. We didn't get far before we were interrupted.

"Hey! You!" a grubby man on a beat-up motorcycle yelled at us in Farsi. We didn't respond to this rude person and kept practicing.

The man got off his motorcycle and strode up to Abdullah, yelling, "Forbidden! forbidden!"

A second man rode up on his motorcycle, stopped, and quickly joined the first. The two of them were gesturing and speaking loudly to Abdullah. They were acting like police, I thought, but they wore sagging, threadbare, black clothes instead of uniforms. Both were middle-aged, with weathered faces and scruffy beards.

I walked toward them but stopped twenty feet away, uncertain. They deliberately paid no attention to me and were obviously negotiating with Abdullah. I realized these men were Basijis.

The first man said something in Farsi and then spoke in broken English, "No play. You man. You woman. No play here."

"But she's my wife!" Abdullah exclaimed. "Why can't I play tennis across a net with my wife? We sleep in the same bed every night!"

My blood pressure was rising, and I felt the heat in my face. Abdullah was arguing better than I could, and I knew these hoodlum cops wouldn't listen to a woman. I bit my lip.

"No play. You play here. Woman play there," the Basiji pointed to a location hidden behind a wall.

"I play here, alone? She plays there, alone? Ridiculous!" Abdullah retorted.

Angry words rose to my tongue, but I held it. Abdullah and I both knew that the Basijis would not relent. They had power, and we had none, like all civilians in Iran. Disgusted, Abdullah and I collected the tennis balls and rackets and turned to go home. I was silently enraged...

> *Mullahs hate, imprison, entangle women:*
> *Insecure and ignorant,*
> *Mullahs say women must not do this. Must only do that.*
> *Their cops constrict, constrain, control us.*
> *It's not Islam, not Qur'an nor Prophet,*
> *But oppressive, destructive, wrong.*
> *My throat tight with anger,*

"Hey. Aisha, are you alright?" Abdullah asked.

I looked around, momentarily disoriented. We were walking toward a high-rise apartment building. We lived in that building. In Iran. I shook my head. "Oh yeah, I'm uh, OK. Just pissed off."

I wasn't all right, but I couldn't understand the depth of what I was experiencing, let alone describe it to my husband. My second-class citizen status as a woman in Iran galled me, of course. But there was a deeper problem; I wasn't aware that I was still affected by traumas, first as a young child rejected by my mother, and later as a college student caught in a violent protest. I couldn't rid myself of the flashbacks of the police riot, but I tried to keep them contained. As for the childhood trauma, I had suppressed it completely and wasn't aware of it until much later in life.

At times like this, I struggled to contain the overflowing volcano of combined present and past grief and anger. If I didn't succeed in cooling the fires within, I knew I could easily endanger myself and my family in this alien land. I had wanted to hurl abuse at those Basijis, but it was critical that I keep my mouth shut and cooperate when in the presence of Iranian authorities, regardless of how they acted. If I couldn't be pleasant to the cops, I should at least be impassive and silent, so that I might endure and not end up in jail or worse. I took a deep breath and tried to slow my breathing. I thought about my children and walked toward our destination deliberately, carefully watching each step.

In my time in post-revolutionary Iran from 1983 to 1984, I saw daily oppression of women. Girls who sought higher education were denied the opportunity to study in all but a few "feminine" fields. Among those women who had been educated before the revolution, I met several who were removed from their positions as university professors or scientists and told to stay home. They were frustrated and desperate to work in their fields, and some of them were depressed and suicidal. All women in Iran at that time were forced to submit to Khomeini's ultra-conservative vision of Islam at the cost of their human rights.

Today, the situation seems no better. Currently, half of enrolled university students are female, but once they graduate, they are still limited to specific academic fields that have been judged suitable for women. Discriminatory laws and employer prejudice make it difficult for women to find work; only 16% of the total workforce are female, reflecting conservative attitudes and policies limiting their employment.[14]

But women are not the only Iranians facing oppression in their country. As I write this, men and women from all sectors of Iranian society have risen up against the oppressive regime. According to the Human Rights Watch World Report 2025:

> Iranian authorities have continued their brutal, targeted repression even though the new Iranian president has promised change, Human Rights Watch said today in its *World Report 2025*. The authorities have targeted human rights defenders, women, ethnic and religious minorities, and families of those arrested or killed in the 2022 protests.

My heart breaks for the Iranian people. And yet I'm amazed by their steadfastness: despite the ultraconservative clerics, a corrupt judicial system, and the threats, imprisonment, torture, and murder meted out by security forces, the women and men of Iran continue to speak out against injustice. I'm continually humbled by the courage and tenacity of Iranian protestors, human rights advocates, lawyers, journalists, students, teachers, and many others who demand freedom, justice, and a say in the way their country is being run. I pray that their dream comes true.

Checking to make sure I had rationing coupons for rice and butter, and enough cash to buy salad greens, a couple onions, yogurt, and a handful of raisins, I called out to Abdullah, "I'll be back soon. Taha's asleep. Have fun with the kids!"

Abdullah grunted, "Sure." He was immersed in preparing lessons for the lawyers whom he was teaching. Yusuf, Jamal, and Jubair were playing in their room.

Quickly, before Jubair could notice my absence, I wheeled Jamal and Yusuf's small, kiddie bike out of the apartment, closing the door quietly behind me. I looped my shopping bag over the handlebars of the bike,

---

[14] https://irannewsupdate.com/news/news-digest/women-in-the-iranian-labor-market-persistent-barriers-and-gender-inequality/

adjusted my long head scarf, and tucked the cuffs of my pants into my socks so they wouldn't get caught in the chain of the bike. Taking the elevator down to the ground floor with the bike by my side, I felt cheerful about my planned ride to the grocery store. I had always loved biking. I happily recalled the different bicycles — old, comfortable friends — which I had ridden in my childhood, youth, and adulthood.

Outside of the apartment building, I hopped on the bike and pushed off. It was way too small for me, and my knees barely cleared the handlebars as I pedaled. I found it easier to stand up to push the pedals, at least until my legs tired and I had to return to a sitting position. Still, I was in my element, with the wind in my face, moving along on my own power, and quietly slicing through empty spaces in sleepy neighborhoods.

It was unthinkable in Iranian society for a grown woman to ride a bicycle, and the Basijis were strict about removing all joy from women's lives, including bicycling. But having previously ridden the kids' bike to the grocery store, I knew that anyone who noticed me would assume I was a young girl in hijab. The Basijis never bothered me as I rode the bike, though on a couple of occasions I had whizzed by them in the street. I smiled at my deception.

The line of customers waiting in front of the shop wasn't very long. I was early enough to get rice and milk before they ran out of this rationed commodity. Looking at the baskets of vegetables at the side of the shop, I saw that there were still a few onions, which were expensive, like all vegetables. Unfortunately, I couldn't afford a small chicken, which cost the equivalent of thirty dollars.

Tonight, I would make a special Iranian dish for the family. A friend had taught me how to make "addis polo," a rice dish with lentils, raisins, spices, and plenty of melted butter, served with yogurt on the side. This would be a step above the various bean and rice dishes I concocted to cheaply feed the family every day. Tomorrow, I would use the salad greens to make "coocoo subzee," savory pancakes of finely chopped greens mixed with an egg or two.

Laboring back to the apartment on the tiny bike with the heavy bag of groceries hung on the handlebar, I felt grateful that I didn't have to walk the mile back home. And of course, I was happy to be on a bike, no matter how hard the uphill slog. If, at that moment, I had been able to look thirty-two years into the future and hear the fatwa issued by Supreme Leader Ayatollah Ali Khameni regarding women riding bicycles, I would have been dismayed that so little had changed. According to Iranian state media, Khameni proclaimed in 2016:

> "Riding [bicycles] often attracts the attention of men and exposes society to corruption, and thus contravenes women's chastity, and it must be abandoned."[15]

Food shortages and rationing were one of the impacts of the bitter war with Iraq from 1980 to 1988. The conflict began with Iraq's invasion of Iran in an attempt to seize oil-rich Iranian land along the Persian Gulf. During the first months we lived in the Islamic Republic, the war seemed remote to me, but that illusion was quickly dispelled one evening. A friend was visiting us, and our after-dinner conversation was interrupted by the sound of men all over the city calling out "Allahu Akbar" – God is Great – from the balconies and roofs. Looking out the expansive windows in our living room, we saw lines of brilliant color that looked like fireworks in the sky.

"Is there some kind of celebration tonight?" Abdullah asked his friend.

"No, not at all. Tehran is under attack from Iraq's forces, and our forces are using anti-aircraft guns against the enemy. The streaks of lights you see are the tracers for the guns."

Suddenly, I was sobered, thinking of the danger to my family, and thinking also of my parents and siblings, who worried about us being in Iran.

The war intruded into what should have been an ordinary activity, my accompanying Jamal and Yusuf to their first day of school. They were attending a private international school, which taught Farsi as well as English, math, and Islamic studies to the children of foreign diplomats or professionals. Although we could barely afford the tuition, public schools in Iran had no means to teach Farsi to students of other nationalities. We hoped the boys would learn the language quickly so we could place them in a free public school.

Walking into the large front hall of the building, our attention was immediately drawn to a huge mural splashed the length of a wall.

"What's that, Ummi?" Yusuf asked.

---

[15] https://www.dw.com/en/iran-women-bike-against-female-cycling-fatwa/a-19570005

"Uh. It looks like a battle," I didn't know what to tell him about the gory scene featuring young Iranian soldiers with the light of religious fervor in their eyes, fighting against a soulless enemy. In the foreground, a young, martyred soldier fell mortally wounded, his flesh torn open and scarlet blood gushing from his wounds. I was repulsed.

The poster was likely part of the mullahs' despicable effort to recruit children, mostly from poor families, to join the war effort. At the front, groups of boys, ages twelve to seventeen, were instructed to rope themselves together and walk unarmed into a heavily mined area to clear the way — with their bodies — for regular troops. Identified by their red headbands, they were taught that they would become martyrs and would be admitted immediately to heaven. According to the *New York Times Magazine* on February 12, 1984:

> "An East European journalist who witnessed one of these human-wave assaults, in which tens of thousands of young Iranians have gone willingly to their deaths, could hardly believe what he was seeing, as first one boy, and then another, detonated a mine and was hurled into the air by the explosion. 'We have so few tanks,' an Iranian officer explained to the journalist, without apology."[16]

I was revolted at this extreme child abuse perpetuated in the name of God. I cried as I thought of the mothers who had sent their young sons to war, never to see them alive again. I felt sickened and guilty to be a bystander to this crime against humanity.

One day Abdullah received a call from the principal of the boys' school. "Mr. Khalid, your son Jamal has been injured while playing."

Abdullah was alarmed. He asked, "What happened? Where is he?"

The principal replied, "He fell while playing and hurt his head. He's at the clinic now."

While Abdullah got directions for the clinic, I asked Yazmeen if she could watch Jubair and Taha. We drove to the clinic, not knowing what to expect.

---

[16] https://www.nytimes.com/1984/02/12/magazine/iran-five-years-of-fanaticism.html

"He's fine, really," explained the doctor, who spoke flawless English. "I've just been cleaning the wound."

Jamal was lying on an examination table. Abdullah leaned over him, "Hey, tough guy, what happened?"

Jamal's eyes were red from crying as the doctor finished wiping sand out of the cut. "I was running, and I tripped over something and fell down," he said. He had an inch long gash in his forehead. I comforted him and held his hand.

"I'm going to stitch this up now," said the doctor, "but I apologize that we have no anesthetics of any kind."

"No anesthetics?" Abdullah and I spoke at once.

"All medicines have gone to the war front," the doctor was grim. "There's nothing left for civilians."

Abdullah and I stepped close to Jamal on either side, encouraged him, and held him tightly. The doctor sewed the edges of the wound together as poor Jamal squirmed, yelled, and cried. Unable to prevent or lessen my son's pain, I wept, too.

It was an ordinary morning. Abdullah had gone to work, and Jamal and Yusuf were at school. Nine-month-old Taha and two-year-old Jubair were happily playing with their toys on the living room floor. To let some fresh air into the apartment, I opened the sliding glass door and stepped out onto the balcony. What a view! I never tired of the beauty of the huge mountains surrounding the city.

Casually, I looked down at the ground, where people and cars appeared as tiny as ants from my perspective on the 24th floor. Suddenly, my old fear of heights kicked in hard, making me dizzy and nauseous. Panicking, I turned back to the doorway and found Taha crawling out to join me on the balcony.

"Hey, pumpkin! Let's go back inside." I scooped him up and stepped toward the doorway, but at that moment, Jubair, who had come over to investigate, proudly pushed the sliding door shut. The door was now closed and locked from the inside, and there was no way to open it from the outside. Taha and I were trapped on the balcony.

"Jubair, come open the door," I called through the heavy glass, trying to stay calm. I pointed to the door handle, "Pull it like this." But he didn't understand what I wanted him to do, though I tried again and again to show him. He began to cry at being separated from me. Taha, on my side of the door, began crying, too. With my heart beating wildly, I sat down with my back to the wall of the balcony and soothed Taha. Trying to suppress my rising panic, I analyzed the situation.

Abdullah, Jamal, and Yusuf wouldn't be back for five or six hours. Inside the apartment, Jubair was now screaming relentlessly. He was too small to get food or water for himself, but he was safe. On the balcony, I could nurse Taha when he got hungry. And I could do without food and water for several hours. But there was a major problem. Although the balcony was cool now, it would be dangerously hot when the afternoon sun shone on it in a couple hours. I had to get help quickly.

I sat Taha down by the wall and I stood up. Swallowing my fear, I looked down at the ground below, where a few people were walking between the buildings. With all the strength I could muster, I screamed for help repeatedly. But no one heard me. Then I saw a man washing windows a few floors below me on an adjacent building. His back was turned to me as he worked his way along each window. I yelled again and again, but he didn't hear me.

I set aside any thought of our distance from the ground and the narrow ledge that separated Taha and me from disaster. Concentrating, I focused my mind silently on the window cleaner's back. Gathering power from unknown depths, I poured a single thought into his soul:

"Turn around. Turn around," I call silently. "Turn around!"
Over and over, I repeat the words,
Picturing him turning around,
Seeing him see me,
Believing the truth of it,
I feel his muscles working to turn,
His irresistible urge to look my way.
He hesitates and looks over his shoulder.
I wave YES! Help me, help me!
He waves weakly and turns back to his work:
Damn crazy lady, waving like a schoolgirl.
I start over, sending the idea into his back,
Expanding my power into a gigantic drill:
TURN AROUND TURN AROUND TURN AROUND!
Finally. He turns around. He looks at me.
Quickly I point to the closed door,

To the baby on the balcony.
The locked door again.
Help me, help me, help my baby!
He pauses, nods, knocks on the window he's washing.
He talks to someone, turns, and nods again to me.
He signs to me: someone will come.

Within ten minutes a building manager was letting herself into my apartment and opening the balcony door. I burst through the doorway with Taha in my arms as Jubair rushed me. The three of us collapsed on the floor in a messy, sobbing hug. The lady who rescued me wanted to talk, but I was unable to manage any conversation, even in English. I just kept thanking her profusely, and eventually she returned to her duties. Exhausted after my harrowing experience, I needed to rest, but Jubair was hungry, and Taha needed his nap. I got myself together and tended to them.

After the children were settled, I made ablutions, set my prayer rug on the floor, and stood in prayer. Though my nerves were still raw, my heart was full of gratitude and thanks for the safe rescue of Taha and me. Understanding now, more than ever, how much could go wrong in our lives, I prayed for continued protection of my family.

During our nearly two years in Iran we met people of diverse cultures and languages. While Persians are the predominant ethnic group in Iran – about 65% of the population – we also met Iranians who were Kurds, Gilakis, Azerbaijanis, Balochs, Arabs, Armenians, and Qashqai. The Persian language, Farsi, is the official language and is spoken by all the educated Iranians we met, but in different regions we encountered local dialects and languages.

There were also many refugees who had fled to Iran during the Soviet invasion of Afghanistan. Suffering discrimination in Iran, the Afghan men found work in Tehran as laborers, but were paid very little. They and their families lived in flimsy hovels constructed with scrap wood, plastic sheeting, and tin. In the bitter cold of the mountains, their children lacked shoes and warm clothes.

Afghans were not the only ones to experience racial discrimination. Arriving home one day, Abdullah was tense and angry, "You won't believe what happened today!"

"What happened? Are you OK?" I asked. He had been running errands.

"I parked on a side street. Not for very long," Abdullah began. "And when I came back there was this old man yelling at me for parking in front of his house. I told him sorry, I was leaving."

"What was the problem?"

"He didn't want anyone parking in front of his house. I started to leave, but he began yelling at me in English. He said, 'I know all about you people! I lived in the U.S. You people are filth!'"

"What did you do?"

"I went up to him, said 'What the fuck you mean?'"

"He screamed at me, 'You negroes you scum!' I punched him in the face and shut his fucking mouth," Abdullah raged. "Broke his fucking glasses, too."

"Oh, Abdullah this is trouble," I worried.

"He called the police, and I called Hossein," Abdullah said. "The government told the police to stand down. But Hossein told me to replace the guy's glasses and apologize to him."

In these circumstances, we were fortunate to have an ally in the government. I thought about the dark-skinned Iranians or Africans in the country, who didn't have any recourse to racist mistreatment. I thought about the Afghan refugees pushed to impoverishment at the fringes of society. Even in the Islamic Republic, racism was alive and well.

Although this ugliness existed in Iran, we also found Iranians who showed us friendship and generosity. We were welcomed into many homes and found these people to be hospitable and friendly. They loved entertaining guests with good food and conversation, and they were especially interested in meeting the American Muslim family who had come to Iran.

Through Hossein, we had a chance to visit the home of a deeply religious family in South Tehran. Driving into the narrow streets of the area, Abdullah followed instructions he had written on a piece of paper. The narrow, uneven streets of this densely populated area were lined with a jumble of unpainted, gray concrete buildings of various sizes, with occasional shops at the ground level. The people here were poor but fervent supporters of the mullahs.

Abdullah drove slowly, scanning the area for a landmark and avoiding pedestrians who were walking in the street. He took a turn into a nondescript alley and came to a stop. "I think this is it."

At Abdullah's knock, a short man with a full, black beard and heavy eyebrows opened the door, smiling broadly. As he ushered Abdullah, Jamal and Yusuf deeper into the narrow entry hall, a middle-aged woman in a black chador appeared. She stepped forward and welcomed me into the house, lifting a protesting Taha from my arms and cooing to him. Her teenage daughter took Jubair's hand. They showed us into an unpainted room decorated only by a picture of Imam Khomeini taped on one wall and a threadbare but clean carpet on the floor. I smiled at the woman, and in my halting Farsi I tried to thank her for inviting us.

The daughter, Fatima Zahra, came to my rescue, speaking basic English, "My mother says welcome to our home, and welcome to our country. She says how you like Iran?"

I was relieved I wouldn't have to spend hours trying to communicate in my broken Farsi. "I am happy to be here. It's a beautiful country."

"Praise God. And you from America? And your parents?"

"Yes, I'm American and my parents, brother, and two sisters live in America," I replied.

"They Muslim, like you?" The questions came fast now. These ladies were very curious about me.

"No, they're Christian."

The older woman's expression was one of consternation. She conveyed a question to her daughter, who asked me, "But your parents stop you Muslim? Your parents stop you... I don't know word... they don't see you?"

"Oh no, my parents didn't cut me off because I became Muslim," I replied, oversimplifying the nature of my relationship with my family. "They believe each person chooses her religion. I chose Islam. They accepted my choice. They still see me and my children."

Their questions and their facial expressions revealed so many aspects of their culture to me. I gathered that if one of them chose a religion other than Islam, they would be disowned and shunned. I saw from their smiles that they were surprised and happy I still had a relationship with my parents, which in Iranian culture was a vital part of a person's life. I also saw their confusion about how a society could allow free choice of religion, which wasn't the case in this country.

They served sweets and tea and continued to deluge me with questions. Were there other Muslims in America? And mosques? Did the government try to prevent Muslims from practicing their faith? How did I meet Abdullah? Why did we come to Iran? What places in Iran had we visited? Had we visited other countries? What were those places like? I felt like I was being interrogated. But these women were generous and kind. I knew they didn't mean any disrespect, even when they asked me why I married Abdullah, how much money he earned, and whether I was satisfied with him. I wondered if these questions were culturally appropriate in Iran, or if they were just naïve queries from humble women who had no experience with the broader world, inside or outside of Iran.

One evening, we visited a middle-class family in Tehran who were celebrating a special occasion with their friends and relatives. Their living room was a swirl of women and men greeting each other, exchanging news, and hustling to bring food from the kitchen to a long central table. Small children, joined by Jamal and Yusuf, ran through the crowd, giggling.

A young man introduced himself to us in English. "I'm so sorry we don't have any music and dancing," he began. "Before the revolution, we would dance to both Western music and Persian music, but now any music, even in our own home, is illegal."

"You mean even traditional Persian music is illegal?" asked Abdullah.

"Yes. The regime is unbelievably repressive. These mullahs are even more conservative than we imagined possible," he said. His glanced around the room. "Our neighbors and even family members might feel obligated to report us for playing any music. Any one of these people."

Abdullah and I looked at each other, unsettled. But the man stood and moved toward the kitchen. Looking back toward us, he called, "I'll bring you plates of delicious Persian food. You'll like it."

"I'm surprised he actually spoke out against the government," I said to Abdullah. "Isn't that dangerous? He doesn't know anything about us."

"Maybe opinions of the government aren't illegal, only actions," Abdullah guessed.

"I don't know. It seems risky to me."

Abdullah had met many of the people whom we visited during his drives around Tehran to find the best prices on groceries. An outgoing, sociable person, he enjoyed meeting people, and nearly everyone liked him. I'm not sure how he met a wealthy man from North Tehran, but I'll never forget our family's visit to his home.

From the outside, their villa was small and unpretentious, with faded, painted walls, and a garden comprised of dusty, untended bushes. At the entry to the house, we were warmly welcomed by Abdullah's friend, Farzan, an older man with white hair. We removed our shoes and followed him into the living room, where I immediately noticed the soft, well-cushioned carpet under my feet.

"Ah, you feel it!" Farzan said to me. "My family was in the carpet business before the Revolution." Lifting a corner of the hand-knotted textile I was standing on, he showed us one lush rug after another layered beneath it. "This is where we hide our carpets. When the mullahs are gone, we'll be able to sell them."

Looking around the large living room, I noticed that the beautiful Persian carpet under our feet extended to cover the entire floor. It had to have been dizzyingly expensive. Around the edges of the room were pieces of heavy, ornate furniture – solid wood bureaus with intricate carved detail and upholstered chairs and couches. In the center of the room, a long table capable of seating at least twelve people was set for dinner. The wealth of this family was concentrated inside their modest villa rather than on the exterior. In these times, it was safer to give the outward appearance of being middle class.

"Come, come in, meet my wife, my sister…" Still speaking English, Farzan introduced us to at least eight adult members of his extended family. We were served perfectly prepared, delicious Persian food, and while we ate, each member of the family satisfied their curiosity by plying us with most of the same questions that the poor family in South Tehran had asked.

Taking control of the conversation, our host asked, "So you've lived in North Carolina and New York, but have you ever lived in Los Angeles? We have family members there."

"No, unfortunately," replied Abdullah.

"You must miss them being so far away," I added. "Have you ever visited LA?"

"A few years ago, yes. But now travel is impossible for us," Farzan said wistfully. "But you must enjoy traveling. It's too bad you didn't come before the revolution. Ah those were good times!"

Our host regaled us with stories of the great days before the Revolution, when Americans were a major presence in Iran. He told of enjoying the family's summer house on the Caspian Sea, drinking wine with his dinner at a luxury hotel in Tehran, and attending formal cocktail parties at the British and American embassies.

"But all of that is gone now," he lamented. "Alcohol is forbidden, the British and Americans have left, and there are no full-dress parties anymore. Worst of all, the moderate government of the Shah has been replaced with frenzied mullahs..."

"Farzan!" his wife objected, adding some strong words in Farsi.

He ignored her and continued, "Replaced by extremists who are determined to destroy our civilization!"

There was dead silence at the table. Farzan's wife glared at him stonily. The other members of the family, distressed, looked away from him. Dangerous words were being spoken. Dangerous for the whole family. But Farzan had more to say.

"Please," he pleaded with Abdullah and me, "tell your government to come back!"

Shocked at the implication, I protested, "But we're not associated with the U.S. government in any way."

Abdullah elaborated, "We are strongly opposed to many of the things the U.S. government is doing at home and in many other countries of the world." Emphatically he added, "And we came here to help the Islamic Republic."

"Of course! Of course, I know you have to say that," Farzan replied. "You can't tell us why you're really here..." He paused as his wife sharply interrupted him, but he was unstoppable.

"I know you're CIA. Just tell your CIA bosses. Please," he begged. "Tell the Americans to come back."

It was clear he would not be persuaded, and we let the matter drop. His wife tactfully changed the subject, but a cloud had been cast over our visit.

In our time in Iran, there was no U.S. embassy or consulate. There were no American companies and no American expatriate community. In the thirty years prior to the Revolution, over 800,000 U.S. citizens had visited or lived in Iran. Other than the foreign-born wives of Iranian men, only a handful of Americans lived in Tehran. This small community consisted of

Black American converts to Islam, who had come to Iran to participate in the building of an Islamic society. Our arrival doubled the size of this community to six adults and six children. If there were any other U.S. expatriates living in Tehran in 1983, they were well hidden.

We first met Hassan Abdulrahman, formerly Daoud Salahuddin or David Belfield. He was notorious in the United States for carrying out, at the behest of the Iranian government, the 1980 assassination of an Iranian dissident living in Maryland. To escape prosecution in the U.S., Hassan fled to Iran. Despite his history and public reputation, I knew him as a mild, good-humored man who became like an uncle to my children. Hassan and Abdullah became good friends.

"Salaamu alaikum Bro, come on in!" Abdullah invited his friend into our apartment.

"Wa alaikum salaam. Hey, nice digs!" Hassan admired our spacious high-rise apartment with wall-to-wall carpet.

"Heh, well, we've been promised something better in South Tehran."

Hassan whooped, "Yeah, that would be a step up!"

Jubair ran up to him, trailing his blanket. Hassan turned to him, "So who's this? What's your name?"

"Bair," replied Jubair. Then holding up his blanket, he said, "Gum." Inexplicably, that was what he called his beloved blanket.

Taha crawled, then stood, looking up at Hassan, who spoke to him, "And who's the little bro?"

"That's Taha," replied Jamal, who had been observing the tall, friendly stranger. "My name is Jamal, and this is Yusuf," he pointed to his younger brother, who was a bit tongue tied.

"Glad to meet you." Hassan shook each boy's hand in turn. "Alhamdulillah! I bet you're a big help to your mother and father."

"Food!" Jubair stated what was on his mind.

We all laughed. Abdullah spread the tablecloth on the living room carpet and Jamal and Yusuf put out plates and silverware. From the kitchen, I brought some of the food I had prepared for dinner and placed it in the center of the tablecloth.

"Jubair, no! Jamal, get him," I exclaimed as Jubair reached to sink his hand into the nearest bowl of food. "Abdullah, could you grab Taha?" The baby had started to crawl across the tablecloth, scattering plates and utensils.

Hassan was closer to Taha and scooped him up, "Whoops! Wait just a minute buddy!" Taha's eyes widened, and his lip quivered as he looked into the stranger's face. Hassan smiled and winked, and Taha giggled. I returned to the kitchen to fetch the rest of dinner.

Abdullah was the happiest I had seen him in a long time, as he and Hassan got to know each other. The kids were attracted to Hassan's warm, friendly demeanor, and they clamored to tell him about themselves and show him their toys. Bless Hassan! He had brought light to our home and to all of us. As I shepherded the kids off to bed amidst their grumbles and complaints, I observed Abdullah and Hassan deep in discussion. My husband now had a friend and brother, alhamdulillah.

Within a few days, the rest of the American Muslims in Tehran held a little party to welcome us. Hassan introduced us to Zainab and Abu Bakr, who were in Iran with their two children, Muhammad, a teenager, and a little boy named Abdullah. The party was also an occasion for the birthday celebration of Abdullah and Jubair, both of whom had just turned three years old. My kids loved the cake, decorations, games, and the festive atmosphere, while the adults enjoyed the opportunity to socialize with Muslims who shared the same culture and language. The other adult at the party was a quiet, single man, Ali, but he mostly conversed with the other men.

Subsequently, I visited frequently with Zainab and her family, who lived in a small apartment in South Tehran. I loved talking with her about Islam, the children, and our experiences in the U.S. and overseas. She helped me understand Iranian culture and taught me some Farsi. She also showed me how to make some Persian recipes using ingredients that were commonly available, despite the food shortages. But most of all, I appreciated Zainab as a friend. Together we spoke our hearts, shared joys and uncertainties, and prayed together.

While Zainab and I chatted and cooked, Jubair and Abdullah, and even Yusuf and Jamal loved playing together, oblivious to adults. But I noticed that Muhammad was listless and bored. At fourteen, he was too old to hang out with the little kids or even nine-year-old Jamal, and unlike Iranian teen-age boys who would be engaged in the conversations of men, he was irked by tiresome adults. He was isolated and lonely.

Muhammad was not the only one in our community having difficulty adjusting to Iran. All of us were isolated from others who spoke English and understood the culture we grew up in. We were distant from friends and family in the U.S. and from our community of Muslims there. Iran was far from the ideal Islamic society we had hoped for, and we were unable — and perhaps unwilling — to integrate fully into it. All of us were stressed by the dangers of the volatile political situation in Iran. Although Zainab made the best of her life in Iran, she was not happy, and eventually she and her family returned to the U.S. Of all of us, Hassan was best integrated into Iranian society, and he has continued to live in Iran until now.

Though I was a foreigner in this land, I had talked to enough Iranians to know many were anxious about high unemployment, food shortages, and the continually rising cost of living. Poverty was an ever-present threat for middle class families and a grim reality for the poorest Iranians. Most people seemed unsettled by the constant shifts in policy as powerful mullahs jockeyed for power. The Iran-Iraq war exacerbated the pressures on society by increasing inflation and scarcity of essential goods. Even worse was the war's cost in human lives, and those deaths added yet another burden to distressed families.

Iranians living under constant stress sought different ways of alleviating it. Traditionally, they would put on relaxed dinner parties for friends or family, visit each other for afternoon tea and pastries, window shop at the bazaar, or travel to scenic locations some distance from Tehran. What I didn't expect was that some people would use illegal drugs to relax and escape, despite the government's draconian punishments for drug use — public flogging, lengthy prison sentences, or even execution. According to the Islamic Republic's figures in 2022, over 1.6 million Iranians, almost two percent of the population, have sought treatment for addiction at drug rehabilitation programs.[17]

One winter day, Abdullah and I were invited to visit a home where a congenial group of professionals was gathered. In the chilly living room, men and women were sitting on benches surrounding a central table, which was covered by a very heavy blanket. Two women invited me to sit between them, and they showed me how to pull the blanket up over my chest to keep warm. I felt a wonderful heat coming from under the table, where there was a kerosene heater. My feet were hot, my stomach was very comfortably warm, and my head and back were freezing.

Those who were talking fell silent, expectantly watching a man handle a long, black wooden tube. When he deposited a sticky, black substance into a tiny bowl in the end of the tube, I realized that he was preparing a pipe. He touched a lighted match to the bowl, placed the pipe to his lips, and

---

[17] https://iranopendata.org/en/article/one-in-52-iranians-seeks-out treatment-for-drug-addiction/

inhaled deeply. He passed it to the person on his left. I had never seen this type of pipe, but I knew it held opium…

> *My eyes find Abdullah across the table,*
> *He won't look.*
> *I think at him: hey we gotta go,*
> *He ignores me,*
> *Watching the pipe circle*
> *Hand to hand.*
> *Uh. If I refuse,*
> *Will they think I'm a cop?*
> *What then?*
> *The pipe is in my hand:*
> *I pause, uh.*
> *Well, one hit won't hurt.*
> *Probably.*
> *Here goes.*

I sucked hard on the long pipe and inhaled deeply. The smoke was unexpectedly mild, and I rolled it around in my mouth, tasting it. Exhaling slowly, I gauged my reaction to the drug. I didn't really feel much. It certainly didn't have the kick of hash or even grass. The woman beside me gave me sweets to prevent nausea, since opium supposedly causes a sudden drop in blood sugar.[18] As each person took a turn, I looked at their intelligent, cordial faces. They were just ordinary, white-collar workers and family people seeking relief from the stress of life in Revolutionary Iran.

Abdullah and I dealt with the pressure of life in the Islamic Republic by taking the kids on short, weekend trips to different areas surrounding Tehran. Outside of the capital and away from the center of politics, the atmosphere was much more relaxed. People were open, friendly, and not plagued with the paranoia of social life in the city. In the late spring, we took a week off for a vacation in the southwestern provinces of Qom,

---

[18] This is evidently not scientifically proven: https://www.ncbi.nlm.nih.gov/pmc/articles/PMC5061814/

Isfahan, and Fars. With our camper trailer pulled behind our car, we headed out on our exploration of the countryside.

Only an hour and half drive from Tehran, Qom is a sacred place steeped in Shia history and scholarship. But we found that the houses, mosques, seminaries, and even the air, matched the color of desert dirt. On some other day it might have been lovely, but Abdullah and the children were hot and impatient to get out of cities and onto the open road. I had to agree with them, though in retrospect, I would have enjoyed taking the time to visit the Shrine of Fatima Masumeh, named in honor of a female Shia saint to whom many Iranians make pilgrimage.

At the end of our first day of traveling, we arrived at the ancient city of Isfahan. We were cheered by the lush gardens and trees, which nestled along the banks of the broad Zayanderud River. Crossing the clear waters were several beautiful bridges built between the third and seventeenth centuries. The city was a mix of modern buildings and centuries-old mosques, churches, and palaces.

But our family loved Isfahan not for its beauty but for its "Gaz," the exquisite pistachio nougat that was made there. A friendly man gave us a box of the candy, which I hid it in a secure place in the camper where the children wouldn't find it. After leaving the city, we found a suitable place to pull off the road and camp for the night, with the foothills of the arid Zagros mountains surrounding us. After dinner, I took the Gaz from its hiding place.

"Does anyone want a piece of candy?" I teased.

"Yes!" was the unanimous reply.

I handed a piece to each of the children, "Now wait until we all have one!" The children grumbled but waited. I handed Abdullah a piece of the nougat and took one myself. "Bismillah," I said, and brought the nougat to my lips. The family did the same, eagerly.

While the children exclaimed, "Mmmmm!" and "Ooooooh!" I let the candy dissolve on my tongue, chewing it gently to release the heavenly flavors of rose flower water and pistachio. I don't think I have ever had a candy so delicious.

"Can we have another one?" Yusuf asked.

"Yeah, 'notha one!" chimed in Jubair, pleading.

Without waiting for me to reply, Abdullah answered, "Sure! Let's have another one."

We repeated the ritual again. And again. As it turned out, we couldn't stop eating this addictive sweet, and before long, the box was empty. The children weren't the only ones who were disappointed that there was no more Gaz.

If we were impressed with the greenery of Isfahan, we were astonished by the vast green fields and orchards surrounding Shiraz, and the countless gardens and trees that shaded and beautified all areas of the city. Like Isfahan, Shiraz had an ancient past, with its history displayed by the architectural gems throughout the city. It had always been a place that welcomed artists, scholars, scientists, and poets, including the mystic, Hafez (d. 1390), who wrote with spirit and humor of the joys of life, and the ironies. Today, he is one of my favorite poets, but in 1983 I hadn't heard of him.

After refreshing ourselves in Shiraz, we continued our journey. Our destination was Persepolis, or Takht-e-Jamshid, the ruins of the ancient capital of the Achaemenid Empire, built from 550 through 330 BCE by the great Persian kings. When we arrived, the children burst out of the car and ran to explore the broad plazas, columns, large stone blocks, sculptures, and carvings.

"Look! pictures on the wall!" Jamal begged me to look. "Some of the people have round hats and some have crowns."

"And they all have beards," said Yusuf. "They look like they're talking with each other."

A young Iranian man, who was looking at the bas-relief depictions, told us in basic English, "They're people from different country. They come see Great King. They talk and work together with King."

As we wandered through the ruins, trying to make sense of various artifacts, the young man accompanied us. "This," he pointed out, "is Homa."

"What's Homa?" asked Jamal.

"It's a bird..." our informal guide struggled to describe the two-headed, mythical creature in English. "It flies always. Not stop. Not come down."

Yusuf ran ahead and called us, "Come look! A lion eating an animal!" Indeed, the lion in this bas-relief had hooked its paws into the flanks of a bull and sunk its teeth into the victim's hindquarters. Our new friend said something about Nowruz — the Persian New Year on the first day of spring — but I didn't understand his explanation. Later, I learned that in Iranian mythology, the Earth is symbolized by the bull, and the Sun is represented by the lion. In the struggle between the two one dominates and then the other, but on the day of the spring equinox, the two entities are equally matched.

Meanwhile Jamal and Yusuf had run ahead to explore more of the ruins, followed by Jubair. Tired, I lagged behind with Taha on my hip. Turning slowly in a circle, I scanned for Abdullah and found him sitting at some distance on a block of stone, smoking a cigarette pensively. All around me were columns decorated with fantastic carvings of strange, winged creatures and two-headed bulls. Far ahead of me, I spotted my boys darting from one column to another and calling to each other. I sighed, hoisting Taha onto my shoulders and trudging toward his brothers.

"Ummi please?" Jamal really wanted me to agree.

Yusuf and Jubair joined his brother, "Please?"

"No. I'm sorry but that is a tomb," I said. "The dead kings are buried there. We're not allowed to go in there."

"But why?"

"Because people can't be going where dead people are buried. That's just the way it is." I wished I could think of a better explanation. "Come on, let's see what Abu is doing. I'm thirsty. Are you?"

The kids ran to Abdullah, and I slogged on back with a sleeping toddler on my shoulders. After leaving Persepolis, we drove through an area with green pastures interspersed with dry, rocky ground. Stopping by the side of the road to have a snack and check out a possible camp site, we noticed horses and black nomad tents about a quarter mile away. As we drank water and munched on cheese, bread, and fruit, we were approached by a boy riding a horse and wearing the brightly colored clothes of Qashqai nomads.

The nomad boy, who was no older than Jamal, rode up to our camper and dismounted. Speaking in his tribal language, he handed me a bag of fresh, warm horse milk as a gift to travelers. Noticing we didn't understand, he used sign language to say, "It's good! For you. Drink. Milk of horse. My family over there."

We smiled and thanked him in Farsi, which he evidently didn't understand. I signed, "Thanks from my heart. I'm happy. Thanks to your family. Peace."

The Qashqai boy smiled, bowed, and leapt up into the saddle, turning the horse back in a gallop toward his family's encampment.

Jamal watched the boy as he faded into the distance, "I wish I had a horse."

"I know," I replied. "If you did, you could learn to ride like that boy. I'm sure he works hard. But they can go anywhere they like. Wherever there is grass for their horses and herds of sheep."

"Like us," Yusuf reminded us. "Except we have a car. And no animals."

Yes, I reflected, but they lived according to the ancient, natural rhythms of life. They might experience hunger, thirst, or danger, but they were free. We, on the other hand, were immersed in a sea of forty-five-million people in Tehran. We were tied to passports, paperwork, jobs, rules, expectations, and the kind of danger that is hidden behind smiles and pretenses.

The children and I drank the horse milk with enthusiasm, treasuring the rich flavor of the warm liquid. This was a thoughtful gift to our traveling family, far from our country of origin...

Feet on earth,
At home under sun and stars,
We wake under dawn sky,
Wash, pray, eat,
Pack up,
Move on.

After breaking camp, we drove nine hours straight, back to Tehran. Our twelve-hundred-mile vacation trip had reminded me that, for us, home was not a specific place. For us, home was wherever we were, whether nights at different roadside camping spots or months at a high-rise apartment in Tehran. We weren't happy to be back in the city, but we enjoyed hot showers and comfortable beds. However, we were soon to discover just how temporary our city abode was.

After the Revolution, Iran had seized U.S. assets in the country, and the U.S. had seized up to $12 billion in Iranian assets in America. Negotiations for the return of assets were ongoing between the two countries at the International Court of Justice at the Hague. Since the legal maneuvering required skilled, English-speaking Iranian lawyers and assistants, Abdullah and I were hired to teach them. My students were highly educated, intellectual women who had been lawyers or law students before the Revolution.

"Hello, my name is Asiya Saidi," I looked at the dozen students in my class, gauging their expressions to see how much English they understood. "My husband and I are both English teachers, and we came to Iran to be part of the Islamic Republic."

"Welcome teacher!"

"Please call me Asiya. Can you tell me something about yourself?" I nodded to the student who had spoken.

"I'm Reyhan and I studied English at Tehran University. I graduated with a law degree and began working at a law office before opening my own law practice. That was before the Revolution."

"Thank you, Reyhan." I replied, nodding to the woman next to her. "And you?"

"You've all been selected to study English in this class," I said. "How will English help you in your work? And what do you need to learn most"

"We will edit briefs that our lawyers will present at the Hague," said one student.

"Yes, but we are not allowed to research and actually develop briefs," added another woman with frustration. "We can only correct the English."

A third student raised her hand. I nodded to her. She clarified the discussion, "We used to be lawyers, but now, because we are women, we can be only legal assistants or secretaries. We aren't allowed to use our legal skills, our minds, our..."

The other women stared at her pointedly, and she stopped speaking. She muttered to the others in Farsi. There was a fine and dangerous line between describing their work objectively and criticizing the edicts of mullahs who severely curtailed the career opportunities of women.

It was clear that every one of these women were angry with their demotions based on gender, but if they wanted to work, they knew they had no choice. They chose to do what it took to keep their jobs, despite the boredom and frustration. The alternative was to sit at home, depriving their families of sorely needed income.

One day, Zainab caught up with me at the office, "All of the employees are going to see Imam Khomeini next week. It's a great honor! You're going, aren't you?"

"Oh! I hadn't heard. That will be wonderful!" I acted more enthusiastic than I felt.

"All the women must wear chadors. I can loan you one to wear for the occasion," Fatima offered.

"That's so nice of you. Thank you, Zainab," I replied.

She and her husband expected that I, as a guest of the Islamic Republic, would be honored by this opportunity. But unlike devout Iranians, I did not see him as a holy, infallible leader. Nor did I agree with his ultra-conservative stand on the status of women or his repression of dissenting views among Iranians. But it would be interesting to see the most important man in Iran, Imam Khomeini. Perhaps, when I saw him in person, I would feel his charisma and understand the devotion that he aroused in his followers.

The day of the event, I arrived at the office wearing a long skirt, over-blouse, and full head scarf, with the chador draped over my head and held with one hand under my chin. Though annoyed at the inconvenient garment, I managed to keep it from slipping off my head. On the bus transporting us to the event, the other women from the office chatted with great excitement. One woman I knew explained that only certain people were allowed to see the Iman, and we were very lucky to have been chosen.

At the entrance to the building where Khomeini would be speaking, several female Revolutionary Guards frisked female attendees before allowing us into a balcony overlooking the main floor of an auditorium. There was standing room only in the sweat-soaked crowd of women. The level below us was packed with men, and the combined noise from the voices of the crowd was deafening. As I wondered if the balcony could hold all of us, I fell into a vision...

> *Floor collapses, crashing down,*
> *Spilling black clothed women from sky,*
> *Screaming, hurtling toward male heads below.*
> *Deadly rain of women, a bloody mess of black and red,*
> *Women and men mixed, merged, obliterated:*
> *Fatal union.*

I shook my head and cleared my eyes of this disturbing mirage. I saw in this vision my abhorrence of the black chador and its symbolism of female submission. It mirrored my deep discomfort with the overt male dominance of this culture. As in a nightmare, the women sacrificed themselves in satisfying, bloody revenge. I shook myself into reality and tried to stuff this vision back into my subconscious. Trying to breathe in the stultifying atmo-sphere of the balcony, I wondered how likely it might be for this desperately overcrowded space to collapse on the men below. This line of thought was no better than the macabre vision and I consciously tried to shift my attention below.

At the front of the hall, there was a small platform. Standing at the back of the stage was a line of clerics in their severe black or grey robes. These were among the most powerful mullahs in Iran, the drivers of the Islamic Revolution. Some had white turbans and others had black. I knew that in Shia Islam, white turbans indicated an ordinary family line, while black was a sign of the lineage of the Prophet Muhammad. In Revolutionary Iran, the latter commanded more respect and had more power.

Suddenly the murmuring of the crowds surged to a huge, collective shout as Imam Khomeini walked onto the stage and greeted his followers. The entire audience of several hundred people gasped, sighed, moaned, and prayed in devotion. As Khomeini began to speak, I was disappointed to find I couldn't follow his discourse at all because of the loud exclamations among the women on the balcony.

Khomeini worked the crowd, touching people with his words. The people's love for him was palpable. I tried but failed to feel his spiritual aura. I felt nothing spiritual from him. Perhaps my experience would have been different if I had been able to hear and understand him, but I saw only a very old man with a white beard and black turban. I saw the Supreme Leader, a charismatic man with the greatest political power in Iran. I saw the man the devout called Imam, a title of historical significance in Shia Islam. But I did not see a divinely inspired savior. To me, he was only a man.

After work one day, Hossein stopped to talk with me. "Asiya, the man who assaulted you, the border guard… would you consider forgiving him?"

I looked at him, startled. He had never spoken of this to me. He spoke carefully, not wanting to discuss the details of what had happened.

I was puzzled, wondering why Hussein was asking this of me. Shouldn't that man be punished for what he did? He would have jail time, eventually be released, and hopefully never repeat his crime. Still raw from the trauma of the deeply personal, painful event, I found myself unable to ask Hossein what he meant by this request. In retrospect, I wish I had done so.

I told Hossein I'd think about it. He nodded and turned away.

Five months since our entry into the Islamic Republic of Iran, Abdullah and I no longer talked about that fateful day. If he had kept informed about the case of the border guard, he didn't share with me what he knew. One night when the children were finally asleep and Abdullah and I had gone to bed, he spoke, "The punishment had been carried out on the border guard."

Suddenly awake, I asked, "What punishment?"

"He was convicted of highway robbery," Abdullah began. He paused, seeing the shock on my face. Highway robbery was a very serious crime in conservative Islam. "They amputated his right hand and left foot."

I caught my breath and nearly fainted, despite lying in bed. Breathless, speechless, and too shocked to cry, my heart seemed to have stopped for a long second or two. I was wracked with horror, grief, and guilt, deeply traumatized now for a second time by that incident at the border.

> *That man:*
> *A sleaze,*
> *But deserving this?*
> *No no no no.*
> *Oh my God forgive me,*
> *And forgive him.*

Now I knew why Hossein had asked me to forgive the border guard. If I had known the sentence, I would have forgiven him on the spot and prevented this miscarriage of justice. "Why didn't you tell me before, Abdullah?"

"I didn't know," he replied. "I just found out."

Something in his calm demeanor told me this was not true. It would be like him to want the worst punishment carried out against a man who had wronged his wife. After all, at the time of the incident, he had wanted to kill the perpetrator.

When my emotions had fallen to a simmer, I thought about the court's sentence. How could sexual assault be framed as highway robbery? How could robbery, a property crime, include a crime against the privacy of a person's body? The obvious answer outraged me. The mullah(s) who judged the case evidently saw my body as property. And who was the owner of this property? I didn't know what the mullahs would have replied, but I had well-founded suspicions. My resulting rage joined heartache and torment in the cauldron of nightmarish emotions.

Over the course of my life, I've painfully relived the predator's assault at the border and my intense aversion, disgust, and sense of violation. But much worse for me has been the torture of recalling the atrocity inflicted on him. It was an extreme violation of the man's physical body that in no way corresponded to the level of his violation of my body. I've never recovered from this, and I deeply regret the part I played, even unknowingly, in the brutality meted out to the border guard. Forty-two years later, I continue to be troubled by the fact that the man who touched me lost two limbs as the cost of his crime.

Abdullah and I were disenchanted with life in Iran and discouraged about the directions of the Islamic Republic. Instead of the modern Islamic society we had expected, we found a repressive, ultraconservative, authoritarian regime. Many people had abandoned the Islamic practice that had previously given them comfort, but they gave an outward pretense of piety in order to protect themselves and their loved ones from persecution by religious extremists. Here, under the leadership of the mullahs, organized religion had killed spirituality and replaced it with fear. In this vacuum, my spiritual life evaporated...

> *Peace eludes me:*
> *My prayers dreary*
> *Burdens cast into nothingness.*
> *Love recedes*
> *As I wander*
> *The desert of my soul.*
> *Where is the One?*
> *And does it matter?*

The office where we worked was now embroiled in unseen but deadly power struggles between extremists and the moderate administration that Hossein exemplified. Our English classes were cancelled, and lawyers who were suspected of being "Westernized" were losing their positions or even disappearing. Many Iranians believed such people were taken to the notorious Evin prison, tortured, and executed. Rarely was any notice given to their families about their fate. One lawyer we had known socially in Tehran went missing, and his wife came in secret to Abdullah, asking if he had any information about her husband's whereabouts. As far as I know, she never saw her spouse again. Equally troubling, it was clear that Hussein was losing his grip on power.

Iran was unpredictable and dangerous for all citizens, but especially for us as Americans, since we would make a convenient scapegoat for violent factions within the country. If Iranians could disappear, what about us? Abdullah and I understood that our migration to Iran had been a serious mistake. We had now lost our jobs and felt at risk of losing much more. Although we wanted to leave Iran immediately, we didn't have enough money to travel. On top of everything, I was heavily pregnant. I needed a calm place to allow the child to grow within me in peace. I would also require a safe place for the childbirth in a couple months.

When our sponsor, Hossein, was fired from his job, he strongly recommended we move away from the political tensions and perils of the capital. Using his remaining authority, he arranged a teaching position for Abdullah at the University of Gilan, a couple hundred miles from Tehran. We hastily packed our belongings into the car and camper and drove north. Shortly thereafter, Hossein moved his family hundreds of miles across the country to the relative safety of his ancestral home.

Barely six months after our arrival in Tehran, we had lost the security of official government support. We were now on our own, unprotected. It was up to us to try to safely navigate our way in the mercurial, unstable world of Revolutionary Iran. If we faltered, there would be no one to help steady our steps. More than ever, we were strangers in this land.

6

CASPIAN RETREAT
1983 – 1984

"If you can feel that staying human is worthwhile, even when it can't have any result whatever, you've beaten them."

George Orwell[19]

Driving from Tehran through Gazvin, we saw the usual dusty, dry towns and truck stops, but once we entered Gilan Province, we were surprised by an entirely different environment. Before us spread a verdant landscape of rice paddies, orchards, farms, and forests. My heart woke up from its desiccated slumber as I felt the warm, humid air on my face. My feet tingled, reminding me of my roots in the forests and farmlands of America. This beautiful, lush landscape, just two hundred and fifty miles northwest of Tehran, could not have been more different from the semi-arid, mountainous, densely populated, and tense capital of the Islamic Republic.

"Wow! Is this where we're going to live?" Jamal exclaimed as he saw the modern, one-story, wood framed house, surrounded by flower gardens, vegetable beds, and fruit trees. Our new home was in university faculty housing outside of Rasht, near the coast of the Caspian Sea.

"Look at this!" Yusuf yelled as he bounded toward the edge of a thick forest.

"Hold it, Yusuf and Jamal," Abdullah commanded. "You've got to help unload the car and camper. We'll take a look at that later."

When we investigated the forested gully next to our house, we discovered it was home to numerous birds and animals, most of which we

---

[19] *Nineteen Eighty-Four,* George Orwell, 1949.

could hear but not see. The thick underbrush made it nearly impossible to explore the area, but the forest – or jungle, as Iranians called it – echoed with the grunts, whines, howls, chirps, whistles, and calls of the hidden creatures. That night, as Abdullah and I were falling asleep, we heard the eerie cries of a pack of jackals running close to our house. With this clear danger to young children, we forbade the boys from going into the ravine.

The house was constructed by an American builder in the days of the Shah. The three-bedroom ranch-style home was spotless and furnished with modern chairs and couches. The kitchen had an electric stove, large refrigerator, plenty of cupboards, and an easy-to-clean tile floor. I was thrilled to have a working washing machine and even a dishwasher. The latter however, along with the kitchen sink, emptied wastewater into the yard outside the kitchen window. The builders had evidently been interrupted before they finished their work.

Our neighbors, other faculty members and their families, were markedly unfriendly and even hostile toward us. I assumed they resented having a new faculty member installed by the central government rather than through university procedures. I tried but wasn't able to establish a relationship with any of the Iranian women in the compound. However, when Abdullah began teaching English at the university, he made friends among staff and students there, and we began to socialize with them.

One couple, a university professor and his wife, took us on a picnic out into the countryside, a favorite Iranian pastime. While the children ran laughing across a field of flowers, Abdullah and I enjoyed the stimulating conversation – in English – with Hamid and Sarah. After a while, Hamid set up a small charcoal grill, set a teapot on it, and began to grill savory ground beef kabobs. Sarah and I went out into the field to pick flowers for a vase she had brought. In this idyllic setting, my worries receded, and I was able to enjoy myself fully for the first time since we had come to Iran.

When we were invited to Hamid's and Sarah's home, I looked forward to learning more about them. Unfortunately, I discovered that their main interest was smoking marijuana and opium, to which Sarah was addicted. Under the haze of smoke, I learned that Hamid grew cannabis for his wife on a hidden plot some distance from his home. Though he said he had taken pains to disguise the plants and hide his entry to the area, I thought this was extremely risky for a man in his position. He could lose everything if he was discovered. I also wondered whether replacing his wife's opium addiction with weed would really help her.

Almost all our new friends in the Gilan area had a marijuana habit in common with Abdullah. Rahim lived with his wife in a lovely walled villa that had a large, lush garden nestled within the walls. He grew healthy, seven-foot-tall cannabis plants grown from seeds he had brought to Iran after a visit to the U.S. While Abdullah and our host smoked grass and talked, Azar and I made lunch, and the children played in the garden, well away from the precious plants. This grass was a very powerful strain, and it became Abdullah's favorite.

Smoking cannabis was also central to the relationship between Abdullah and his friend Hassan. During one of Hassan's many visits to our home in Rasht, the two men hatched a plan to visit the ancient Alamut Castle in Qazvin province, not far from where we lived. The castle was the fortress of Hassan-i Sabbah, who in the early ninth century founded a ruthless sect which was informally called the Hashishin, meaning "outcasts" or "hashish users." In modern times, the word "assassins" derives from the name and murderous activities of the Hashishin. For two hundred years, the highly trained, secretive devotees were said to have wreaked terror across much of the Middle East, assassinating those they deemed enemies – Muslim and Christian leaders, European crusaders, and even caliphs of vast Islamic empires[20].

Two men with a dark past in common with each other and with the Hashishin, Abdullah and Hassan looked forward to visiting the fortress of the famed hash-smoking assassins. When they approached Alamut, they saw that it was built on a rocky peak with steep sides which made it nearly inaccessible. People in the village at the foot of the lofty fortress were astounded that anyone would try to climb the two-hundred-meter cliffs to reach the top. But Hassan and Abdullah were determined to make their pilgrimage.

The climb was demanding and risky, and it was nearly sunset when they summitted. What they found was rubble. Although little remained of the castle, they had completed their challenge. Before descending from the ruins, they sat on an outcropping overlooking the valley below, smoking hashish in solidarity with the Hashishin and with each other. Abdullah came home very late that night, exhausted after the strenuous climb.

---

[20] https://en.wikipedia.org/wiki/Alamut_Castle#Legend_and_folklore

One day as I was washing dishes after supper, Yusuf ran up to me, "There's somebody at the door!"

I dried my hands and went to the door. There stood a young but haggard woman, her dirty, threadbare clothes hanging on her bone-thin frame. A grimy scarf was draped haphazardly over her head. Her crooked smile and her dull eyes did not put me at ease. She was obviously poor, but there was something odd about her manner. I couldn't put my finger on it.

"Abdullah," she said.

I turned to Yusuf. "Go get your father. There's someone who wants to see him." I couldn't imagine what she wanted with him.

Abdullah approached the door, "Galia! Salaam alaikum." The woman looked at him without speaking. She scratched her arms.

"Who is this?" I asked him.

"This is Galia," he told me. Then, he turned to the woman and said in Farsi, "Not today. I'll see you tomorrow." When the woman paused, confused, Abdullah repeated, "Tomorrow. Tomorrow." She nodded, turned, and disappeared.

After she was gone, I turned to him, "Abdullah, what did she want? Why are you going to see her tomorrow?"

"Oh, she's a friend," Abdullah said. "She wanted to meet you."

"Why?" I stammered.

"What's your problem? Too snotty to meet one of my friends?"

I walked away from him. If I argued, he would become louder and meaner. I wondered at his interest in the strange, unkempt woman, who had asked to speak to him, not me. Her image was opposite the one that Abdullah cultivated for himself. He was always fastidious, with clean, pressed clothes and articulate manner, and he insisted that his wife and kids always dress neatly in spotless clothes.

A week later, when Abdullah suggested we go for a drive in a nearby rural area, I was glad to get some fresh air and a change of scenery. The children happily piled into the car. As we drove through a hilly green area interspersed with small farms and woodlands, I relaxed into the beauty of the rural area.

Abdullah was silent, as he usually was when driving. Then he turned onto a dirt road, saying, "I want to check on Galia. I haven't heard from her in a while."

I protested, "Abdullah, can't you do this some other time? I really don't want to visit her."

"No. I have to see if she's OK." He turned onto another dirt road without hesitation. He seemed to know the area well. When we arrived at a small, dilapidated house he stopped the car, saying, "You need to come in with me."

"No, Abdullah I don't want to go in."

"You have to."

"I have to? Why? You go on ahead." I protested.

He gave me a dark, threatening look that said he would not accept no for an answer. Intimidated, I followed him into the hovel. While the children waited in the car, Abdullah led me through the abandoned house, checking each dirty, bleak, unfurnished room of what appeared to be a crash pad for addicts. We found only two people, a young man and woman huddled in a corner, incoherent and high on heroin. Galia was gone.

Abdullah turned around and drove home, silently. I realized, then, that his sole purpose for our outing was to come to this place. If we encountered police, he hoped they would believe his assurances that he was just a family man who had gotten lost on a drive in the country with his wife and children. Bringing us along on this ride endangered us, and I was angry. But anger was not an emotion I dared reveal to him.

Galia did not return to our door, and as far as I knew, Abdullah did not hear from her again. But even if she had moved on, I knew I was losing him. Although I saw occasional glimpses of light in his eyes when we had an intimate moment together or if the children made him laugh, there were more days when he seemed enveloped in a gray pall. On those days, he wouldn't speak with me or interact with the children.

Now heavy with my pregnancy, I felt rejected by my husband and immersed, as usual, in thankless housework, chores, and cooking. Our diet was too low in protein, whole grains, and fresh vegetables, and as a result it was impossible to cook fully healthy meals for the family. I was home-schooling Jamal and Yusuf while trying to provide preschool activities for Jubair. Though Taha was weaned, he was still deeply attached to me. Constantly fatigued, I had no time to myself during the day, and the nights were never long enough.

Spiritually, I felt drained, without direction. My few acquaintances in Rasht had no interest in religion, other than surviving the Islamic Revolution. I mourned my loss…

Duller than soot,
I'm a rootless tree dying,

I was in this state when Abdullah came home one evening with a highly disquieting report about one of his university students. Heading home after classes, the young student had gotten a ride with a group of people. When the car was stopped and searched by Revolutionary Guards, anti-government pamphlets were allegedly found in the trunk of the car. The driver and passengers were all arrested and accused of working with the Mujahedin Khalq, an active guerrilla group fighting against the regime.

The student, who had no interest in politics and cared deeply about his studies and family, was never heard from again. He had caught a ride with the wrong people. Or perhaps they were innocent and the Pasdaran had planted the inflammatory materials in their car. I didn't know the young man, but I felt keenly how grief-stricken his parents must have been, knowing that their promising son had met a violent end to his life. With my pregnancy hormones at their height, I felt those parents' heartache as my own, and I broke down weeping.

With six or eight weeks remaining before I expected to deliver my fifth child, I needed to find medical support for the childbirth. Abdullah and I had already seen appalling conditions at the local hospital, where we took Yusuf for an emergency. Sitting in the dirty, crowded waiting room, we had been keenly aware of the man next to us, his diseased foot in a bucket of bloody water. The halls were filled with people lying on pallets on the floor, moaning or suffering silently. This was definitely not a safe place to give birth.

Fortunately, we had heard of a private prenatal and birthing clinic run by skilled midwives. On our visit, a midwife showed us around the clean, professionally run clinic. I felt it was important that Abdullah stay with me during the labor and delivery of our child. The midwife assured us that this would be no problem, though Iranian fathers were never present at the birth of their children.

Then the day arrived. "Abdullah, I'm having contractions," I announced. "But there's no need to go to the clinic yet, not this early in labor."

"Babe, just let me know when," Abdullah replied. He seemed nervous and protective of me.

After I cleaned up the kitchen, I gave instructions to my older boys, "Please take care of your brothers while I'm gone," I told them. "And don't go outside. Sister Soraya will be here with you." She was the only one of our neighbors to reach out to me as my pregnancy progressed, and I was truly grateful to her.

When my contractions began to intensify, signaling the onset of the transition stage of labor, I told Abdullah to take me to the clinic. He dropped me off at the door to the building and parked the car as I slowly ascended the stairs to the second-floor clinic. As the pains came faster and stronger, I paused on each step. When I got to the door, I couldn't open it, so I waited, bent over with a strong, painful contraction. Abdullah bounded up the stairs and tried to open the door. It was locked, and no one answered his urgent knocking. A man in the neighboring apartment who heard us opened his door.

"The clinic is closed," he told us.

"When will they be back from lunch?" Abdullah asked.

More emphatically, the man repeated, "The clinic. It's closed. The government closed it."

Abdullah and I looked at each other. "To the hospital?" he asked me.

There was no way I was going to that filthy place to have my baby. "Take me home, Abdullah," I replied.

I had already given birth four times, including one home birth — my firstborn, Jamal — so I knew the process of labor and delivery. First, I took a moment to monitor the state of my body and the baby within. I felt nothing that was unhealthy or portended any risk. My intuition told me that all would be well, and the baby and I would be all right. Back at home, I gave Abdullah instructions to protect the bed with newspaper and put fresh sheets on it. He should start a pot of water boiling, find my sharpest sewing scissors and a brand-new shoestring, and put them in the pot to sterilize. I had him thoroughly wash and dry the baby nasal syringe, and bring me my travel bag, which contained baby clothes and receiving blankets. Then, Abdullah called a doctor he knew who could give him advice on the birth, if necessary.

I hunkered down on the bed, did pelvic tilt exercises to move the baby into position, and let my laboring body bring the baby. Using childbirth breathing, I worked with the strong contractions, which were coming one upon another now. I didn't want to push too soon, but it was hard to stop bearing down.

Finally, Abdullah kneeling at the foot of the bed, called out to me, "The baby's head! I see the hair!"

I took a deep breath and pushed with all my might. Over and over, I breathed and pushed, for what seemed like a very long time. And then suddenly, I felt the baby slide out.

Abdullah exclaimed, "It's a boy!"

I directed him to use the syringe to suction out the baby's nose and mouth, and then place him on my belly, covering us with a blanket. Reconnected with my newborn, I communed with him…

My sweet newborn soul:
I see your deep eyes,
Small cherished being from another realm.
For the first time you are of this world:
Little one, my love surrounds you.

There was one more thing to be done. Following my instructions, Abdullah tightly tied one piece of sterilized shoestring on the umbilical cord two inches from the baby's belly, and a second piece one inch beyond the first one. Using the sterilized scissors, he cut the cord between the strings. And so Shamail, our youngest son, was born in fall of 1983 at our home in Rasht. He had a healthy sucking reflex, and I put him to my breast to nurse, which stimulated the contractions to start up again, delivering the placenta. To ensure there were no pieces of placenta left inside my womb, I examined the afterbirth carefully; there were no breaks or tears as far as I could tell. I was relieved, happy, and very tired.

Abdullah brought the other children in to see their new brother. Searching my face, Jamal and Yusuf looked scared and worried about me. Jubair and Taha were unusually subdued, reflecting their older brothers' concern. Unfortunately, because we had made no plans for a home birth, I had not prepared the children for it. Before the labor and delivery, Abdullah had sent all the boys outside. I didn't know they had been huddled outside my bedroom window listening to the sounds of my moaning and then roaring as I pushed the baby out. I felt so sorry for my beloved children. I assured them I was all right, smiling and giving hugs all around. Though each child got a chance to hold the baby, they weren't too impressed with the little stranger who had caused their mother pain.

To satisfy a legal requirement for the birth certificate, Abdullah rounded up four neighbor women to witness that I had borne the child. They looked very uneasy as they entered the room. Later, I learned that they thought they were going to witness the birth — and childbirth is considered a truly awful experience by Iranian women — so they were relieved when they saw the baby safe and whole in my arms. They sent soup to me afterward, marking a tentative thaw, I hoped, in some of our neighbors' attitude toward my family.

After Shamail's birth, the rainy season was upon us, and the winter skies opened up and dropped torrential rain on Rasht for a biblical forty days and forty nights. This was no moderate rainfall. In the subtropical climate, water poured from the sky like an ocean falling to earth. The children were restless, as they could only go outside to play during short periods each day when the rain let up. I wished we had an automatic clothes dryer for the volumes of laundry generated by the seven of us. Throughout the house, I strung clothesline to dry the clothes I had washed, but it seemed they never got really dry in the damp air. In fact, our skin always felt sticky with the humidity of winter in Gilan. Much as I love rain, the loud drum of constant rain on the roof of the house began to get on my nerves long before the season was done. The area got an average of fifty inches of rain a year.

One day in January, we woke up not to the endless rain but to silence. Jamal popped his head into Abdullah's and my room to see if we were awake. "Ummi, guess what?"

"Uh I don't know..." Just waking up, I was not in the mood for a guessing game.

"It snowed! A lot!"

Yusuf and Jubair joined him in the doorway. "Let's go out and play! Snow!"

"You'll have to wait until I finish nursing Shamail," I answered.

After I put Shamail down to sleep, I looked out the front door. Jamal was right. Six to eight inches of pristine, fluffy snow covered the world. I hadn't expected there would be snow in Iran. Abdullah came to the door.

"Wow! it's deep." He put on his jacket, fetched the dirt shovel he kept in the camper, and started shoveling the front path.

"OK boys, go get dressed in warm clothes," I told them. "Jamal, you help Jubair. Yusuf, you help Taha get dressed."

Pulling string and several plastic bags out of a kitchen drawer, I grabbed clean socks from the laundry line and stood at the front door. Though the family had winter jackets, we had no snow boots or gloves, but I had a temporary solution. After each child put on his coat, I tied plastic bags over his shoes and ankles and put socks on his hands.

When Jamal and Yusuf stepped outside, a giggling snowball fight erupted as Abdullah bombarded them with fists full of snow and they responded in kind. For Jubair and Taha, their first exposure to snow was a surprise.

Jubair flinched at the cold snow on his face, "Ummiiiiii," he whined. "It's cold!"

"Go ahead Jubair, throw some snow back at them," I urged.

He scooped up a handful of snow and threw it into the melee. Then he tried to catch the soft snowball Abdullah tossed at him. "Snow!" he squealed, getting into the spirit.

Two-year-old Taha, meanwhile, was crying to go out and play with the family. He was the only one with a snowsuit, so I knew he would stay warm and dry. I fitted him with the makeshift mittens and shoe covers and let him go out. Slipping on the snow and sitting down abruptly, he wondered at the strange, cold, white stuff. He laughed at his father and his brothers in their wild snow dance.

Feeling the cold in his hands and feet, Taha began to cry, and I took him inside, but not before Abdullah whooped and threw another snowball. Slipping on ice, he succumbed to a volley of snowballs from the boys. I smiled at the uproar of a new year snow celebration. It was a good beginning to 1984.

As the year unfolded, I reflected on George Orwell's classic novel, *Nineteen Eighty-Four*, a well-worn, contraband copy of which Hassan had brought us. I recalled reading it as a college student in 1970, when it was a cautionary tale of possible futures. Reading it again in 1984 in Iran was a revelation.

I could see why the book was forbidden in the Islamic Republic. Not only was it an example, in mullah-speak, of the pollution of Western thought, there were striking parallels between Orwell's dystopian future and the political and social realities of Iran in 1984. As in the fictional world, independent thinking in Iran was discouraged, and a cult-like worship of Imam Khomeini was encouraged. People were under totalitarian control in which their private lives were not their own, even among family members.

But despite the similarities to Orwell's nightmarish vision, the reality of life in Iran was more nuanced. Official control was not total throughout the country, and opposition to the government was widespread, if only among certain groups. When religious extremists commandeered control of the country during the Revolution, the ideals that had inspired the people – and Abdullah and me – were trampled. The new government blocked the people's vision of a just government that allowed for diversity of religious views and personal expression. Instead, the regime followed the playbook of Orwell, who tells us:

"One does not establish a dictatorship in order to safeguard a revolution; one makes the revolution in order to establish the dictatorship."[21]

In post-revolution Iran, Abdullah and I were disillusioned, but worse, we were afraid. The only thing standing between us and disaster was a letter from Hossein on official government stationary that stated, in effect, that Abdullah Khalid and his family were devout Muslims and guests of the Islamic Republic. Any official or guard reading the letter was urged to offer assistance and hospitality to Brother Khalid and his family. Whenever we were stopped by Pasdaran, Abdullah presented the letter. Upon reading it, the guard's initial hostility was instantly replaced by an apologetic bow and fervent well-wishes.

However, since Hossein was no longer in an official position, we knew that if the Pasdaran decided to telephone our former government office, we would be in trouble. The longer we remained in Iran without the protection of a powerful sponsor, the more we risked being subject to imprisonment, disappearance, or worse. For now, Abdullah needed to keep working so we would have enough money to leave the country and travel to our next destination.

---

[21] *Nineteen Eighty-Four*, George Orwell, 1949.

The winter rains finally let up, and spring arrived suddenly, with trees bursting into bloom and warm weather chasing away the dampness. My heart lightened a little. The kids, who had no idea of the burdens their parents carried, were overjoyed that they could finally go outside to play. Jamal, Yusuf, and four-year-old Jubair kicked a soccer ball around, played hide and seek, or took turns riding their small bicycle. When toddler Taha begged to go outside with his brothers, I relented and asked Jamal to take care of him so I could finish up cooking dinner.

After the children came in from playing, Taha seemed more subdued than usual and went to bed without eating supper. I thought perhaps he had a touch of flu, and I let him sleep. In the morning, his left arm was swollen to twice its normal size and he was favoring it.

"Did anything happen to Taha yesterday when you were outside?" I asked Jamal.

"Not really."

"Do you know how he hurt his arm?"

"Well, he wanted to ride the bike," Jamal admitted. "I put him on the seat, and I pushed the bike, but he fell off."

"Ah. OK. He's too little for the bike," I said mildly. It was clear Jamal felt terrible about the accident.

Taha, who ordinarily cried frequently throughout the day for any reason, was not crying now. When Abdullah and I took him to a pediatrics clinic, the X-ray showed that his left upper arm bone was broken. Throughout the examination, and even when the doctor put a cast on Taha's arm to the wrist, he didn't make a fuss. I felt I had been negligent...

It must have hurt so much.
Why didn't you cry?
How could I not know?
Oh my little Taha,
I'm so sorry.
You cry for me, you cry for your brothers,
But I'm too busy, and your brothers too big.

In the deep shadows of midnight, a circle of happy faces turned toward the center, where the flames of a campfire flickered. It was the first day of spring, Nowrus, and people were celebrating.

One man emerged from the ring and ran toward the bonfire, shouting, "Take my yellow and give me your red!" He flung himself over the blaze in a wild leap of joy. He had asked the fire to take his yellowed, winter complexion and replace it with rosy cheeks and good health. Cheers and laughter greeted him as he merged back into the crowd.

One after another, people took turns chanting the ancient refrain and leaping over the bonfire. This was the Persian New Year, an ancient holiday dating back thousands of years, long before the coming of Islam. This popular holiday encompassed a two-week period of festivities celebrating spring, new life, and health.

During Nowruz, all Iranians — even the elderly and infirm — went outside to enjoy the springtime, rain or shine. Families took picnic lunches out to the fields, riversides, and mountains. On the last day of the holiday, each family cast sprouted wheat or lentils into a river or stream. While government officials firmly discouraged the celebration of Nowruz as un-Islamic, they couldn't forbid such a widespread and popular holiday. Everyone, it seemed, loved Nowruz. I marveled at the courage of Iranians…

I can't shed my fear,
But they laugh, sing, jump the fire!
They honor earth's renewal,
Praise family,
Strong together.
Despite grim mullahs,
They look ahead,
They survive.

As the wheel of seasons turned, our family felt restless, confined in our house and the limited grounds of the compound. "Hey what do you think about camping by the Caspian Sea?" Abdullah asked me.

"Sounds great to me," I replied. "You mean, this weekend?"

"Sure, why not? Let's take the camper and set it up in a good spot," Abdullah suggested. He had bought a used camper to replace the now broken-down trailer that had accompanied us to Iran.

"Let's do it!" I responded enthusiastically. To be outside in the fresh air, with plenty of room for the kids to run sounded wonderful. I also was encouraged by my husband's cheerful mood. Perhaps by the sea we could breathe new life into our relationship.

We went for a weekend, and we ended up staying the whole summer at our camp on the shore of the Caspian. Taha and Jubair loved excavating holes in the sand and burying treasures they had found on the beach — shells, stones, driftwood, and tiny crabs. While Jamal and Yusuf collected dried cow dung for the evening fire, they explored the pomegranate orchard and hunted for lizards and insects. Six-month-old Shamail bounced happily in his baby seat, which hung from a tree in our camp. Spinning around, he could watch the whole family as we played or did camp chores. All of us enjoyed long walks along the beach and swimming in the semi-salty sea.

One evening, I stood watching the sunset cast its rosy glow over the gentle waters, which greeted me as the waves lapped my bare feet. I felt nurtured by the earth, sun, and sea...

Free:
Sea breeze whisking skin,
Sun shining my world,
Orchard fresh pomegranate seeds on my tongue,
Sweet red juice running down my chin.
Healing. For me. For all of us.

Heading back toward our camp, which perched on a knoll in the orchard two-hundred feet from the shore, I felt the breeze drop. Clouds of mosquitoes descended on me, so I hurried toward the campfire, which we kept stoked with dried cow manure, creating heavy smoke that repelled the bugs. The smoke also caused everyone near the fire to cough and gag, but we chose that over bloodthirsty mosquitoes. The baby was already asleep in the screened camper and the other children were dozing off in the roomy tent, protected from insects by the fine screen door and windows. The sound of locusts singing in the pomegranate trees was a summer lullaby. I stood listening to the sounds of the night and the pulse of the sea.

Abdullah was sitting by the fire quietly smoking a joint, and I joined him there. Talking softly, we connected and felt peace together.

He handed me the joint. Abandoning my scruples, I took a deep drag. It felt good to share this time with him. "It's peaceful here," I said, releasing my breath slowly. "Look, the moon is coming up."

"It's a good place to be, for now," he replied. "But we need to plan for leaving Iran."

"When can we leave?"

"The university owes me my pay from last semester. And then there's the pay for the summer classes. We need that money to travel."

He fell silent, and we both gazed at the fire. The moonlight silently skipped across the gentle waves that nudged the shore. The night was serene, but we knew we needed to remain alert in the coming weeks. The next change in our lives could happen soon.

Our family lived a seemingly idyllic life on the beach as we swam, played, and collected useful items that had washed up on the shore. The large, wooden cable spool that Jamal and Yusuf found became our campsite table next to the fire circle. Various driftwood logs were repurposed as seats.

One day, when the boys found a few straight, heavy logs floating close to shore, they tried, unsuccessfully, to ride the rolling broncos in the surf.

Watching them, Abdullah suggested, "Hey, let's make a raft!"

"Yeah!" Yusuf responded enthusiastically. "What's a raft?"

"How?" asked Jamal.

"Go ask Ummi for some rope," Abdullah said. "I'll show you." Abdullah and the boys worked to lash the logs together, periodically testing the raft. At first, it rolled uncontrollably, tossing any rider off into the water. With the additions of a couple cross pieces, the craft was finally stabilized.

Putting Shamail on my hip, taking Taha's hand, and calling Jubair to come with me, I walked down to see how the builders were doing. Abdullah was now sitting on the raft, straddling the long, narrow vessel and paddling with his arms. But his weight made the waterlogged platform sink under the water.

Jamal tried next, "Watch me, Ummi!" Kneeling on it and using a pole, he pushed out into the surf, rising above each small wave and dipping down into the trough between waves. His longish hair blowing in the wind as he looked seaward, Jamal's face radiated joy.

"It's my turn!" yelled Yusuf. Since Jamal couldn't manage to turn the raft back toward shore, he hopped off and swam and dragged it back to Yusuf. Watching them and smiling, perhaps recalling his own boyhood, Abdullah relaxed on the beach, drying off in the sun.

Every night, hundreds of pretty, white shells washed up on shore, leaving a white band in the sand. In the morning, the children and I collected these shells in large buckets and hauled them up to the campsite, where we covered the ground in the center of camp. This blanket of shells kept sand from migrating into the tent and camper. Seen from up and down the beach, our campsite gleamed shell-white in the Caspian sun.

Abdullah continued to teach at the university a few days a week and bought groceries on the way back to our campsite. As usual, I supervised the kids, kept the camper, tent, and campsite clean, prepared our meals, and nursed the baby. It was not practical to return to our house in Rasht to use the washing machine, so I washed our clothes in sea water and hung them to dry on a line strung between two trees.

When Abdullah returned from work in the afternoon, he would watch the kids so I could go for my swim along the coast. Of course, this was a public beach and I still had to maintain hijab, so I was fully clothed in long pants, a knee-length, long-sleeved tunic, and a headscarf. Swimming against the drag of my clothes in the water, I gained endurance over the course of the summer…

> *Swim far and farther,*
> *Stoke pull,*
> *Power the kick,*
> *Over wallowing waters.*
> *Rolling over I gaze upward,*
> *Clouds and I floating together,*
> *Then onward,*
> *Fifty more yards!*
> *Oh fish-in-clothes,*
> *Swim!*

Jamal had been waiting for me to finish. "Ummi! Mike stinks awful. He found a dead seal on the beach."

"Oh no! Let's go get him," I replied. Mike was the new member of our family, a German Shepherd dog who was given to Abdullah by a friend. Mike was friendly and loved playing with the kids, but he was also protective when strangers came around. Mike's presence made our campsite more secure at night, but he also added more chaos to the family scene.

"Mike, come!" Mike looked up at my command, ignored me, and threw himself onto the rotting carcass of the seal, rolling back and forth. Gagging at the stench. I decided Mike shouldn't come anywhere near me, the little kids, or the camp.

Abdullah had come looking for us. "Dumb dog! Hey Jamal, bring the leash quick," he yelled, grabbing Mike by the collar. "And the dish soap too!"

Mike whimpered, knowing he had done something wrong. Abdullah took the dog into the sea, poured dish soap over him, and scrubbed and rinsed him several times. After tying the dog up, Abdullah and the boys pushed the dead seal back out to sea, where it eventually floated away from our beach. Finally, the three of them scrubbed the foul odor from themselves in the surging evening sea.

The Caspian was a prime vacation spot for Iranians seeking to relax in a beautiful location, so our campsite became a destination for our friends from Tehran and Rasht. The cares of their stress-filled lives fell away as they walked barefoot on the beach, collected shells, and splashed in the shallows with rolled up pants. The women pushed their headscarves onto their shoulders, feeling the wind in their hair. We all stayed alert for any Pasdaran, who would harass women deemed to be inappropriately attired. Fortunately, with the broad, open beach and limited road access, we could see anyone approaching from a distance.

Our visitors enjoyed taking the kids, particularly Jubair, for a walk on the beach.

"Jubair so funny!" Yasamin exclaimed. She knelt to give him a hug. "We had very cute talk."

"Really?" I wondered what Yasamin and four-year-old Jubair could have talked about on their walk. He didn't speak Farsi.

"We saw crabs in the water," said Jubair. "They went down in the sand!"

Yasamin explained, "He talk very much. In English. I don't know what he say. I talk Farsi. He talk English."

I laughed, "Did he understand you?"

"He not understand me. But OK. We talk and walk like this."

My oldest, Jamal, had become fluent in Farsi as he interacted with teachers and kids in his school in Tehran. Then, in Rasht and at our Caspian camp, he honed his use of the language with our visitors and local shopkeepers. Over the summer, he became friends with a young man whom I tutored in English twice a week at our camp. Following the class, Cyrus would take

Jamal for rides on his motorcycle along dirt tracks in the area. My son was delighted and looked forward to each time Cyrus came to our camp.

After several weeks, Cyrus invited Abdullah and me to watch Jamal drive the motorcycle. Jamal stood next to his friend, grinning.

"But Jamal doesn't know how to ride a motorcycle!" I objected. I was floored at the thought of my ten-year-old child handling a heavy, highly mobile, dangerous vehicle. This was long before helmets and other protective gear for motorcyclists were common.

"Just wait. Watch!" Cyrus said.

"Watch, Ummi! I can do it," said Jamal. "I've been practicing."

I suddenly realized that Cyrus hadn't just been giving Jamal rides in the countryside. He had been teaching him to drive the motorcycle. Reluctantly, I nodded. The demonstration was on a short segment of the dirt orchard road. Jamal drove Cyrus' motorcycle up and down the road, navigating turns skillfully. He shifted the gears with confidence, braked smoothly, and steered without hesitation or mistakes. He was even able to avoid sliding on the sandy road. I was so proud of Jamal, but I still thought he was too young to be driving a motorcycle. However, Abdullah disagreed with me, stating emphatically that Jamal had shown us he could drive, so he would be allowed to do so, at least on back roads. This was the beginning of Jamal's lifelong enjoyment of motorcycles.

We interacted frequently with fishermen who came down to the sea to launch their boats. They were of the Gilaki ethnic group and spoke a distinct dialect, but most of them also spoke standard Farsi. Abdullah made friends with Giv and Arman, who had a fishing shack on the shore where they kept and repaired their equipment and relaxed after working. Often, they came to our smoky campfire and shared hash or grass joints with Abdullah, talking long into the night. Other evenings, they quietly took their boats out fishing — poaching, I assumed. Because of government restrictions, the fishermen could no longer make a living legally.

On one quiet nightfall, I heard murmuring just beyond the faint light cast by our dying campfire. "Abdullah, come look," a man spoke quietly in Gilaki. It was Giv. Keeping his voice low, he added, "Bring your family." Abdullah followed Giv to the beach.

Jamal and Yusuf, listening from the tent, whispered, "Can we go too?"

"Sure," I replied. Peering into the tent, I saw that Jubair and Taha were sound asleep. In the camper, eight-month-old Shamail breathed softly in a dream, his eyelids flickering and his mouth twitching a slight smile. The older boys and I headed in the direction Abdullah had gone. I would return in a few minutes to check on the younger kids.

Our fishermen friends had come in from night fishing on the Caspian with a rare catch — an extraordinary seven-foot-long sturgeon, which was cause for intense but quiet jubilation. This threatened species fetched high prices on the black market, and the proceeds from it would enable the family to survive through the fall and winter, when fishing was often impossible. Giv, Arman, and some family members were processing the fish quickly, without speaking. Above all they wanted to avoid alerting the Pasdaran, who patrolled the shoreline by boat and on foot, watching and listening for poaching or other illegal activities.

Pointing to the sturgeon, Abdullah mouthed "Wow!" to me as I arrived. I gawked at the largest fish I had ever seen. Yusuf and Jamal leaned close to touch the tough skin of the sturgeon and examine its eyes and gaping mouth. Giggling silently, they opened and closed their mouths, mimicking the creature.

Giv and Arman were expertly cutting the flesh of the fish into chunks, which they loaded into large baskets. When each basket was full, a teenager hauled it onto his back and hurriedly returned to the village. A second youth waited for his basket to be filled with the valuable contraband. Finally, the task was done, and a couple men of the family loaded the carcass into the boat and rowed far out to sea to surreptitiously dump the remains. I felt regret about the loss of an endangered sturgeon, but on the other hand, this catch meant life for a poor fishing family.

Our friends built a small fire in a sheltered spot on the beach, screened from the prying eyes of the police. Then they skewered chunks of sturgeon steak and barbecued a feast for us all. Quietly celebrating what was the best catch of the year, they wanted to share their good fortune with us. Despite having no salt, seasoning, or marinade, the kabob was intensely flavorful. The dark, firm flesh was similar to swordfish but more delicate in flavor. My boys were elated at having all the delicious meat they could eat, Abdullah was smiling with a full belly, and I was grateful for this delicious, nourishing bounty. Without speaking, we enjoyed this magical moment with our friends. Then, Giv and Arman brought the secret feast to a close, put the fire out, and faded into the darkness with a soft goodbye, "Khuda hafez."

Our friend Soroush was an early rising farmer, unlike his night-fishing friends. He appeared at our camp one day as I was cleaning up after breakfast, keeping an eye on the little kids, and supervising Jamal's and Yusuf's studies.

"Is Abdullah here?" Soroush signed.

"Abdullah drove to Rasht," I signed back, moving both hands as if holding a steering wheel and pointing in the direction of the city. "He should be back in a couple hours." I tapped an imaginary watch on my wrist and held up two fingers.

Soroush was completely deaf and mostly mute. While he could say some words, he couldn't hear them, so the sound of his voice was often distorted. He had his own, expressive sign language, which I was learning. Strangely, I could comprehend and communicate with him better than anyone I'd met in Iran, other than those who spoke English.

Taha and Jubair came running up to him, "Roush! Roush!" He laughed and squatted down to chat with them for a minute.

Yusuf popped his head out of the trailer with a question about his assignment, but seeing our visitor he asked, "Ummi can we go to the farm with Soroush?"

"Not now, you've got to do your schoolwork."

"Are they studying?" Soroush signed to me.

"Yes," I replied. "I teach them here. Reading, writing, and math."

Soroush looked thoughtful, then said, "I went to school when I was little, but then I got sick."

"Sick?"

"Yes. I had a high fever when I was eight years old. When I recovered, I had lost my hearing completely," he explained. "After that, I couldn't go to school anymore."

I felt sad that this intelligent, warm person had been deprived of an education due to his loss of hearing. There were evidently no schools for deaf children in rural Iran.

He saw my wistful expression and told me, "It's OK now. I help my family raise vegetables on our farm. And my family and friends know how to speak my language. You, too!"

"Only a little bit!" I protested. "I'm like a child speaking your language."

Soroush laughed and signed to the children, "I'll come back to see you later." Then he headed back to his village.

After nursing the baby and putting him to sleep in the camper, I stepped outside into the still morning. Shading my eyes from the sun, I looked far down the beach where the kids were kneeling on the sand, sifting items that had been washed up by the waves.

The day was promising to be beautiful, and the setting was perfect, but I was worried. The problems in my marriage had been temporarily eclipsed by our healthy outdoor life, but my husband had now become more remote from me than ever. For the past couple weeks, he had spoken only in monosyllables to me, if at all. He ignored me as if I weren't there.

"Babe, you've been awfully quiet lately," I remarked. "Want to go for a walk? There's a nice breeze along the shore."

"Nah, I'll pass."

"What's wrong, Abdullah? If I've done anything wrong..." I started.

He interrupted me abruptly, "No! You haven't done anything wrong!"

"Well, what then? If there's a problem, I should know about it. We're in this together!"

"There's nothing wrong!" He was shouting now, "Just leave me alone!"

My tears welled up, and I stifled a sob. Shamail, in the camper, awakened with a cry and I went to him. Holding the baby close, my silent tears fell on his little T-shirt as he leaned back to scan my face, wondering. I struggled to contain my emotions, for Abdullah often became furious when I cried. At these times, he scared me. I was glad the older kids weren't around.

Gradually quieting myself, I took comfort in the love of my youngest child. Still, I knew that Abdullah and I had to repair our relationship before it was too late. I felt I was reaching a breaking point, beyond which my trust in and love for Abdullah would not recover.

Our sandcastle succumbs
To the tide.
Fearing him, not trusting,
I can't love.
Every rejection burns, every silence silences.
Step by step he disconnects from me,

Over the next week, I waited fruitlessly for an improvement in his mood. But his state of mind seemed to be more entrenched than ever. Again, I approached him. "Abdullah, our relationship is dying. I don't know if this is what you want, but if we don't do something now, our marriage will be dead."

Turning away, he shrugged and didn't speak.

"Habib, our love is like a tree, alive and growing," I continued. "But when it receives no water, the tree will die. My love is slowly withering away. Our marriage is dying, Abdullah. Let's save it together."

Abdullah turned toward me, and I felt hope that he was responding to my plea. But when I saw his face, my heart quivered. His hard, pitiless expression exuded sub-zero cold. I recoiled from his hatred and rejection. To protect myself I began the painful process of closing my heart to him. I might feel love for the man he used to be, but not for this man. And I knew I would never trust my heart to him again.

We were in a situation from which we couldn't escape as long as we were in Iran. I understood that he wanted me to leave him, but he needed a wife and children to maintain his image as a family man. Here, as in most places, a strange man alone often raised suspicions among people, especially among police. As for me, I wanted to separate from him, but restrictions on the movement of women in Iran would be a problem. Even if I were able to borrow money from family in the U.S., I would probably be prevented from leaving Iran without Abdullah's permission, and I was sure he would not do that if I planned to take the children with me. I was certainly not leaving any of my precious ones behind, so we were trapped in Iran together, and I would have to wait until we left the country.

Several times a week now, Abdullah brought to our camp a twenty-one-year-old university student, Neda. Fourteen years her senior, my husband was clearly infatuated with the young woman. The two of them walked hand-in-hand on the beach, played in the shallow water, and cuddled together on a log in front of our campsite. I was hurt and outraged but not yet willing to confront my husband.

Breaking his silent treatment of me for a moment, Abdullah mentioned he was interested in marrying her. Wordless, I stared at him. He was telling me, not asking me for permission, which in Islam is required of a man taking a second wife. I didn't reply and turned away.

Neda was evidently considering his offer of marriage, but she knew she would be a second wife and that Abdullah would be leaving Iran soon. This was not preferable for a young woman. She could easily be the first and only wife of a Persian man and live near her family. But I knew from experience that love is blind, so I waited, while my husband resumed shunning me with the coldest, most remote silence.

Meanwhile, I tried to keep my pain and anger in check. Then one afternoon, I had a rare moment alone. Abdullah was at work, and Jamal, Yusuf, and Jubair had gone off with Soroush to see his farm. Taha and Shamail were napping in the tent. It was then that my emotions broke through the floodgates…

Why does he do this?
I've loved and cherished him,
Waited out his years in prison,
Kept his home, borne his children,
Followed him to the ends of the earth.
Howling, I rage and grieve love lost.
I scream and wail,
Legs trembling,
Eyes swollen, face dripping tears and snot.

My core meltdown was interrupted by a sound, an insistent knocking on the side of the camper, and then a voice, "Madam, are you alright? Madam, please, do you need help?"

I stopped and wiped my face. A worried man was at the door. I had never seen him before. Perhaps he was picnicking nearby with his family. "No. I'm OK," I replied, knowing I was clearly not. Then I heard something else, my babies crying in the tent. I straightened up and went to comfort them.

A couple days later, I learned that Neda had decided against marrying Abdullah. I felt dull relief. My husband was now talking and acting normally with me, and he did not discuss what had happened. Instead, he acted as if we could go back to the way we had been, as if I would forget the intense pain I had experienced in the face of his repudiation.

Our marriage was precarious long before Neda came on the scene. But now it was shattered. If any good came of the past four years, it was that I now had seen a hidden side of him. And more importantly, I was beginning to understand my own weaknesses. I had been naïve and had ignored early warning signs in our relationship. I had abandoned my principles and my religion not only because of disillusionment with the Islamic Republic of Iran, but also because I put my relationship with Abdullah above my relationship with Allah. Instead of turning to the One for compassion and direction, I turned to my husband, who, like any human, could not meet my spiritual needs. I wandered in a wasteland of despair instead of working to bring Spirit to my life and to my children.

One day as I swam in the sea along the coast, I was roused from my concentration by a disturbance in the rhythm of the waves. Then I became aware of the sound of a motor as a small boat pulled alongside me. Two men in the skiff yelled repeatedly at me to go ashore. I realized they were Pasdaran, who had a reputation of harassing anyone they pleased, for any reason. But I was going to finish my swim. I was fully covered according to Iranian law, and I didn't believe they had any right to stop me from exercising in the water. Stubbornly, I ignored them and kept swimming.

After I had swum half a mile, I turned toward the beach and emerged from the sea, dripping gallons of water from my long clothes. Without looking at the Pasdaran, who had beached their boat and stepped onto the shore, I walked casually back toward our camp. Though I was seething, I tried to act as if I didn't have a care.

Fortunately, the men following me were met by one of our Iranian visitors, who had seen the cops' interaction with me. She placated them by explaining that I was a guest of the government and didn't speak Farsi.

The Pasdaran declared that women were forbidden to swim in this area. I was not to swim unless I went to the women's beach at Bandar-e Anzali, a small, crowded piece of sand and a wading area screened off from public view. These ignorant men made a rule just for me, because they couldn't tolerate a woman acting like an equal human being…

> *My fury rises, frothing whitecaps.*
> *I churn foaming loathing.*
> *They do not own me. I'm free.*
> *Sea whispers: Wait. Watch those malicious men pass.*

Sea soothes: Peace, sister. Shush, shush, my waves roll.
Sea urges: When coast is clear of human debris. Then come to me.

This wasn't our only encounter with the authorities at our beach camp. One morning I had just finished washing the laundry in the sea and hauling the heavy, wet clothes back from the shore. Setting the laundry basket down next to the camper, I went inside to fetch some clothespins. Abdullah was there, standing at the wide front window and intently watching something outside. Turning, I saw two cars quickly descend on the campsite and come abruptly to a halt in the sand. Men dressed in military fatigues piled out of the cars with weapons in hand and surrounded the camper. Abdullah sized up the situation and handed me his stash of marijuana. "Hide this," was all he said, and he went out of the camper to talk to the Pasdaran.

Swallowing my fear, I pushed his plastic-wrapped stash into the bottom of the laundry basket and carried it behind the camper to the clothesline. Bending to lower the heavy basket to the ground, I surreptitiously glanced at the guards. Abdullah had tied Mike up and was talking with the men in a friendly way, inviting them into the camper. As I hung up the clothes, I made sure no one was looking my way. Then, as I moved to hang up a pair of socks, I dropped them, seemingly by accident. When I stooped to retrieve them, I extracted the bundle of grass from the basket and pushed it deep under a nearby bush.

Heart pounding, I finished hanging the laundry. Then I busied myself with cleaning up the campsite and keeping the children occupied, while the Guards talked with Abdullah. I acted calm, but inside I was boiling. Abdullah had placed me in harm's way, and if he and I had been arrested for drug possession, our children would have been taken away, never to be found again in dark Iran.[22]

After a half hour or so, the Pasdaran left us with wishes for good health, much to my relief. Abdullah had leveraged his considerable charisma, impressing the men with his openness, honesty, and piety, and of course, with his connection to the central government in Tehran. The guards had been suspicious about our shortwave radio since Russia, situated directly

---

[22] My friend Zaynab had told me of her friend, an American Muslim widow in Iran whose only child, a boy, was taken away from her to be raised by the mullahs. Her repeated requests for the return of her son were refused.

across the Caspian from Iran, was considered a major enemy of the Islamic Republic. They seemed disappointed to find that our radio was just a commercially available device with no transmission capabilities. Then, they questioned Abdullah about some cryptic markings on the calendar. When he told them that his wife marked the days of her menstrual period for birth control purposes, they were abashed, and the interrogation quietly ended.

Abdullah's charm saved us in this encounter, but I was alarmed by the unnecessary risks he was taking in a country which was inherently dangerous to him and his family, even without the crime of possession and use of an illegal drug. I was beginning to see that for him, smoking marijuana was not just a pleasant diversion or way to relax, but something he could not do without, despite the perils.

By early September, the white shells we had collected to adorn our campsite had stopped washing up on the shore. Nights were a bit longer, fewer vacationers walked the beach, and it was clear that summer was coming to an end. The last friend to visit us at our camp was Hassan. As usual, he spent time with the kids, splashing in the sea, building sandcastles, and engaging them in long conversations as they walked on the beach. I was gratified to see my kids develop this kind of relationship with an adult outside the family. But I was also pleased with Hassan's impact on Abdullah. When his best friend was around, Abdullah was closest to being the man he was when I met him: mellow, generous, and thoughtful. After the increasingly abrasive behavior I had witnessed in him during the summer, I was relieved to see the change in him. But though I could breathe easily now, I was not reassured, for I hadn't forgotten what I had learned.

On this visit, I had a brief glimpse into another side of Hassan's character. When I went looking for Abdullah to announce that dinner was ready, I found the two of them leaning on the side of the car and laughing. Hassan prominently displayed his nine-millimeter pistol like an American thug in some movie. Though he was joking around, that outlaw pose and its implication of lawless, vicious violence shocked me because it contrasted so starkly with my experience of Hassan as an easygoing and compassionate man. I knew of his radical past and had heard about the murder he had committed in the U.S. I wondered if he, like Abdullah, had a dark, hidden side.

Opening the camper door, I stepped outside and paused to sniff the cool, morning air that heralded autumn. Overnight, it had rained, washing away the dust from the leaves of the pomegranate trees. The orchard glistened with moisture, and some of the leaves had curled and fallen from the trees, littering the ground. Jamal and Yusuf were already awake, dressed, and kicking the leaves into piles.

"Hey Jamal and Yusuf," I called, "help Jubair and Taha get their shoes on so they can play, too."

"Sure! Hey Ummi watch this!" exclaimed Yusuf as he took a running leap and landed on a small pile of damp leaves, sliding to a halt on his back.

"Cool! Look, you've got a few more minutes, and then it's time for chores," I said.

"Awww."

"After breakfast," I finished. All the kids perked up at that.

I put the coffee on and began to slice the previous day's bread and dip it in a mixture of egg and milk. I set it aside while I made some strong green tea, added a cup of sugar, and boiled it for a few minutes. This was our "syrup" for the French toast I would fry for breakfast.

"Mmmmm, smells great!" Abdullah had returned from a trip to the local grocery store, bringing fresh bread, milk, eggs, cheese, and of course his cigarettes. "It was cold last night. We need to be moving off the beach and getting ready to for the trip."

I noted he was in a good mood. "What about your pay from the university?" He had been waiting months to get paid for his work.

"They told me the check would be ready this week. I really hope they're right."

Over breakfast, I nursed Shamail while Abdullah and I continued the discussion as we ate. The kids silently devoured the French toast along with small cups of milk, a special treat.

"So, we've got to get out of here," Abdullah said. "But where will we be safe and able to get jobs? Preferably a Muslim country. Not a developed country with computer security systems. A country we could get to without going through Europe." He paused, thinking. We had managed to avoid problems while traveling in Western countries on our way to Iran, but we didn't want to push our luck.

I cleared the table and directed the older boys to take the little ones out to play. Shamail had fallen asleep, and I gently laid him on the front bed of the trailer.

"You know, Abdullah," I said, "a few weeks ago, when Azar and Rahim visited us, they brought a guest, a young woman from Malaysia. Do you remember? I had a chance to talk with her and her English was excellent. She says that Malaysia is a beautiful, culturally diverse country, and very welcoming to foreigners. It's a Muslim country, but not conservative like Iran. And many people speak English besides their native language. She's returning to her country soon and gave me her phone number and address."

"Hmm. Sounds interesting," he said as he pulled out our collection of maps and opened one on the table. "From Pakistan, we could travel across India, Burma, Thailand, and into Malaysia, by land or sea, depending on local conditions. Maybe we could get jobs there." Abdullah was thoughtful.

"A while back you had talked about East Africa," I said. "What about that option? If we can't go through Europe, how would we get there?"

"Look here." He opened two maps and laid them side by side. "Karachi is the major port of Pakistan. We could drive across Iran to Pakistan and then south to Karachi. Perhaps we could catch a ship, with our car and camper, sailing southwest across the Indian Ocean to East Africa."

"To what country? Somalia? Kenya? Tanzania?"

"Well, any port would do, but our goal would be Tanzania. It's independent, socialist, stable, and there are plenty of Muslims there. Politically, Kenya's too close to Britain and the West. Somalia is mostly Muslim, but it's unstable."

"That sounds cool." I was beginning to feel hopeful about our plans to escape Iran. I sensed the strengthened bond between us as we faced the challenges of the immediate future together. "How do we know there's a ship from Pakistan that goes to Africa?"

"We'd have to go to Karachi and find that out," Abdullah replied. "That's it Habiba! We've got Plan A for Malaysia. If that doesn't work out, Plan B will take us to Africa."

I felt myself relaxing into the moment...

He smiles, calls me beloved,
And something stirs,
Hope thawing me.
Something else says:
Be careful, remember!

As soon as Abdullah got paid, we cleaned out our faculty housing unit in Rasht, loaded up the car and camper, and moved to a "beach house" he had rented not far from our campsite. Though it had parking for the car and camper and running water, the windowless concrete building with a steel door was cold and cheerless. This was to be our staging area as we prepared for our next, long journey. Abdullah got busy doing maintenance and repair on the car and camper.

Meanwhile, I organized all our belongings, packed them into the camper, and bought provisions for the long trip ahead. Jamal and Yusuf were spared from their studies and set to the task of supervising Jubair and Taha. With Shamail strapped to my back, I toiled among the stacks of belongings in the frigid building. In the evenings, we gathered around a small fire we built to keep warm. At night, we huddled in sleeping bags on the hard floor.

It was now October, bitterly cold and rainy, and we shivered despite the campfire. With the sea so rough and uninviting, none of us were interested in walks on the beach. We were saddened that Giv's aging father had to keep fishing in this weather, wading in the frigid surf to cast his fishing nets. Increasingly violent storms swept in from the north and howling winds from Russia roared down over the Caspian.

Finally, with the wind at our backs, we said goodbye to our fishermen friends, Giv and Arman, and the farmer, Soroush. We had two possible plans for our immediate future, but the first obstacle to either plan was getting out of the country. We didn't know if we'd be allowed to leave Iran, now that our sponsor, Hossein, was no longer in power. Without his protection, any official who wanted to bolster his political standing could arrest Abdullah and me as American spies, imprison us, and give our children away to supporters of the regime.

Though there was no one to vouch for us if we encountered problems at the border, it was a risk we would have to take. It was clearly not safe to stay in Iran. We turned toward Tehran for final preparations and more farewells. From there, we would be journeying into an uncertain future.

7
THE COLDEST WINTER
1984-1985

"Serve Allah and join not any partners with Him; and do good – to parents, kinsfolk, orphans, those in need, neighbors who are of kin, neighbors who are strangers, the companion by your side, the wayfarer..."

Qur'an 4:36

Hassan stood in the doorway of his Tehran apartment, calling out to Abdullah, "Hey Bro! Come on in!" Turning to the kids, he welcomed them with the nicknames he had concocted for them, "Hey there Radar! What's up Big U? Come here JoBay, you too Bahbah Taha!" We filed in and set down our overnight bags, looking around the clean, modest dwelling. Hassan went into his kitchen to make tea for us, as the kids fanned out and explored every square inch of the place. Hassan was amused at this sudden invasion and set out some cakes on a low table to attract the troops.

"So have you decided where you're going?" he asked.

Abdullah replied, "Yeah, we have a couple ideas. First plan is to go to Malaysia. If we can't do that, we'll take a ship to East Africa. Take a look and tell me what you think," he said, spreading out a map and describing the details of each trip.

"Do you think you'll be able to get out of Iran?" wondered Hassan.

"I don't know," replied Abdullah. "There's no way of knowing. We'll just have to try."

Hassan looked worried, "Maybe you'll get lucky. Well, if you can't get through border control, just come back here and we'll figure something out. I'm with you, you know that."

After staying with Hassan for several days while we obtained visas for Pakistan and made last minute preparations, we said a poignant goodbye to our friend. I uttered a silent prayer as we pulled away from the curb. Our car was in good shape, but it carried two adults, five children, and a dog, and it would be pulling the heavy camper trailer packed with our belongings. Travel would be slow on our trip southeast across Iran and on to our destination.

Leaving Tehran behind, the terrain gradually gave way to barren steppes and desert. People in this arid region lived in traditional clusters of adobe houses that sheltered the inhabitants from brutally hot summers, freezing winters, and corrosive sandstorms. Graceful, round roofs covered the houses and walkways of the village.

In this part of Iran, we saw ancient qanats — large, regularly spaced mounds that marked the location of hand-dug wells dotting the landscape. Three thousand years ago, the Persians learned how to dig a series of vertical shafts into the hard ground to access the water table deep below the arid earth. While one hole in a series was the primary connection to the water below ground, others were used for digging and maintaining an underground sloping channel which carried the water from the mother well to the surface for irrigation.

Abdullah and I settled into our traveling pattern, relaxed in the monotony of driving long distances and yet alert to any dangers or threats to our security. While traveling, we had defined roles. He was responsible for driving and maintaining the car, as well as security and dealing with visas, border crossings, and paperwork. I oversaw operations — navigating the course of our travel, supervising the kids, feeding the family, setting up camp in the evening, breaking camp in the morning, and packing the car and camper. The children's job was to quietly entertain themselves and refrain from squabbles in the car. Jubair and Taha observed their older brothers and learned to do the same. Baby Shamail would soon learn, too.

My relationship with Abdullah became closer than ever, as we pulled together to face whatever would come on the coming days and weeks...

> *On the road.*
> *Uncertainty but peace,*
> *Moving toward tomorrow.*
> *Survival depends on both of us*
> *Strong, merged as one.*

After hours of driving on the long, two-lane highway, the children and dog were asleep in the back, but I was awake in the front passenger seat, with the baby sleeping on my lap. When Abdullah stopped at a gas station to refuel, he handed me a small bag of grass and some cigarette rolling papers, asking, "Could you make me a couple joints? I'm going into the store to get some cigarettes." Rolling joints was another one of my tasks. It made me nervous that we were carrying grass on this journey, but I knew Abdullah needed it to stay alert and keep his energy high while driving.

Careful to not awaken Shamail, I shifted him into the driver's seat. Then I slouched down in the passenger seat so that my movements were not visible to anyone outside the car, I began preparing some papers and filling them with pinches of grass. When I finished rolling the joints, I glanced to my right, where a large tractor trailer had pulled up to the adjacent pumps. With shock, I realized the driver of the rig had been looking down from his window at me with astonishment as he watched a proper woman in modest hijab rolling marijuana cigarettes. The trucker laughed heartily at catching me, but I was scared, not amused. If the Posdaran discovered us, we'd be in deep trouble.

When Abdullah came back to the car, I was in a panic. "We've got to leave quickly! That trucker saw me rolling the joints!" For the next several hours, Abdullah drove as fast as he could and kept an eye on the rearview mirror in case the trucker followed us, or a car full of Posdaran was gaining on us. But we didn't see the trucker again, and we encountered no trouble from the police. When we realized we were in the clear, we relaxed. I imagined the trucker continuing his long-distance drive, chuckling about the lady who rolled joints. Later, he would have a good tale to tell his buddies. Fortunately for us, he was just a regular Iranian, not a fervent government supporter.

As we approached Zahedan, the last city in Iran before the border, we encountered people called Balochs, an ethnic group that lived not only in Iran but also in Pakistan and Afghanistan. The men wore long robes and turbans, like traditional men in North Africa, and women dressed in long tunics, colorful scarves, and loose pants, a style frequently seen in Pakistan. The Baloch people are mostly Sunni Muslim, a small religious minority among the Muslims in Iran. As we passed a mosque, I heard the call to prayer chanted in the haunting, melodious Sunni fashion. That beautiful sound made tears rise to my eyes.

But all was not peaceful among the Balochs. At one roadside stop we encountered people who were openly hostile toward outsiders and would not tell us where to get water, food, or gas. We thought there might be resistance among the Balochs against the central government in Iran. Whatever the cause of the hostility among the locals, we knew we were not safe in the area and kept driving.

Hot and thirsty and unable to obtain drinking water, we bought a couple dozen bottles of soda at one outpost. At first, the kids were excited to have Fanta and 7 Up, but it wasn't long before they only wanted plain water. Since I was nursing Shamail, at least he had plenty to drink for the moment, but I worried that the lack of water would decrease or stop my milk supply altogether. We could give our poor dog, Mike, little water to drink. And when we opened the car windows to get a breeze while driving in the heat of the desert, hundreds of large black flies filled the car, making us even more miserable. The kids tried to drive the flies out by swatting them with a towel, with little success.

The driving conditions worsened steadily, with blowing sand encroaching on the paved road, and gullies cutting across the roadbed. Our speed slowed to a crawl. At one point, we were shocked to see the truck ahead of us veer off the road onto the hard packed desert and then brake to a stop. Abdullah stopped driving and watched the truck.

"What's he doing?" I asked Abdullah.

"He's waving us to follow him."

"Is it a trap?" I was leery.

"Uhhh…"

The truck driver again beckoned as his vehicle began to move forward. On instinct, Abdullah decided to follow the trucker, whom he felt was taking a known short cut around the increasingly impassable road. The truck driver's good deed and Abdullah's gut reaction saved us from potential catastrophe. We later learned that several vehicles had gotten stuck in sand or broken their axles on the road to the border. Following the trucker, we drove over relatively smooth, hard desert for many miles, avoiding the dangers of the road.

The Iranian soldiers at the border looked listless from the heat. Taking a deep breath and relaxing his face into an open expression, Abdullah gathered our passports, got out of the car, and walked toward the small, dusty building marked with the symbol of the Islamic Republic of Iran. I offered a prayer for our protection as he entered. Keeping the children in the car, I distributed sips of soda to them. They were tired, dirty, and thirsty.

Jamal made a face and refused the syrupy drink, asking, "When can we have water?"

"I don't know. Soon, I hope. As soon as we can find some."

"Where are we?" asked Yusuf, watching the door Abdullah had entered.

"We're at the border between Iran and Pakistan," I answered. "Oh, here comes Abu."

Abdullah got in the car slowly and deliberately, and then pulled out of the sandy lot and onto the road toward Pakistan. We had been cleared to leave Iran. Evidently, no Iranian official had put our names on a list that would result in our detainment and arrest. That was good to know, but Iran was behind us now. At the Pakistan border, we passed through customs easily. I was suddenly cheerful, something I hadn't felt for a long time.

"We made it!" I exclaimed, turning to Abdullah.

"Babe, I am so glad to be out of Iran," he replied. He smiled, putting his arm around my shoulder. "Let's see where we can get some water."

His hand warm,
His smile radiant,
The man I love is back.
World of tension behind,
Our future ahead,
I hope.

We stopped at a major truck stop, where dozens of worn but brightly decorated trucks were parked, with colored lights, dangling mirrors, and Pakistani-style painted designs. The drivers were resting before resuming their travels, either west into Iran with imported goods, or northeast to Quetta and Islamabad, or south to Karachi. Some might even be bound east into India. As Abdullah was inquiring about water and food, we were met by the Pakistani military officer in charge of the border station. Dressed very smartly in his perfectly groomed uniform, the officer's erect posture was a startling contrast to the rough-spoken, grimy truckers who were gathered at the border. He spoke English with a very proper British accent.

"Welcome to Pakistan!" the officer said. "You've had a difficult journey I imagine, with your car — and the camper, too — crossing the sandy desert!"

"Just when the road was getting worse, a trucker helped us," replied Abdullah. "He led us on a detour across hard-packed desert."

"God was with you!" exclaimed the officer.

"Alhamdulillah!" both Abdullah and I replied.

"Come," he told Abdullah. "I'll show you where to fill up your jerry cans with drinking water."

When Abdullah returned, we were all grateful for clean water to drink. Then, as I began to prepare a quick meal for the family, the border officer returned, carrying a tray. He offered each of us a cup of "milky tea" as he called it. The hot black tea with milk and sugar was delicious and refreshing. The children were positively enthusiastic. I reflected that this man had a position of total authority at the post, where he was obeyed without question. Yet here he was humbly serving us tea and talking kindly with the children. What a warm welcome this kind man gave us as we entered Pakistan.

We camped at the border station a couple days, cleaning up the caravan, washing our bodies and clothes, doing maintenance on the car, and resting. One of those days, we heard a commotion among the truck drivers, who had been listening intently to a radio and exclaiming in loud voices. Abdullah investigated and learned that Indira Gandhi, prime minister of India, had just been assassinated by Punjabi separatists who often took shelter in Pakistan. The border of India with Pakistan was therefore closed indefinitely. The date was October 31, 1984, and this international event had just nullified our plan to travel through India and on toward Malaysia. As I recall, the border was closed at least a year following the assassination.

We were now focused on our backup plan to travel to East Africa. After a good night's sleep, we began the next stage of our journey, driving winding roads through a rugged valley surrounded by awe-inspiring, barren, mountainous terrain. The road paralleled a railroad track that climbed upward along the mountainside.

"Look! a choo-choo train!" Jubair was excited. It looked just like the heroic, old-fashioned steam engine in one of his story books. Black smoke was pouring out of its stack as it pulled a dozen rail cars up a narrow track dug into the steep slope.

Jamal and Yusuf looked at the train with longing, remembering that story. "Can we ride on it?" asked Yusuf.

"Sorry, Yusuf…" I began, then gasped as an oncoming truck appeared in front of us.

"What the hell!" Abdullah exclaimed as he quickly swerved to avoid a crash. Driving in Pakistan was hair-raising, with wild truck drivers barreling fast around curves, often on the wrong side of the road.

Gradually the road gained altitude through the mountains, bringing us to the city of Quetta, at over 5,500 feet altitude. Near the Afghanistan border, this large town was a crossroads hosting different ethnic groups, including refugees from the Soviet invasion of Afghanistan. I was pleased with Quetta's produce market, and a bazaar with clothing, perfumes, carpets, cookware, sweets, electronics, and many other goods. Of course, we had little money to spare for anything but food.

We found a plain but clean hotel where we took a room large enough for all of us, except for Mike, who stood watch in the camper at night. It was much safer than camping in unknown territory, and I was grateful for the opportunity to sleep soundly. A bonus was a bathroom with running water and a hot shower. The only drawback was that the room had no heat, and with freezing temperatures at night, we had to bundle up and huddle together to stay warm as we slept.

During the day, the children and I stayed with the caravan, where I cooked meals and the kids played nearby. Abdullah went off to obtain information about the various routes available to us and the conditions we should expect. When he returned, he watched the kids while I went to the market. Several languages were spoken in the city, but at least two of them — Balochi and Pashto — were similar to Farsi, so I was able to do food shopping without having to rely on sign language. Here in Pakistan, I was pleased that fresh produce and meat were much less expensive than in Iran.

At night, we returned to our hotel room, usually with bread, cheese and fruit we would eat at bedtime. We'd then get into bed, and Abdullah would lock the door before we all fell asleep. But one night was different.

In the middle of the night, Abdullah and I were awoken by a loud knocking on the door. Instantly alert, Abdullah jumped up and went to the door, where a woman was speaking in a language he didn't understand. When he opened the door, he saw a woman with a colorful skirt and white blouse holding the hand of a small child — our child, Taha. Somehow, 21-month-old Taha had opened the door and gone exploring the halls of the hotel, where the woman, probably a maid, found him.

Abdullah was adamant about having locked the door before bedtime, but if so, how did little Taha reach the lock when it was at least two feet over his head? There were no objects near the door that he might have stood on. Even if Abdullah had forgotten to lock the door, questions remained.

How did Taha turn the heavy door handle by himself? And with the usual hotel personnel not available at night, how did the woman know which room the child belonged in? I was deeply unsettled by this experience...

> *Sweet Taha:*
> *Thank God he's safe!*
> *But unknown dangers*
> *Beyond control*
> *Occur*
> *Any*
> *Time.*

A month had passed since we left Tehran, and we were ready to travel to Karachi to obtain visas and arrange for transportation to East Africa. However, before leaving Quetta, we celebrated Shamail's first birthday. Abdullah bought him a toy, and his brothers and I orchestrated the festivities. The birthday boy was a bit bewildered at all the noise, laughter, and singing, but he warmed up and joined in the fun.

The four-hundred-mile road from Quetta to Karachi was narrow and rough, with numerous potholes and ditches which slowed our travel. Descending from the cool, lofty mountains around Quetta, we passed into rocky desert. When we stopped at a roadside café to have lunch, we were immediately surrounded by at least forty men and boys who stared silently at us as we sipped our sodas. Not understanding what was going on, we became uncomfortable. Were these people just curious about this family of foreigners? Looking for a handout? Hostile? The café proprietor attempted to disperse the crowd without success.

When we left, the men jostled us all the way to the car, and one guy deliberately spit on my shoe. Interpreting this as a threat, Abdullah and I hustled the kids into the car, jumped in, and quickly shut and locked the doors. The crowd continued to press closely around the car and camper as Abdullah slowly drove through the crowd and pulled onto the road. We were greatly relieved to get away from that place. Much later, I learned that we had been driving through the Baloch region of Pakistan. The members of that tribe in Pakistan, like those in Iran, had been involved in long-standing conflicts with the government.

Around dusk we pulled off the road and set up camp. At night, a thick, black curtain fell quickly over the earth. Stepping away from our campsite, I looked up at the night sky, trying in vain to catch sight of any stars. I walked a few more yards, keeping our lantern-lit camper in view. Hearing a tinkling sound, I turned my head toward it and smelled and then felt the breeze of a very large animal passing within inches of me. In the very faint light, I saw with shock that I had almost got run over by a camel, a bell hanging on its neck. In the next moment, I jumped back just in time to avoid being trampled by the string of camels behind the lead animal. A caravan was traveling in the pitch dark, with the camels' sense of smell and keen night sight guiding them.

The next day, our route took us past irrigation canals, lush rice fields, and grazing water buffaloes. Now and then, a friendly herdsman would wave at us. Eventually we arrived at the outskirts of Karachi, a big, seemingly endless city — today the seventh largest in the world. Home to millions of people, the city was dirty, densely populated, and noisy, with modern skyscrapers and narrow, ancient streets.

Abdullah befriended some men from Saudi Arabia who lived in the city's outskirts, and they let us park the car and camper in front of their whitewashed, single-story villa. Extremely conservative, the men invited Abdullah and the boys to come in, drink tea with them, play ping pong, take showers, and fill up our water containers, but I was forbidden to enter. That had never happened to me before. Even in the most conservative homes in Iran and Algeria, our whole family was welcome, though there were often separate living rooms for men and for women. Eventually, Abdullah persuaded the men to allow me into the house when none of them were at home, so I was able to take a shower.

Unfortunately, all of us got sick from drinking the water in Karachi. While Abdullah and the kids recovered quickly, I was very ill, with a high fever. Too sick to cook, I could barely care for Shamail, who was still nursing. For supper, Abdullah took the rest of the kids to a local restaurant, but the food was so spicy hot that it was inedible, even for Abdullah. Fortunately, he found a Chinese restaurant, and he and the kids ate supper there every day for a week.

Once I was well enough to care for all the children again, Abdullah got busy going into the city to shipping companies, airlines, and embassies. One day he brought me news about our travel plans.

"Well, we can ship our car and camper to East Africa," he began. "But we can't travel on the ship as passengers."

"How do we get there, then?" I asked.

"The family would have to fly," he replied with a pained expression on his face. We both knew that wouldn't be possible for Abdullah.

I looked at him. "Could we all take a passenger ship?"

"No, there aren't any. And anyway, even if there were, or even if we flew, we couldn't afford it. It costs more than all the money we have."

I was silent. This was such bad news. We had traveled all the way to southern Pakistan, only to be defeated, first by the unexpectedly closed border with India, and then by the lack of affordable and secure travel to Africa.

Abdullah continued, "We'll have to go back through Iran and then across Europe to North Africa." Soberly, he added, "We have no other choice."

Having traveled over thirty-three hundred miles in vain, lost a month of travel time, and spent money we could ill afford, we finally found ourselves back in Tehran. Hassan gave us warm hospitality and made us feel at home in his apartment. While the kids played, Abdullah, Hassan, and I discussed the situation. The mountains at the border of Iran and Türkeye were between six and nine thousand feet high, and Mt. Ararat, only ten miles from the Iranian border, was over fifteen thousand feet. The pass through the mountains had notoriously bad weather in winter and was often impassable. Hassan urged us to stay with him until spring, when the pass would be safe and the roads in Türkeye clear of snow.

While we talked, I let Jamal and Yusuf go outside to explore the immediate vicinity of the apartment. They felt the biting winds of winter barreling down the sides of the mountains circling Tehran, with sixteen-thousand-foot Mount Damavand already covered with snow. The boys didn't stay long in the cold streets, but they did discover something interesting. They came back to the apartment with glowing reports of something good to eat that a vendor had given them. Jamal told us he didn't know what it was, but it was hot, sweet, and satisfying. His and Yusuf's fingers were stained dark red. When I went outside to investigate, I found that the vendor was cooking and selling giant, two-pound sugar beets in a steaming vat on his cart. Most people bought a small piece of the beet, but I bought a whole beet and brought it upstairs for everyone to enjoy.

Meanwhile, Abdullah and I had come to a decision. We would leave as soon as possible for the western border of Iran. Once there, we would evaluate the weather and road conditions. If possible, we'd cross into Türkeye, but if not, we'd turn around and come back to Tehran. We were on the road the next morning. The well-maintained road heading west out of Tehran made the miles fall away as we pushed toward the border. About five hundred miles from Tehran, we finally came to the border crossing, which was closed for the night.

We prepared to camp overnight. It was bitter cold, so after a quick supper of heated up beans and rice, we all piled into one of the double beds in the caravan. Abdullah and I slept on opposite edges of the mattress, with Taha and Shamail between us. Jamal, Yusuf, and Jubair also lay between us, but with their pillows at the foot of the mattress and their legs in a tangle with Taha's and Shamail's feet. I was last into the bed and covered all of us with our warm sleeping bags. Sometime in the night, Mike, our German Shepherd, decided that the floor was too cold for him, and he made himself comfortable on top of the rest of us. I was grateful for his added warmth.

In the morning, I attempted to heat up the camper by boiling water for tea, coffee, and hot cereal. Jamal and Yusuf went outside and noted a thin layer of snow on the ground, but they didn't linger. Our cotton clothes, which had been sufficient for living in Tehran in the winter, were not nearly warm enough in the mountains, with temperatures well below freezing. Inside the camper, I managed to get the temperature up to 45 degrees or so, certainly not cozy, but at least not freezing. Still, the floor was frigid, despite the cardboard and old blankets I put down to stand on while I cooked. This rudimentary insulation was already frozen solid and would remain that way until we reached Istanbul, nearly nine hundred miles away.

After gulping down his coffee, Abdullah took our passports into the border station to wait in line. When he finally came back, he was accompanied by guards who needed to inspect the contents of the camper. The kids and I stood outside shivering and stamping our feet. When Abdullah accompanied the guards back into the building, the rest of the family rushed back into the camper, which I heated again by cooking beans. To pass the time, I read stories to the children as we huddled in blankets on the bed. Finally, Abdullah returned and silently signaled us to break camp. I turned off the cooking gas, secured all pots in the cupboards, and made sure Mike had water to drink. The family dog didn't like traveling in the camper, and he whined when Abdullah locked the door. We arranged ourselves in the car, and Abdullah slowly drove away from the border station and crossed into Türkeye.

Breathing a sigh of relief as we left Iran, we could see that traveling conditions were more dangerous here than on the Iranian side of the border. Snow was falling, and the roads were slippery. Although Abdullah had put chains on the car tires, the weight of the camper and the icy road surface made driving very difficult. Abdullah's extraordinary driving skills saved us from the fate suffered by numerous crashed cars and jackknifed tractor trailers that we saw on the highway.

As travel conditions worsened, the camper slid off the side of the road. Every effort Abdullah made to drive forward ended up with the camper sliding further toward the embankment, threatening to pull the car with it. There was nothing to be done but stop there, cook something to eat, and wait for conditions to improve.

While Abdullah and the kids stayed in the car, I went into the camper to warm it up, but I couldn't get the stove to work. Then, trying repeatedly to light a match, I began to have trouble working my fingers. When Abdullah came back to check on me, I was confused, shivering uncontrollably, and unable to speak due to hypothermia. To warm me up, he put me in the back seat of the car with all five kids and layers of blankets.

Meanwhile, Abdullah determined that the pipe from the gas can to the stove was frozen. Fortunately, a trucker with a similar problem had parked nearby and was thawing his diesel line with a butane torch. Abdullah borrowed the torch to carefully thaw our line, warm up the camper, and cook dinner. We ate the hot food, drank hot tea appreciatively, and got in our crowded bed to stay warm. It was even colder than the night at the border.

In the morning, we saw we weren't alone, as many motorists and truckers had slid down the steep banks of the road into fields of snow. Our whole family was crammed in the parked car for hours, since it was too cold to go outside, and we couldn't spare any more cooking gas for heating up the camper. If we ran out, it would be disastrous.

"How long do we have to stay here?" asked Yusuf.

"When will the police come to help all these people?" Jamal wondered.

At this point, I didn't think any help was coming, but to both questions, I just answered, "I don't know."

Taha whined, "Jubair has my toy!"

Jubair complained, "I gotta pee, Ummi."

"OK, let's make it real quick, Jubair," I responded, opening the car door and shutting it as soon as we climbed out of the car. Shamail, awakened by the cold blast of air, was now crying. When Jubair and I got back in the car, there was much grumbling until I quieted the baby and started teaching the kids a song from my childhood, "She'll Be Coming Around the Mountain." Abdullah made a face and sighed, getting out of the car to confer with a trucker who was walking toward our car. After a few words, Abdullah returned to our car.

"He's going to try to pull us off this icy spot and up the rest of the hill," Abdullah said, watching the trucker maneuver his tractor trailer.

"Where's he going?" I cried in alarm as I saw the man drive his huge vehicle over the embankment and down into the vast field of snow below the road.

"He couldn't back up to our car because he might slip on this ice and smash into our car," Abdullah replied. "See, he's circling around down there and coming back up to the road!"

I watched in astonishment as the trucker powered up the hill, over the shoulder, and then onto the road behind us. Then, he carefully pulled in front of our car. I couldn't imagine the courage it took to drive that truck out over a field of snow of unknown depth with undetectable obstacles under the snow, with no help if his plan didn't work out. He and Abdullah worked to fasten chains connecting the rear of the truck to the front of the car, and the trucker pulled us up over the hill. I felt the thanks and blessings we expressed to him were not nearly sufficient for the risks he took to save us from a cold disaster. He said something in Turkish about Allah, and I understood he was just doing his duty to help strangers and travelers.

After saying goodbye to the man who had rescued us, we drove slowly over the still-treacherous road. At the first gas station we saw, we pulled in, refueled, bought more cooking gas, and camped there for the next four days. We learned that not only were people calling this the worst winter in memory, but also that no snowplows were expected. Everyone who was stranded by the storm, like us, would have to wait for the ice and snow on the road to melt.

Meanwhile, I was hard put to keep the little ones occupied with toys, snacks, stories, and coloring books in our confined space. When the children would ask to play Monopoly, I was always happy to agree, since keeping five children from descending into chaos in the cramped quarters was difficult at best. This game was a cheaply made, pirated version we had bought in Pakistan. With the game board laid out on the bed, we sat cross-legged in a circle around it, covered in blankets. Even Jubair and Taha played, with help from their brothers. The game would go on for hours, and all the kids were totally immersed it. It bored me to no end, and I began to call it Monotony. However, this was an important daily ritual that kept everyone occupied and maintained some sort of sanity among the family.

Mike was tied outside during the day, and he spent most of the time sleeping curled up under the camper. One day, though, Abdullah let him come inside while we were playing Monopoly. Always one to enjoy mingling with the children, Mike jumped up on the bed, placed a muddy paw on the game board, and spilled all our pieces – tokens, houses, and hotels. Swishing his tail, he sent the flimsy paper money flying as he tried to wedge himself between Taha and Jubair. There were screams of "Mike, no!" "Oh Mike!" "Down Mike, down!" The game was over, and the campers were not happy, especially Yusuf, who had been winning. I declared it time for dinner, and we picked up the pieces and set aside the mud-stained board to dry. To this day, I have kept that game board, bearing Mike's paw print, as a souvenir of our arduous winter travels.

Eventually, the snowfall ceased, and the temperatures warmed slightly. From what we could see, the road was partially thawed due to the heavy trucks that hauled loads successfully despite the snow and ice. From all accounts, the road was passable. As we drove west through Türkeye, the altitude decreased, the snow began to melt, and the size of the villages increased.

One afternoon we pulled over to the side of the road so Abdullah could fix a flat tire on the camper. Although we had a spare tire for it, our car jack was not tall enough to raise the camper sufficiently. As Abdullah and I considered the problem, four or five burly men walked by on their way home from work. Sizing up the situation, they immediately offered their help. They knocked on the door of a nearby house and asked to borrow a few cinder blocks. Then they took hold of the rear of the heavy camper, and grunting in unison, they raised it high, while Abdullah pushed the blocks under the frame. After he had changed the tire, the men lifted the camper once more while Abdullah removed the blocks.

When we thanked them profusely in Farsi, Arabic, and English, they just nodded, smiled, said something in Turkish, and continued walking down the road. Not only were these Turks hospitable to strangers and travelers, but they were also hard workers and problem solvers. I was fascinated by their blend of eastern and western cultures. To top everything off, a woman who lived in a nearby house gave us the most delicious hot soup made from barley and yogurt.

Back on the road again, the villages gave way to urban areas that no longer showed traces of snow. Finally, we saw the gateway to Istanbul — the sparkling waters of the Bosphorus Strait, dotted with countless boats of all sizes and spanned by a long, graceful bridge. The strait separated western from eastern Türkeye and linked the Black Sea on the north, to the Marmara Sea on the south, which lead south to the Aegean Sea and eventually to the Mediterranean. I was entranced by the sight of endlessly bountiful water, intriguing islands, and more people than I had seen since Tehran.

Crossing the bridge, we passed into to a world of springlike warmth and a busy urban environment with stunning architecture, both modern and ancient. Istanbul was crowded with skyscrapers, modern financial firms, and international businesses, alongside traditional bazaars on narrow streets. My mind was boggled by the layers of over two thousand years of history, architecture, and culture visible in Istanbul — the Roman Empire, the Byzantine Empire, the Ottoman Empire, the republic established by Ataturk in the 1920s, and the modern era. But the land that is now Türkeye was settled even earlier than the historical record indicates, as evidenced by archeological sites that are at least eleven thousand years old.

After asking around at gas stations, we eventually found a peaceful, clean campground in a grove of trees. While I set up camp, Abdullah took the car to an auto repair shop, and the children explored the grounds. The kids came running back to me with fists full of nuts they had found on the ground. I cracked open a nut and tasted the nutmeat. It was a hazelnut! We were excited by this special treat.

I was making lunch for the kids when Abdullah returned. "There's bad news about the car," he announced. "As I suspected, the head gasket is cracked and has to be replaced."

"Oh," I cringed. "That's going to be expensive."

"Very. The auto shop owner said he has to order the parts from Europe. Altogether it'll be over a thousand dollars."

"Oh man…"

"We can't afford it," Abdullah sighed. "We have just enough money to get us to Spain, take the ferry to Morocco, and then make it to Algeria."

I was silent for a moment. "Who can we borrow money from?" Neither of us were comfortable about borrowing from our family, but at this point, there was no choice. When Abdullah called his mother in North Carolina, she told him she couldn't help. I called my mother, who fortunately was able to loan us the money we needed to repair the car.

Meanwhile, the kids were happy at the campground, for they had plenty of room to run and play. They had also met some friendly French children, whose family was camped nearby. Their father was writing and publishing articles about their travels in different countries, while their mother was schooling the children as they travelled. On the surface, we had a lot in common, and the French family seemed to assume that we traveled for the love of it, like them. But of course, appearances were deceptive…

> *Survival is our pursuit,*
> *Where danger awaits*
> *And disaster tracks the hapless.*
> *But our battered wings struggle,*
> *Lift us into flight,*
> *And carry on,*
> *For now.*

For a couple weeks, we waited first for the new gasket to arrive, and then for the car to be repaired. While our new friends at the campground kept an eye on our older kids, Abdullah and I explored the city, with Taha and Shamail in tow. We visited Hagia Sophia, a large Byzantine cathedral that had been converted into a mosque during the Ottoman era. I found it hard to believe that such a large, beautiful domed monument could have been built nearly fifteen centuries earlier.

We also visited the Blue Mosque, a huge, stunning place of prayer, decorated with hand painted blue tile walls. For the first time in a year and a half, I felt deep emotion well up within me as I stood, bowed, and prostrated in prayer. I felt gratitude for our safe journey out of Iran, for our rescue from the treacherous winter conditions of eastern Türkeye, and for being in this Muslim country with an open society, generous people, and a rich history. But we were not truly safe here, and ahead of us we had a risky journey across Europe. Choking up, I continued to pray, tears streaming down my face...

> *Oh Allah, we are in your care.*
> *There's no one to help us*
> *But You,*
> *No one to protect*
> *Our blameless children*
> *But You.*
> *I beg you to forgive me,*
> *Forgive my husband,*
> *And bring our family to safety.*
> *For in this world,*
> *There's no power or strength*
> *But You.*

Though Istanbul had mild weather, we had heard that bitterly cold temperatures and snowstorms were descending on Europe. News reports said that it was the coldest winter in Europe in fifty years. To prepare for the next leg of our journey, we went to the bazaar, a vast covered market sparkling with colorful rugs, clothing, jewelry, home furnishings, spices, fruits, vegetables, and much more. But we were shopping for essential clothing — winter coats, gloves, hats, scarves, socks, and boots — for the whole family. Abdullah drove a hard bargain and managed to stay within our very tight budget.

After three weeks in Istanbul, our car was finally ready to go, and so were we. Much as we would have liked to stay longer in Türkeye, we had to leave and make best use of our limited funds to get to Algeria. The

French family had already said their goodbyes and continued their travels. Now it was time for us to do the same.

From Istanbul we drove west and crossed the border into Greece on December 31, 1985. The border guards, roaring drunk on New Year's Eve, barely looked at our passports and with great cheer, waved us through the crossing. We traveled along the Aegean coast for a while, then headed north into the Balkan peninsula, traveling through Bulgaria and what was then Yugoslavia. The snow and cold weather returned with a vengeance as we entered this mountainous region.

Equally cold was our reception by the people of this area, who shunned us and treated us with suspicion, in stark contrast to the friendly hospitality we found in Türkeye. I realized my family looked disreputable, wearing several layers of clothes under our coats to protect against the bitter cold and unable to bathe except for the single time we were forced to stay overnight at a motel. Our car and camper were crusted with dirty ice, and we were slowed to a crawl by icy and unplowed roads.

As we entered Italy, we encountered increasingly negative attitudes from people we met. There, the border guards were certain that we were carrying drugs or other contraband and detained us for several hours while they attempted to search all our belongings. As it happened, before leaving Iran, Abdullah had stashed two pounds of Rahim's prime Iranian marijuana in the camper, along with an illegal firearm that Hassan had given him. While the guards were busy, he passed me his traveling hashish to hide in the baby's diaper. I couldn't refuse without endangering the whole family. On the other hand, doing so also endangered us. Inwardly, I was in turmoil, anxious at the danger to the family.

When the police brought a drug sniffing dog to search the camper, our dog Mike threw an outraged, snarling, snapping fit at the intrusion of this strange canine on his territory. Abdullah made an unsuccessful attempt to control Mike, or so he made it seem. In the face of a violent, uncontrollable German Shepherd, the police decided they couldn't risk damage to their valuable dog, so they backed off and allowed us to cross the border. Fortunately, they didn't have information about Abdullah's fugitive status, or they certainly would have detained us. Relieved, but still worried about the border crossings ahead of us, I clamped down on my feelings and soldiered on.

In southern France, we discovered that people were hostile toward us because they thought we were Roma, the nomadic people of Europe who are pejoratively called "gypsies." With extremely cold conditions in the

Riviera, Roma travelers had hunkered down in their cars and trailers in every campground we saw.

By the time we passed into Spain on this marathon journey, we were perpetually cold and exhausted. On the rare occasion when Abdullah asked me to drive because he was tired, I was also too sleepy to drive. If we pulled over for a nap, the younger kids would wake up from their naps and noisily demand attention.

There was only so long we could keep this up, and the inevitable happened. Dozing, in a dream, I felt myself being bounced up and down. Suddenly, the bouncing woke me up. "Abdullah!" I screamed, as I saw weeds and brush rushing toward the windshield.

"Shit!" he exclaimed, awakening at the same time. Seeing that he had driven off the road into a field, he carefully slowed the car and drove it back up the embankment. He brought it to a stop at the side of the highway, noting that the camper was still attached. "Is everyone OK?" he asked. The kids were wide eyed and crying.

The family piled out of the car, and I examined each child. "The kids seem OK, and I'm fine," I said. "But Mike?"

We all stared at the camper, which looked lopsided. The left front corner was cracked open, and clothes we had stored under the front bed were dangling out of the opening. Suddenly, Mike nosed his way out of the crack and bounded into the field. Jamal, Yusuf and Jubair ran to give him a hug.

Abdullah inspected the car. "It seems fine," Abdullah said. "There are some weeds stuck underneath, but I don't see anything broken. But the camper is another story."

While I made coffee and nursed Shamail, Abdullah and the older boys got busy covering the crack in the camper with sheet plastic and duct tape to keep out the rain and road dirt. Though the frame under the camper was bent, it was still possible for the car to pull it. We got on the road again, limping slowly onward, toward southern Spain.

It was February when we finally reached the warm haven of Almeria, a port city along the Mediterranean coast of Spain. There, we found a convenient campground on the beach. As soon as Abdullah parked the camper, the whole family burst out of the car and went wild…

Collapsing on sunlit sand
Sun soaks my bones
Cold be gone!
Kids dancing crazy sun dance
Dog joy jumping
Abdullah quiet touching sea.
We're warm at last
And almost
Home.

The Mediterranean welcomed and entranced us. Jubair and Taha waded in the sea, Shamail played in the sand, and I sat on the shore relishing the early spring breeze and the waves lapping gently on the shore. Yusuf and Jamal swam and hunted squid beyond the shallow water with snorkeling gear and a spear gun.

When the boys brought the squids ashore, a local fisherman demonstrated how to kill and flay them on rocks to tenderize the meat and remove the skin. The young fishermen were proud to contribute to the family dinner, and we were all happy to have some protein after our arduous travels. Abdullah would go to the market in Almeria and buy fresh bread and vegetables to accompany the fried squid. After months of a monotonous diet with little protein and few fruits or vegetables, we were deeply grateful for delicious, healthy food.

We also made some friends at the camp: a Canadian couple, who were in Spain on vacation. During the day, Jamal and Yusuf often accompanied them on hikes in the surrounding hills. At other times, Abdullah and I enjoyed long conversations with them. And critically, Ray helped Abdullah to fix up the camper so we could get back on the road.

I reveled in this much needed break from the cold and the stress of the past four months. But we were running out of money, and we couldn't afford to stay any longer. When the camper was wired together and patched, we said goodbye to our friends and made our way to Algeciras, a port city on the southernmost peninsula of Spain. There, we loaded ourselves, our car, and our caravan onto the ferry, which would cross the Mediterranean bound for Ceuta, a Spanish enclave on the northern Moroccan coast.

As the ship got underway, I thought about the significance of this crossing, the last link in our journey to North Africa. In my arms, Shamail grew quiet and gazed at the expansive waters around us.

Jubair was excited, "Ummi, it's a huge ship! And loud!"

Taha giggled and jumped up and down in a wiggly dance.

Jamal and Yusuf had prepared tightly capped bottles containing messages, and now they became pensive.

"What would it be like to be inside a bottle floating in the ocean?" Jamal reflected. "I wonder who will find it. I asked them to write me."

"Where will it go?" Yusuf asked. "It could go that way, to Italy," he said, pointing west. Then he turned east. "Or that way to America, across the ocean."

"Or maybe to Morocco or Algeria," I suggested, looking south.

Yusuf was poised at the railing, "Should I throw it now?"

"Not yet," I replied. "Wait until we're out in the middle, halfway between Spain and Morocco." I had given the boys my mother's address to put in the bottle. Perhaps one day she would receive a letter addressed to Yusuf or Jamal from someone who had found one of the bottles.

My mother's address was the only one we had. But it was her home, not mine. The country in which I was born seemed so alien to me, with its intense commercialism, the rapid pace of existence, the lack of personal direction other than the accumulation of money, and worse, the lack of meaning in life. I didn't miss it at all.

I reflected on my life since I had brought Jamal, Yusuf, and Jubair to North Africa to join Abdullah. Since then, young Taha and Shamail had become part of our family, too. The past five years had been full of stress and upheaval, and my relationship with Abdullah had been difficult at times. But I had chosen this way, instead of an existence spent fulfilling middle-class American expectations. I smiled as I recalled my naïve childhood dreams of adventure. Those dreams had been realized in my life overseas, hadn't they? This was what I had wanted. But these adventures were not just exciting but dangerous for me and my family. This life was full of risk. Gazing at the living, blue-green waters of the Mediterranean, I reflected on my real-life journey…

> *Almost safe*
> *But not,*
> *Not until Algeria,*
> *Maybe not even then.*
> *Fugitive life is unsafe,*
> *But the far shore beckons.*
> *If home is anywhere*

The ferry delivered us without mishap to Ceuta, and from there we easily crossed into Morocco. But now our situation was precarious because purchasing the ferry tickets had consumed the rest of our money. We planned to drive the eighty miles to Algeria the same day, cross into Algeria, and borrow money from friends there so we could pay for gas to drive to Oran. Unfortunately, travel was much slower than expected on the narrow, twisting road in the mountainous terrain, and the car was using more gas pulling the trailer in these conditions. It was clear we wouldn't make it to the border before we ran out of gas.

This wasn't to be the worst of our problems. Staring into his side view mirror, Abdullah suddenly exclaimed, "The camper!" I looked back just in time to see the vehicle soar down a steep ravine. The trailer hook had broken as the car rounded a curve. Abdullah screeched to a halt, and we piled out of the car. After a moment of stunned silence, we all cried, "Mike!"

We carefully made our way down a hundred yards of the steep mountainside to the camper, which was crushed and overturned, with its wheels in the air. The repaired front end had cracked all the way open again, allowing Mike to scramble from the wreckage. He was obviously shaken, and Abdullah rushed over to make sure he was all right, stroking him and comforting him. The children were crying. I was numb for a moment, staring with a sinking feeling at our belongings scattered around the site. Not allowing myself to dwell on the latest disaster, I told myself the situation could have been much, much worse. None of us were hurt, our family dog was fine, and the car seemed undamaged. Belongings could be replaced when we started earning money again.

We got to work salvaging what we could. While Abdullah pulled our things out of the camper, Jamal and Yusuf carried them up the steep mountainside to the car and dropped them in a pile. I began choosing essential items that would be loaded into the car. I packed cooking and camping supplies in the trunk of the car and lined the interior of the car with bedding, jackets, and clothes. I bundled the rest onto a wood panel from the camper.

Meanwhile, residents of this mountainous region had been gathering to watch us work. One man helped Abdullah lift the heavy bundle onto the roof of the car and tie it down. Other people were interested in buying items we were leaving behind. Abdullah busily sold off our discarded gear and the camper sink, benches, mattresses, cupboards, and wheels. The money would hopefully pay for gas and food until we got into Algeria.

"Ummi, Abu found this," Yusuf handed me the three-quart, copper-bottom pot which my mother had given to me one Christmas. This essential pot was used daily as I cooked for our large family.

I smiled, "Thanks Yusuf! This is my favorite pot." It was now dented and had lost one handle, but it was usable. I tucked the pot into the last, small, unused spot in the trunk of the car.

Finally, we loaded ourselves into the heavily laden vehicle. In the back seat, the children and dog sat on the layers of bedding with their heads touching the ceiling. In the front seat, with Shamail on my lap, I was encapsulated by clothes and baby gear. Abdullah was cradled in a space just big enough to allow him to drive.

Travel was slow in the heavily laden car. When we stopped to refuel, we discovered that gasoline was more expensive than we expected, and we were again penniless. By the time we got to the Moroccan border, it was closed for the night. I fed the family the last of the bread and cheese, and we all had to sleep, uncomfortably, in the car. In the morning, we all piled out and stretched our legs. The border post was still closed.

"Ummi, I'm hungry!"

"Me too!"

The only food we had left was a small packet of cookies, and there was no money to buy food. "OK, drink some water, and then you can have a cookie," I told them.

Abdullah shook his head, letting me know he wouldn't have any.

I gave each child a cookie and took one myself. "This is all we have. Eat it slowly. We don't have any more food, so after this, we'll all have to wait."

"How long?" asked Yusuf.

"I don't know," I replied. I felt guilty that my children were hungry. But my kids surprised me. They didn't complain, not even the youngest ones.

When the Algerian border opened, we had a stroke of luck. A border guard recognized Abdullah from his trips to Morocco three years earlier. He eased our crossing into Algeria, not requiring us to unload, unpack, display, and repack our car. Even better, Abdullah was able to borrow money from the man. Breathing a sigh of relief, we drove across the border into Algeria.

It was February of 1985, and our family had traveled approximately 8,086 miles since leaving the Caspian four months earlier.[23] We had lost our camper, and we had no money, no jobs, and no place to live. But we had arrived in this safe haven, and we had friends here. When we stopped at a grimy roadside café to fill our empty stomachs, the chatter of the other customers made me realize how much I had missed the sound of Arabic over the past two years.

As we drove on, my eyes feasted on the distant mountain ranges to the south, the rolling green hills, the humble farming villages, and finally the shining Mediterranean Sea beyond the cliffs of North Africa. Thank God, we were home.

---

[23] From October through December 1984, we drove approximately 3,618 miles from Rasht, Iran to Karachi, Pakistan and back to Tehran. Then we drove 4,621 miles from Tehran west across Europe, south into Morocco, and finally east into Algeria.

8

ALGERIA, THE EDGE OF CONFLICT
1985-1986

"Life is a train that stops at no stations; you either jump
aboard or stand on the platform and watch as it passes."
Yasmina Khadra[24]

A gentle breeze ruffled the tall grasses of the meadow and brushed my face
as I stood basking in the heavenly warmth streaming from the sun. Shamail
held onto my leg and looked up at me to gauge my reaction to this strange
environment. Squatting down, I smiled and showed him how to run his
hand through the grass. Three-year-old Taha had already left my side and
begun to imitate his older brothers, who were dramatically prancing, falling,
giggling, and rolling in the grass. Feeling residual tension in my face, I
consciously relaxed the muscles, surrendering to peace. With a sigh of
contentment, I offered silent thanks to the One, who had delivered us from
the perilous conditions we had endured in Pakistan, Iran, Türkeye, Europe,
and Morocco.

We had set up camp at this uninhabited spot in western Algeria, not far
from the Mediterranean coast and within driving distance of Oran. With
the destruction of our camper, all seven of us now had to sleep in the tent,
but that was a small inconvenience compared to our grueling travels of the
past few months. The situation before us, however, was critical. The money
Abdullah had borrowed was dwindling, and we urgently needed to find
work and housing. Although the skies were currently clear, we knew the

---

[24] *Ce que le jour doit à la nuit.* Yasmina Khadra, 2008.

springlike weather was only a temporary reprieve from the cold winter rains of North Africa. We couldn't continue tent camping for long.

While I organized our belongings, supervised the children, and started cooking dinner, Abdullah explored a nearby town for food, water, and cooking gas. He talked to people and gathered information about potential job contacts, housing, residence visas, and more. His social talents amazed me. It had never been easy for me to reach out to strangers and make friends. If his and my roles had been reversed, I would not have been able to do half of what he achieved through his social contacts. On the other hand, he would have struggled if tasked with the work I did day in and day out, along with nurturing the family. When our marriage was working, we were a good team together.

On one local excursion, he met an Iranian couple who lived near our campsite. With unflagging warmth and hospitality, Anoosh and Mitra invited us to stay at their apartment. Having fled Iran during the Revolution and settled temporarily in Algeria, they planned to go to Vancouver, Canada so they could rejoin family members there. I was relieved to have shelter in their home, where I could bathe the children, wash our clothes, and relax. Best of all, I appreciated getting to know them, talking about Iran, and sharing meals together.

Meanwhile, Abdullah had begun visiting the city of Oran, where he began searching for work. He told me he met devout Muslims who welcomed him to their community. He returned late one evening with good news.

"We've got a place to live!" he said. "It's a two-bedroom apartment in the old part of the city."

"How did you pay…" I began.

"It belongs to the brothers I met," Abdullah said happily, "and they're letting us stay there until we get back on our feet."

Our third floor, walk-up flat was on a narrow but busy lane in the *souk* or traditional marketplace. Two windows and a small balcony overlooked the street, while a rear window faced a small courtyard. Little natural light filtered into the apartment, and I felt closed in and restricted after our ten months of camping and traveling. But it was home for now.

Abdullah found a part-time job in the late afternoon and evening writing copy for the English language program of a local radio station. The opportunity to earn some money, however little, was welcome. Meanwhile, I worked for many hours a day to tend to the needs of the family – caring for the kids, keeping the apartment clean, scrubbing clothes, buying groceries, and cooking three meals each day. Making nutritious meals was difficult because of our tight budget, prohibitively expensive meat and dairy products, and limited, low-quality vegetables. In addition, I tried to teach the boys, each to his level, in reading or pre-reading, writing or drawing, and math or numbers.

Managing our water needs consumed much of my time. Like Arzew and Boumerdes, Oran had a shortage of fresh, drinkable water. Water ran from the taps in our apartment only from midnight to 2:00 A.M. However, the water was salty, undrinkable, and not suitable for cooking. Regularly, I had to stay up late so I could fill up five-gallon jerry cans with the brackish water and wash clothes and dishes with it. Then, I would take a shower, even though my body would be coated with minerals afterward. To obtain fresh water for drinking and cooking, Abdullah and I spent one evening each week standing in a long line of residents at a local spring. There we would fill up more water cans. With our car, we transported the heavy containers to the apartment, and Abdullah hauled them up the three flights of stairs.

Always looking for places to take a walk with the kids, I asked Abdullah for directions to his office, which he had told me was a twenty-minute walk from our place. We wouldn't disturb him at work, but we could at least see where he worked. But instead of encouraging me, he gave me a vague description of the location and said it was not a safe neighborhood to walk in. Something in his cryptic reply made me pause, and I realized he had never talked about his work, the news he was writing up, or his boss or coworkers. He must have sensed my suspicion, for then he admitted that he was working secretly with the Muslim Brotherhood, and he could not reveal any details of their activities to me.

My instincts warned me. If he didn't have a job, where was he was getting the money that he brought home? And if he was collaborating with this underground organization, we would all be in deep danger. I would try to figure out what was going on, but for now, I didn't pursue it.

Living in the city was hard on the children and the dog, who were used to playing outside near our house or campsite. Abdullah and I allowed Jamal and Yusuf to explore our small corner of the city as long as they stayed together. Always looking for open spaces to run and explore, they found what they called "the dirty park." When I asked them to show me this park, I took the younger kids and Mike along, too. It was not a park but a steep hillside under a bridge, the hard-packed clay dotted with dry bushes, trash, and a few tired trees. The empty lot was an adequate place to walk the dog but otherwise offered nothing but dirt. However, the kids happily dug holes in the ground and created little forts under bushes.

Another day, Jamal returned from his and Yusuf's latest exploration of the city to tell me of a new friend, a boy whose family raised pigeons on the roof of their apartment building. The boy was a bit older than my sons and sold single cigarettes on the street to help support his family. Abdelkader was unable to walk, since his legs were permanently twisted beneath his body, and to move about, he sat on a wooden platform on casters. But that wasn't what Jamal talked about when he mentioned his friend. He was impressed with how friendly Abdelkader was and how welcoming his family was to him and Yusuf.

Jamal was quickly picking up Algerian Arabic, and he and Yusuf made friends with other boys they encountered. They even joined a local Boy Scout troop. When the troop participated in a ceremony celebrating a national holiday, Jamal and Yusuf were excited to wear Scout uniforms, which were provided by the troop on special occasions. The highlight of their time with the troop was a day trip to a nearby beach with the scouts and their leader. At the end of the day swimming and playing on the beach with their friends, my boys returned sandy, sunburned, and happy.

As the rest of the family slept, I quietly communed with the Divine. Since arriving in Algeria, I had resumed praying in an effort to revive my spiritual life…

> *Night falls,*
> *Cradles my prayer,*
> *Hears my silence,*
> *Expands my heart.*
> *This space forgives*
> *All my rushed*
> *Daylight prayers,*
> *And in this moment,*
> *I release my cares.*

Sometimes these moments brought me lightness and ease. But unfortunately, the feeling would dissipate all too soon. I would fall back into the spiral of depression in our dark apartment. Outside in the city, I missed the green trees, open spaces, and fresh air that could revive me. Abdullah also seemed depressed, remote, and worried about our lack of money.

Before we knew it, Ramadan had arrived, the month of fasting. All adult Muslims — except for pregnant or nursing mothers, children, and the elderly or infirm — refrained from eating or drinking from early dawn to sunset. Fasting offered an important spiritual discipline for Muslims and a reminder to feel compassion for the poor.

Each morning around three o'clock, Abdullah and I got up to eat a small meal before the daily fast began. If I had been tired before Ramadan, I was exhausted as I fasted while doing my usual housework and managing the energetic children in our small apartment. At sunset, Abdullah and I broke our fast, performed the early evening prayer, and then enjoyed a late meal with the children.

After dinner, Abdullah would go with his friends to the mosque for the special Tarawih prayers. I was determined to participate in these prayers and boost my spiritual practice, so one evening a friend took care of my kids, while I accompanied Abdullah to the mosque. Despite feeling elated to be standing shoulder to shoulder with other Muslims in prayer, sleep threatened to overwhelm me. Without realizing, I fell asleep on my feet. The two women on either side of me caught me as I swayed and nudged me awake. With their help, I managed to get through the long prayer.

During Ramadan, we frequently visited other families to break the fast, enjoy a meal together, and let the children play. I was glad to be part of a Muslim community again. I especially liked to visit with the families of Abdullah's Palestinian friends, Farid and Rashid, who spoke English. Their wives gave me tips on where to purchase the best produce at the lowest prices, and we shared recipes and home remedies. But I was not skilled at making conversation, so I never really got to know these women. I also keenly felt the cultural differences that marked me as an outsider. These women had grown up in a traditional Muslim society, married young, and had never worked outside the home, let alone done any of the wild things I had done in my independent youth. And they didn't know the real reason Abdullah and I had come to Algeria. Thus, I didn't reveal much about myself.

I found that I was not alone in my struggle to adjust to the culture and language. I met another woman who spoke English, an Iraqi refugee who had just arrived in Algeria with her husband. As other friends had done for me, I now showed Umayma around the souk, pointing out grocery stores, street stalls with carrots, potatoes, and anise, and carts piled high with oranges.

"Can you ask him how much this is?" Umayma asked me, holding up a carrot from the nearest stall.

I stared at her, surprised. "Uh, sure." I turned to the vendor, "Shal hadha?" He told me the price and I conveyed it to my Iraqi friend.

Noting my quizzical look, she explained, "I don't understand anything these people are saying! Their language is so different from mine."

"Really!" I exclaimed. "I had no idea." I was amused by the fact that I, who knew so little Algerian Arabic, was translating it into English for an Iraqi Arab.

After Ramadan, my schedule became less hectic, and I was mostly able to catch up on my sleep. The next holiday was Aid al Adha, the Islamic Feast of Sacrifice, in which Muslim families ritually sacrifice a lamb and donate a portion of the meat to the poor. Because such an expense was beyond our means, I had set aside money each week so I could buy a pound of stew beef for the Aid meal for my family. On the day of the festival, I was in the kitchen preparing a beef and vegetable stew when a young boy knocked on the apartment door and without a word delivered a whole leg of lamb into my arms. By the time I stammered my thanks, he had already bounded back down the stairs. This was an anonymous gift of lamb from a Muslim family in accordance with Islamic custom. I was startled by a realization that my family was considered poor here in this North African nation. I felt humbled and grateful.

We rarely had visitors, so when Abdullah brought home some young men from Rwanda who were studying at the University or Oran, the kids were excited. They were eager to enjoy the treat of tea and cookies and the opportunity to talk to someone new. After the students left, I gathered up the teacups and carried them to the kitchen. I was returning to the living room to finish tidying up, when I saw twenty-month-old Shamail perched precariously on a rickety chair, reaching for the last cookie on the tea table. Before I could act, the chair toppled over and he crashed down with a cry, the cookie gripped tightly in his hand.

Shamail was in pain and couldn't stand on his left foot, so we took him to the local hospital. The doctor there declared that the foot was broken, but there was no need to splint it because Shamail was young. He said the break would heal on its own. We didn't quite believe that, so Abdullah asked his doctor friend, Farid, to look at the injury. Farid was shocked at the bad medical advice and insisted on putting a cast on the foot. He personally took Shamail to the hospital to make sure the cast was done correctly. Health care in Algeria in those years was primitive at best.

For a couple weeks, Shamail was confined to his crib, and he was vocally unhappy about that. When he took a breath between shouts and whimpers, I heard knocking. I opened the apartment door to find a well-dressed young Algerian woman.

She spoke English. "May I come in?" she asked.

I had no idea who she was. I hesitated and then invited her to step through the doorway.

She spoke plainly, "My name is Zahra, and Abdullah has promised to marry me."

She uttered two more words, and they crushed me, as if I had suffered a heavy blow. I nearly fainted. As a loud roaring assaulted my ears, my legs turned to jelly, and I collapsed onto the living room couch. I couldn't speak. Zahra remained standing silently, her worst fears confirmed. She saw by my reaction that Abdullah had not told me of his relationship with her or received my consent to marry her.

At this moment, Abdullah came out of the bedroom and stood at the entrance to the living room. The two lovers stared wordlessly at each other.

Finally, Zahra said in a tight, barely controlled voice, "You lied to me, Abdullah. I know you're never going to marry me. I have to go to France, of course. Don't try to contact me. Goodbye." She turned and quickly walked out of the apartment. I sobbed, devastated by the suddenness of this news delivered simply and powerfully by this woman.

Zahra's and Abdullah's relationship must have been serious for him to promise her marriage. To get to that point, I realized, he must have been spending a lot of time with her. It was clear that he had never had a job but had been with her on so many afternoons and evenings. I understood that the money he was receiving for the family came not from his work but from the Muslim community, and I felt ashamed that I was part of the deception.

⌒⌢

Our precarious married life disintegrated. I was furious and hurt, and he exploded into tirades against me. I feared him and was acutely conscious of the nine-millimeter pistol Hassan had given him, loaded and hidden under the mattress, within his reach.

When Abdullah left the apartment the next day, I took the gun, concealed it in my clothes, and walked over to Farid's apartment. I instinctively felt I could trust him.

"Brother, I have something I want you to keep for me," I said, handing him the pistol. "Abdullah has cheated on me with another woman."

Farid replied softly, "I'm sorry, Sister."

"I'm afraid of him," I continued. "He became so angry. I'm not safe with this gun in the apartment."

Farid looked at me with compassion. "I'll keep it here until you feel safe enough to pick it up," he told me. "But why would he be angry with you over his unfaithfulness? Surely, it's natural for you to be angry with him." He gently implied that I was so angry that I didn't trust myself not to use the gun on Abdullah. Although shooting my husband had not crossed my mind, I didn't contradict Farid. Thanking him, I left.

Before Abdullah discovered the gun was missing, I needed to tell him what I had done. I found him in bed, gazing out the window.

"What?" he asked, looking at me blankly.

"I didn't feel safe with the gun in the house," I replied. "I took it to Farid for safekeeping."

Abdullah was strangely silent as he kept looking at me. Without a word, I turned and left the room. I sensed that he was thinking same thing as Farid. . .

> *Indeed,*
> *Let him think*
> *I have limits,*
> *Beyond which*
> *He shouldn't push.*
> *Soon the time*
> *To act*
> *To break bonds*
> *Comes.*

When I started thinking seriously about leaving Abdullah, I encountered numerous logistical problems. A departure from Algeria would require me to get the children's and my passports from his briefcase, which he kept locked with a key that he kept on his person. To leave the country, I would have to go to the capital, obtain exit visas, open a bank account, get my family to wire money to me, and buy air tickets – all without his knowledge or permission. And I couldn't keep any evidence of my plan, including the money and tickets, at the apartment, for fear Abdullah – who frequently searched my belongings – would find them. So I would need a safe place to keep the tickets and money as well as someone to watch the children while I was in Algiers. All my friends were the wives of Abdullah's friends. I was sure they could never keep a secret from their husbands, who would side with my charismatic spouse in any marital dispute.

Even if I secretly accomplished those steps, I couldn't imagine how to arrange for Abdullah to be somewhere else for the period when the children and I had to leave for the airport, get onto the plane, and fly away. Now that his mistress had rejected him, he was home most of the day, with only brief visits to his friends. I knew that if Abdullah returned home to an empty apartment, he would instantly comprehend the situation and rush to the airport to physically prevent us from leaving.

Altogether, these contingencies seemed impossible without someone to help me and the children. I could envision only one realistic alternative. I could somehow evade him long enough to take the children to Algiers by train, go to the U.S. Consulate, and take refuge there while they helped me and the children leave the country. This would undoubtedly result in the U.S. investigating Abdullah and discovering his fugitive status. The main risk of this plan was that Abdullah was extremely sensitive to changes in my state of mind and behavior. If he suspected I was acting differently, he would not hesitate to respond proactively against me.

However, I dismissed this plan, for I refused to betray my husband, no matter how painful my life with him had become. I was still loyal to him. Though I would leave him if I could, I wouldn't turn him in, because I still felt he deserved to be free. I was still politically radical and opposed to the oppressive U.S. government. I refused to send him back to prison in that racist, soulless country. Without a viable plan to leave him, I felt it best to continue to bide my time and look for my opportunity.

In September 1985, I retrieved Abdullah's pistol from Farid because we were packing to leave our apartment. After seven months without work, Abdullah and I had found teaching positions in Khemis Miliana, a city bordering the Tell Atlas mountain range about a hundred kilometers west of Algiers. Again, we temporarily set aside our marital problems so we could focus on moving into our new house, starting work, and building up our emergency fund.

We were assigned a single-story, wooden ranch style house in a compound for foreigners nestled in foothills above the city. I felt uncomfortable being segregated from the local people, but we had no choice in the housing provided. The compound, surrounded by a high chain link fence, must have been built fifteen or twenty years earlier, when many foreign workers had come to this area. However, in 1985 we found only a handful of people living there – French, English, Bulgarian, and Russian expatriates. After months of cramped city living, we enjoyed the fresh mountain air, the gardens and orchards, and a roomy house to live in. Within the compound, Mike wasn't allowed to roam freely and had to be tied up, but the children could safely play among the fruit and nut trees and hide in the tall, uncut weeds.

This area had seen fierce fighting during the early resistance to the invasion by the French in the 1830s. Emir Abdelkadir, a Sufi who led the struggle in western Algeria, took control of and held Miliana for several years. This national hero was renowned for his moderate yet dedicated practice of Islam, his high level of education and intelligence, and his ability to use effective military tactics in the fight against the French.

Generations of Algerians followed in Abdelkadir's footsteps, resisting the French control of the country for over one hundred and thirty years. Meanwhile, the invaders pursued a policy of settlement in Algeria of hundreds of thousands of Pied Noir – French and other European people. After confiscating Algerian communal lands, the French government gave it to the immigrants, depriving many native Algerians of their livelihood.

The French provided education to children of the Pieds-Noirs, French-speaking Algerians, and some Berber tribes. However, Muslim-Arab Algerians, the majority of the population, were excluded from schools. They were segregated and discriminated against in all spheres of life. They were even prohibited from entering "European" sections of Algiers and Oran.

Over a century of this oppression culminated in the brutal Algerian War, from 1954 to 1962, in which Algerians finally won independence from France, at a great cost in lives.

As a teacher at the Institute of Technology at Khemis Miliana, I saw the effects of French colonialism on my students. They all spoke Arabic, French, and English, which meant they were among a highly educated minority of Algerians. Still, the deaths and maiming of their parents, grandparents, and earlier generations in the struggle against the French was a raw wound that hadn't healed. Social divisions created by the French still resonated among my students. The young Kabylie woman in class was frequently the butt of cruel jokes by her Arab classmates, a backlash against the long-term French policy of favoritism of her Berber tribe over Arabs.

My job was to train these young people to teach English in the Algerian middle schools. I enjoyed my work and threw myself into teaching and understanding my students. I admired their dedication to their studies and eagerness to perfect their English. They loved hearing about American culture, though they couldn't believe that there were homeless people in U.S. cities, even when I brought in a *New York Times* article about the problem. They were sure every American was rich and carried guns like the people they saw in the popular U.S. television show, *Dallas*. They also chose to ignore my advice on how to discipline their future students. While I advised positive reinforcement to mold behavior, my students insisted that Algerian students needed to be beaten to behave. Our classroom was a lively meeting of two cultures.

Abdullah was faced with a very different assignment, teaching English at the local high school. His job was physically and mentally demanding, as he had to enforce iron rule on a large class of tough Algerian teenagers, most of whom could care less about English. Several of the older boys enjoyed creating chaos in the classroom. One day, the rowdiness came to a head.

Driving home together after work, Abdullah told me, "You'll never believe what happened today in class. Pissed me off. One of the tough kids – bigger than me – got up to leave without my permission, gave me an ugly look, and slammed his book down on my desk. Right up in my face."

"My God, Abdullah!" I was shocked at the student's threatening behavior.

Curling his lip, Abdullah continued, "I jacked him up good. Threatened to fuck him up. Threw him against the blackboard. Shocked the hell out of him. He ran out."

"What did the administrator say?" I was worried that this would mean the end of Abdullah's job.

"Oh, he congratulated me. The other teachers heard the noise and came out in the hall and applauded me," Abdullah smirked. "I don't think I'll have any more problems with those guys."

Our car, its suspension wrecked by our arduous journey from Iran, was now having additional problems that would be expensive to repair. We decided to sell it and buy a more reliable used car. However, to my surprise, Abdullah bought a nearly new Volkswagen Westfalia camping van with a nice sound system, sleeping bunks, a closet, stove, and sink. When I asked where he got the money for the car, he told me he had put a deposit on it with a check from a joint account I had opened at a bank in Geneva in 1982. I was furious, for I knew that the account had only $20 in it, and as a cosigner I was legally liable. Abdullah assured me he had arranged for his next paycheck to be deposited in the account, and he told the seller that the car would be paid off in several months. That seemed unlikely, and I was nervous about the whole deal.

The camping van gave us opportunities for travel again in Algeria. From our students we learned that there was a pyramid in Algeria, only about 45 miles northwest of Khemis-Miliana on the coast of the Mediterranean. The pyramid, called Qabr-er-Rumia, was the tomb of King Juba II of Mauretania and his wife Cleopatra, the daughter of Queen Cleopatra and Mark Anthony. The sizable but crumbling edifice was built with large blocks of stone, which were dark grey and weathered with age. As with other ancient sites in Algeria at the time, there were no foreign tourists, no pamphlets, and no tour guides. It was used as a popular seaside picnic area for local people.

While I walked down to the rocky coast with the three younger kids, Abdullah, Jamal, and Yusuf went into the pyramid. When they finally came out of the ancient ruin, the boys were excited.

"Ummi, you've got to see it! It's a real pyramid!" Jamal took my hand. "Come on, we'll show you."

"Uh…" I hesitated before the low, rectangular opening in the side of the pyramid. I hated confined spaces.

"You can see where the dead body was!" Yusuf tried to encourage me. "I mean the mummy."

"What! A dead body? A mummy?"

"Not anymore," Jamal explained. "The room where it used to be."

They were so pleased with their discovery and so insistent that I agreed. I convinced myself that I should really go inside the only pyramid I had ever seen. But I didn't like the idea of being inside that pile of rocks. I decided to make it quick, and I ducked into the dark entrance. Even though I'm a short person, I found myself walking bent over the length of a low, pitch-dark tunnel, following Jamal's flashlight.

"Wait up Jamal! Slow down! I can't see anything," I complained. As we dove deep into the rock edifice, the tunnel got progressively shorter and narrower. My back ached. Claustrophobia assailed me. I called frantically, "Jamal! Yusuf! Come back!"

"It's OK Ummi," Jamal called to me in the darkness. "We're almost there."

"But I can't see!" I could no longer detect Jamal's flashlight, and worried that the battery had died. What if this tunnel branched and I took the wrong way? What if we got lost in a maze of false passageways? Terror began to take hold of me. I took a deep breath to try to calm myself, but that was a mistake. The musty, ancient, unhealthy air that hadn't seen daylight for centuries made me cough and gag. My throat constricted, my heart pounded, and my lungs gasped for air.

I had just turned to flee from the tomb when I heard Jamal announce, "We're here!"

Instead of retreating, I took a few steps forward and saw a vague patch of grey ahead. Trying to be brave for my adventurous boys, I took one step after another toward the sound of their voices. Then, the tunnel suddenly widened. I found I was standing with Jamal and Yusuf in a large room with a flat, dusty floor and unadorned rock walls. There was nothing in the room, not even a sarcophagus. It had been totally emptied of whatever had once been there. The boys and I chatted and speculated on what this burial place of a king and queen might have originally looked like. After a few minutes, I told the boys we had to leave, giving them the excuse that their brothers needed me. When I finally emerged from the tunnel of my torture, I was overwhelmed with relief. But I could now say I had once gone into an ancient pyramid.

Another weekend, we took a camping trip to a beautiful oasis several hours southeast of where we lived. It was lush with plants and trees, nourished by abundant waters from an underground river. Arriving at dusk, we quickly set up our tent, but we weren't fast enough to escape the hordes of hungry mosquitoes that descended on us, filling the tent. We were driven back into the hot van, which had only one, small, screened window. Even as the evening approached, the heat in the van was overwhelming. Bathroom breaks were torture, as we had to quickly exit the van, shut the door, do our business while being attacked by the bloodsucking swarm, and re-enter the van without letting in too many bugs. We suffered all night.

In the morning we quickly took down the tent and drove away, scratching our bites. When we passed into an arid desert area far away from the oasis, we stopped to have breakfast and plaster our bites with ointment. Then we cut short the weekend and returned home. The oasis we visited was named for the river from which it sprang, but that name has been lost to me. In our family lore, we renamed it Oued Al-Namoos, or River of the Mosquitoes.

Our enjoyment of weekend trips was short-lived, unfortunately. Arriving home after work one day, Abdullah and I were met by our anxious children and the adult neighbors, who told us that they had heard rapid, repeated gunfire echoing across the high valley. We learned that the mountains were home to guerillas fighting against government forces. In the coming weeks, we heard more sporadic battles in the mountains, and the people in our compound were tense.

When Abdullah went to the mosque for Friday prayers, he was told it wasn't safe for him there because the mosque was under government surveillance. We had not known there was an armed insurgency in Algeria, though we sometimes had heard grumbling about the military dictatorship, cost of living, food shortages, and the lack of good jobs. With the mosque under suspicion, we understood that the insurgency had Islamic as well as economic roots.

The situation came closer to home when a Bulgarian man living with his wife in our housing compound was shot in his home. He claimed that he had been shot by insurgents who wanted the medical supplies he kept for his employer. Our small expat community was abuzz with speculation and concern. If guerrillas had targeted him, how they could have known he had medical supplies? How could guerrillas have gotten over the barbed wire topping the fence surrounding the compound or past the gate with its 24-hour guard?

"Are we safe here?" I asked Abdullah.

Abdullah's face was grim, "Mike would have raised hell if he smelled or heard any intruders, even if they tried to be quiet. I think the Bulgarian's wife shot him and he's covering for her. Their neighbors often heard loud arguments from that house."

"Well, that's a relief…" I began.

Abdullah continued, "But the bigger picture is the real risk. Everyone here is under surveillance, not just because of the Bulgarian thing, but the gun battles nearby. The police are on high alert."

He paused, and then added, with chagrin, "I was probably spotted at the mosque. They'll be watching me because of that."

His mention of the mosque triggered another worry. I hadn't really thought about how we got our jobs. I had naïvely believed that our résumés had convinced our employers to hire us. But maybe Abdullah's contacts with the Muslim Brotherhood had worked that magic, just as they had probably landed him his first job in Algeria six years earlier. These were matters he didn't discuss with me. But if the police got wind of it, we would be in trouble. Big trouble.

Meanwhile, our German Shepherd dog, Mike, disappeared. His chain in front of our house was unbroken, and he was not to be found anywhere within the compound fence. Neither were there any gaps where a dog could escape to the outside. Our search of the surrounding fields and nearby village yielded nothing. Abdullah's search widened to adjacent farms and hamlets, without success. Mike was an essential part of our security. Since he was the only thing standing between distance surveillance and up-close surveillance of our home, Abdullah became convinced that he had been stolen by the authorities.

Abdullah decided to move boldly by asking those regional military authorities for assistance in finding our dog. If they suspected us as being tied to guerrilla groups, they wouldn't expect us to come to the police station to ask for their help. Perhaps we could ease their suspicion by demonstrating that we were just ordinary foreigners. Of course, we hoped they would order the release of Mike or help us locate him. On the other hand, there was the possibility that they would hold us for interrogation since we had presented ourselves. The thought gave me the chills.

At the administrative military headquarters, we were asked to wait in a hall for what seemed a long time. Abdullah casually smoked a cigarette, while I tried to breathe slowly and appear utterly calm. Finally, we were ushered into a large, bleak office. A deadly serious man in uniform — the commander — sat at an imposing desk. He closed the file he had been reading and looked up at us, searching Abdullah's face. He folded his hands over the folder.

"What can we do for you?" he asked in a flat, brisk voice, glancing at his assistant, who returned the look.

"Thank you for meeting with us," Abdullah said respectfully. "Our dog, a German Shepherd, has been stolen. He is like family to our children."

"The children have missed him so much," I added, hoping to elicit sympathy from the grim military man. He ignored me and remained impassive.

Abdullah described where we lived and the areas that he had searched. "Have you heard anything about a German Shepherd wandering in your jurisdiction? We'd be grateful if you have any information that might help us find him."

Again, the commander's eyes flickered at his assistant, who carefully returned the look with hooded eyes. "We haven't heard of any such dog, but we will let you know if we see him," he said. Without sincerity, he added, "Good luck with your search." He nodded to his assistant, who rose to accompany us out of the office.

As soon as we were back in the car and on our way home, I exclaimed, "They knew!"

"Yes, it was clear they knew who we were, and they knew about Mike," Abdullah replied. "They were either the ones who ordered Mike to be taken, or they knew who did it."

"This is bad..."

"Yeah. I have a feeling that folder that he had been reading was about us. I feel their net closing in," Abdullah said. "We have to get out of Algeria before they decide that we're with the guerillas. Or that they can make us fall guys to cover their asses."

Abdullah and I pulled together in the face of danger to the family. With armed resistance fighters near our home and government officials suspecting our involvement in that fight, we were too vulnerable. Unlike normal American citizens, we could not walk into the U.S. Consulate and ask for help when faced with a dangerous situation. Nor could we leave immediately, because the Ministry of Education was keeping our passports until our teaching contracts were completed at the end of the school year. Abdullah and I began quietly sending out résumés to obtain teaching jobs in Libya.

When we received offers to teach English in the Libyan desert town of Sabha, we immediately made plans to travel to Tunisia, where we would obtain visas for Libya, and then travel to our new jobs. Abdullah and I asked our respective school administrators if we could leave the country for a two-week family vacation in Tunisia during the spring break. Fortunately, the school authorities gave us permission, so we applied for and got our passports back, and then obtained tourist visas to Tunisia. However, we didn't tell our kids, students, neighbors, or local friends about our so-called vacation, because if word got back to the military authorities, they might feel their suspicions about us were justified. They certainly could stop us from leaving, arrest us, and imprison us, and we would have no protection or legal recourse.

One day, Abdullah received a tip that there was a dog barking continuously in a certain neighborhood. When he drove slowly through the area calling for Mike, he heard a couple faint barks. Following the sound, he eventually found our canine friend chained up and too weak to stand. Our dog had either refused to eat or had not been fed and watered, and he was near death. Perhaps the villagers had been notified in advance that the foreigner was coming for his dog, or perhaps they thought the dog would be no use to them dead. In any case, no one objected to Abdullah unchaining Mike and carrying him to the car.

Back home, when the children and I saw Mike, a pandemonium of love broke loose, the kids exclaiming, "Mike! Mike! Mike!" We rushed to hug our best friend, and he hopped from the car only to collapse in a heap. He was extremely thin and weak, but his tail wagged with joy at being home with the family. The first day of Mike's recovery, Abdullah carefully gave him water and only a little bit of food. Gradually over the course of a couple weeks he increased his food until Mike recovered his health, strength, and most of his former weight.

During the time leading up to our scheduled leave, Abdullah and I were very busy. I packed up our essential belongings and Abdullah drove them to another town thirty miles away. There, he put our things into a small trailer he had borrowed, covered it with a tarp, and left it with a friend. He then returned home with the empty van. When the time came, we would leave the country with the van pulling the trailer.

As we talked through our plan, I asked, "But how are we going to return the trailer to the owner?"

"We won't," he replied.

"But those folks trusted us…"

Abdullah spoke harshly, "Look, we need it to escape this country. We won't return it. And by the way, I haven't paid anything for the van. And I won't."

"So, you're stealing the trailer and the van!" I exclaimed.

Abdullah just looked at me. I knew there was no use arguing, but I felt ashamed. It was so wrong to defraud anyone, especially people who trusted us. And the bad check he had written on our joint account had involved me as a partner in the crime. If I had been the decision-maker, we would have sold our old car and bought the only thing we could afford, a cheap used car that wasn't much better. However, when faced with imminent danger and an unreliable car, we wouldn't have been able to travel. I suspected Abdullah was right. My ethical approach wouldn't protect us from the danger that hovered over us.

In the meantime, we continued to teach, attend teachers' meetings, grade papers, plan lessons, play ball with the kids outside, go shopping, and take Mike for walks. Abdullah continued to drive to a nearby store some evenings to get cigarettes or milk. On weekends, we chatted and gossiped with the neighbors and shared food. Our lives looked the same as always to those who knew us.

After finishing the last day of teaching before spring break, Abdullah and I returned home, gave the kids dinner, and made one last sweep of the house, leaving the curtains closed, and the lights on. The belongings we were leaving behind were still in the cupboards and closets. At nightfall, I gathered the children and told them we were leaving, and they would have to be completely quiet so no one could hear us. Together, the kids and I got into the back of the camping van and hunkered down on the floor. Abdullah put Mike in the back with us, whispered a reminder to the kids to not move or make a single noise, and covered us all with dark blankets. I made this a hiding game for the younger children, but Yusuf and Jamal realized this was serious business.

Under the blankets, my heart was thumping loudly, and I was covered with sweat. I tried to clear my mind of anxious thoughts, acting calmly for the children's sake. I could do nothing now but trust Abdullah. I knew he would play his part flawlessly. He got in the driver's seat, turned up the radio, and drove the car to the gate of the compound. He stopped to chat casually with the guard at the gate, just as he had done many times before on his evening runs to buy cigarettes. I could hear the guard's voice as the two of them gossiped; time seemed endless to me, with my neck and back aching from my awkward position on the floor of the van. Little Shamail squirmed, but he didn't make a noise, and I put my hand on him to reassure him. Taha and Jubair were doing very well with hiding quietly, and the older boys were experts at it. Finally, Abdullah ended his conversation with the guard and drove slowly out of the compound. Very quietly, he told us to be still and silent a little longer.

After fifteen endless minutes, he told us we could sit up and take our places in the car. I gave the kids candies for their success at playing the game. The younger ones were happy about the treats, but the two older boys just looked at me, wanting an explanation. They knew from the expression on my face that I wouldn't tell them what was going on. I organized Jamal and Yusuf in the rear seat and put the younger ones to bed in the flat space behind the rear seat. Mike stayed on the floor, and I took the front passenger seat. We had left Khemis Miliana and were on our way.

We picked up the trailer packed with our critical belongings, turned east, and drove all night to the border of Tunisia. It was unlikely that anyone would discover our absence for at least a couple hours, and hopefully not until morning, but there was no sense taking a chance. We hoped it would take a while before they figured out where we went.

We easily crossed the border into Tunisia. With the danger of discovery by the Algerian authorities behind us, I breathed a sigh of relief. But Abdullah and I knew we had to attend to urgent matters. After getting some sleep in the van at the side of the road, we ate a quick breakfast and headed to the Libyan consulate in Tunis, where Abdullah would apply for our visas. He left the van on a side street near a park, where the kids and I could get out and stretch our legs while we waited.

"Bad news, Babe," Abdullah said as he returned.

I looked at him, noting his serious expression. My stomach sank. "What?"

"No visas to enter Libya. The border between Tunisia and Libya is closed, and they wouldn't say why."

"Oh no..." I said, swallowing the lump in my throat.

"I went into a hotel to see if I could get any information about the situation," Abdullah said. "A bunch of foreigners were in the lobby watching the news on TV. Something about diplomatic tensions between U.S. and Libya. Not sure why they closed the border."

We set up camp in a quiet area outside the city and considered our next move. Since we were currently in limbo, we might be able to find jobs here in Tunis. While I stayed with the kids and dog at our camping spot.

Abdullah took the van and made the rounds of language centers and schools in the city, asking about openings for English teachers. At least for now, there were no available positions. And the border with Libya seemed to be closed indefinitely.

Our situation was difficult. Tunisia is a small country bordered on the north and northeast by the Mediterranean Sea, on the southeast by Libya, and on the west by Algeria.

We seemed trapped, unable to go forward or back. "We can't stay in Tunisia without jobs. And we can't get into Libya from here." I looked at Abdullah. "The only way we can get into Libya is to cross back into Algeria, but that's dangerous..."

"I think we'll have to do that," replied Abdullah. "Drive southeast through Algeria to the Libyan border. It's not too far."

I was worried. "How do we know the Libyan border will be open there? If it's open, how do we get in without entry visas?"

Abdullah answered, "Once we get to the border, maybe the school administrator in Sabha can get us visas into Libya. If the border is open."

"Going back into Algeria is a risk. If the authorities in Khemis-Miliana have already discovered we're gone, they'll be sending out bulletins about us..."

Abdullah frowned, "Yeah. Well, hopefully they won't know where to look for us."

I felt a migraine invading my skull. "And the Algerian police will also be looking for you and the stolen car."

Abdullah stared at me pointedly. "Look, we have no choice. And we have another problem to deal with." His face was grave.

I looked up, alarmed. "Another problem?"

"Our visas," Abdullah replied. When he saw I didn't understand, he continued, "We can go back into Algeria using the travel visas we got to leave Algeria for our 'vacation.' But when we try to leave Algeria again to enter Libya, they won't let us because we no longer have a valid travel visa. We will either need our employers to issue another travel visa or cancel our work visas." He shrugged, "Obviously that isn't going to happen. But I have a plan."

Heading south through Tunisia, we entered Algeria on a dusty highway near El Oued. Stopping to camp for the night, I cooked supper, while Abdullah worked carefully on our passports. He removed the pages containing his and my Algerian work visas and travel visas. Then he smudged the date on the visas with which we had entered Algeria in 1985, so that it appeared that we had only recently entered as tourists. Hopefully, the Algerian border guards wouldn't notice that alteration, or the odd configuration of pages in the passports. This meant, however, that we would never be able to take the altered passports to an American consulate or embassy for any reason.

Nervously approaching the border near Ghadames, we hoped we would be allowed to cross into Libya and reach the jobs that were waiting for us. But as we approached the border crossing, we were stopped by Algerian police. They informed us the Libyan border was closed, and they required us to set up camp in the parking lot of the police station. They took our passports to screen, as we waited overnight anxiously. I made breakfast and tended the kids, my mind elsewhere…

Burning fear:
Will they arrest us
As suspected insurgents?
Swindlers, car thieves?
Will they leave my kids alone
In this land,
Our family broken?
Panic boils under the lid
Of my calm, decisive,
Façade that steels me
To keep us safe.

Finally, around noon the next day, the police returned our passports and informed us that we had to stay in the parking lot for our own protection. They didn't say why we needed protective custody. They were friendly, but deadly serious. Sensing a way out of the situation, Abdullah told them we had decided not to go into Libya. He asked for and received permission to leave the border and travel west to continue sightseeing in Algeria.

Stopping for fuel at the first gas station away from the border, we learned of the dangerous situation into which we had blundered. A day or two before we had tried to enter Libya — April 15, 1986 — the U.S had bombed the capital, Tripoli, killing scores of civilians, including the infant daughter of the Libyan leader, Muammar Gaddafi. The U.S. claimed this was in retaliation for Gaddafi's sponsorship of terrorists who had bombed a German nightclub. At the gas station, angry Algerian men gathered around a radio, listening to the horrifying news and shouting curses at President

Ronald Reagan and Americans in general. They were not necessarily fans of the despotic Gaddafi, but they were outraged at the foreign aggression on North African soil and the loss of civilian life.

Listening to the radio with them, Abdullah understood the danger to our safety. From then on, we would no longer admit we were Americans to the Algerians we met. Abdullah would represent himself as Jamaican – "like Bob Marley"– and I would be a Canadian. This would make us safer from possible retaliation by ordinary people, but the police at checkpoints, unfortunately, would know us as Americans by our passports.

Together, Abdullah and I developed a plan. The roads south through the Sahara were notoriously bad and often impassable, so going further into Africa was not an option. Our only option now was to travel west to Morocco. We would get jobs there, obtain work visas, and get our family resettled. Still, the country was a friend and ally of the U.S., and we would have to be very careful about our security. There would be no protection for Abdullah if the American authorities discovered him there. But even if we had had another choice, we didn't have enough money to go any further than Morocco.

We decided to avoid traveling through the populated coast of Algeria, where the authorities might be looking for us. The Algerian police at the Libyan border hadn't found anything suspicious when they presumably telephoned a more central authority with our passport numbers. But we had no guarantee that the slow wheels of Algerian bureaucracy wouldn't eventually connect the dots.

Our southern route took us through barren semi-arid and desert landscapes dotted with occasional small villages where we had to stop for police checkpoints. We assumed that the police who had kept us in protective custody had contacted their counterparts along the travel route we had indicated. That way they could track our movements. Each stop was nerve wracking as we waited to either be arrested or told to go on with our journey. Fortunately for us, the lack of computerized security systems in this part of the world worked in our favor.

But we wouldn't leave Algeria unscathed. Months after we left the country, we received word that the owner of the camping van had gone to court and received a judgment against Abdullah. The court required Abdullah to pay the victim the full amount owed for the car plus court costs, and he was sentenced to two years in an Algerian prison. Of course, Abdullah didn't pay anything or serve any time. But he could never return to that country, one of the few places where he would have received refuge if he had not committed this crime.

When we finally reached the northwestern Algerian border with Morocco, we faced a long wait while the customs officers processed travelers leaving the country. When our turn finally came, we were told that as tourists in Algeria, we were supposed to have documented the exchange of $700 U.S. dollars for Algerian dinars while in the country. Since we hadn't done so, we would have to pay the customs officers that amount now. Abdullah argued that we had no knowledge of this requirement and didn't even have that much money. He didn't elaborate, but in fact, we had only two hundred dollars left, and that would have to cover gasoline.

Unfortunately, none of Abdullah's old customs friends were on duty to help him out now. He spent hours trying to persuade one or another of the officers without success. The children were hot, tired, and hungry, and I was worried. Figuring that a relentlessly screaming baby might make the guards change their minds, I secretly pinched two-and-a-half-year-old Shamail as hard as I could. My poor toddler was an easy going and cheerful child, and even this insult only caused him to whimper. Guilty and defeated, I didn't try it again. I had no idea how we were going to pass the border. The guards were adamant.

One of the guards came over to our family for another try. He suggested our family in America could send the money. When Abdullah explained that his family were poor and had no money, the guard turned to me. He said, "Tell your family to send the money and then we can let you go!"

I thought of the death of my father, my mother's declining health, my unstable marriage, and the danger and stress I had endured stoically for years. The steel barriers I had built to stay strong now twisted and fell away. I couldn't stop the painful emotional flood that burst out of my heart.

In this utter breakdown, I wailed, "My father is dead! Dead! My mother's old and sick. She's so far away and I can't see her! We have no money! No money!" I collapsed in the dirt, sobbing...

> *My sacrifice unheeded,*
> *Love unloved.*
> *In smoldering pain,*
> *Endless tears flow to earth.*
> *I can't*

> *Can't go on.*
> *Little ones you gather around me,*
> *Weeping, holding me,*
> *Holding my broken heart.*
> *Except for you, I'd no longer exist.*
> *I am broken,*
> *But you breathe love into me,*
> *And once more*
> *I try to stand.*

Abdullah seemed shocked. He tried to comfort me and the children as we wept and held each other. The tide of tears turned the hearts of the customs officials, and they let us go. Into Morocco.

9

CLOUDS IN SUNNY MOROCCO

1986-1989

"Plant the love of the holy ones within your spirit;
don't give your heart to anything
but to the love of those whose hearts are glad.
Don't go into the neighborhood of despair:
there is hope.
Don't go in the direction of darkness:
suns exist."

Jelladin Rumi[25]

Emotionally exhausted, I was lulled by the steady rumble of the road rising to meet the tires of the speeding van. As we traveled through the Moroccan countryside, the two-lane paved road continuously sprang westward, leaving behind the dangers we had evaded but not truly leading us to safety. I allowed myself to be numbed. My breakdown at the border had allowed painful, suppressed emotions to surface. Now I felt wounded and fragile, with uncertain recovery. I trod the edge of depression and felt despair hovering just beyond. I wondered how I could proceed from this precarious position.

I knew with absolute certainty that we were in a struggle for survival, and my children needed me to be strong. For their sake, I tried to steel myself and wall off my pain again. But this time, I wasn't sure the wall would hold.

---

[25] *Love's Ripening: Rumi on the Heart's Journey,* "The Laughter of Pomegranates." Kabir Helminski and Ahmad Rezwani, 2008.

Our destination was Rabat, the capital of Morocco, poised on the edge of the Atlantic. Before reaching the city, we stopped at the shore of the vast ocean, its large, dark waves piling onto the earth relentlessly. Though the spring weather was still cool, the kids ran barefoot along the sandy beach, squealing and dashing into the icy shallows, ignoring my warnings not to get wet. Abdullah, who had scored some hash in Oujda, rolled it into a joint mixed with tobacco, and smoked quietly, staring at the waters that extended from this North African shore all the way to the Americas. Hash was cheap here in Morocco, though we could ill afford anything other than food and gas. But if it kept him happy, it made life easier for all of us. Or so I thought at the time.

Drawing a deep breath from the cool sea breeze, I kicked off my shoes and let my toes taste the surging waters. Regardless of what had happened or what would happen, I felt calm in this moment as I connected with earth, sea, and sky. I murmured a prayer of thanks as I stood at the western edge of the most western land of the Arab world – al Maghreb. But all too soon the moment passed, and my thoughts turned to the mundane. We needed to find a place to camp and buy basic groceries. Then, I would set up camp and cook a decent meal for the family. And of course, Abdullah and I urgently needed to find work.

In the city of Salé, across the Bou Regreg River from Rabat, we pitched our tent at a campground that had running water, toilets, electricity, a large grassy area where the kids could play, and 24-hour security guards. The next morning, and every day afterward, Abdullah showered, dressed, and took the van to look for a job, while I prepared meals, washed clothes, and managed the kids. Then, one day our luck turned.

Abdullah pulled up and hopped out of the car. Smiling, he exclaimed, "We got job offers, both of us!"

"Alhamdulillah." I felt hope surge within me, though cheer was elusive. "Come tell me about it while I cook," I said.

"We'll be teaching English at the American Language Center," Abdullah said. "It's part-time at first, but the ALC director assures me more hours will open up next semester."

"That's great," I said, relieved that we would begin earning money again. The little we had was dwindling fast. "But if we're both working, what about the kids?"

"We both have to work so we can save money to rent an apartment," Abdullah said. "Meanwhile we'll stay here at the campground. The kids… well, Jamal and Yusuf will have to take care of their brothers."

I felt uneasy leaving twelve-year-old Jamal and ten-year-old Yusuf in charge of the little ones, ages six, four, and two-and-a-half. They were a handful, even for me. But if I stayed with the kids while Abdullah worked part-time, we'd have only enough income to pay for camp fees, food, cooking gas, and gasoline so he could drive to work. Both of us needed to work so we could eventually move into an apartment. Abdullah spoke to the camp guardian about our concern for the children, and the man promised he'd make sure they didn't leave the camp.

The ALC offered English language classes for adults, teens, and children, as well as advanced reading and writing for Moroccans preparing for study in the U.S. The syllabus, lesson plan, and materials for each course was provided, so I focused on improving my teaching skills and interacting with the students. I enjoyed teaching the diverse students who came to the center, but I worried about the children while I was at work.

Two weeks after we had started working, Abdullah got a phone call at the ALC. The guardian at the campground reported that one of the kids had been hurt. Abdullah had trouble understanding the man, since Moroccan Arabic differs from the Algerian Arabic dialect we spoke. We wound up our classes, notified the administration of the emergency, and left work.

"Who got hurt, Abdullah?" I asked as we drove to the campground.

"The guardian said the youngest, Shamail. He said he was all right, I think, but hurt," Abdullah replied.

"What does that mean?"

"I don't know. We'll find out when we get there."

At the campsite, Jamal ran to meet us, "Shamail burned his neck!"

"How?" Abdullah asked as I bent to attend to my toddler. He was subdued but did not seem to be in pain, except when I touched the ugly, second degree burn to put ointment on it.

"Jubair and Taha and Shamail were running around the tent," Yusuf explained. "Shamail ran into the tent and fell on the heater."

"The electric heater was on?" I looked at Jamal. I had turned it off when I left for work that morning.

Looking at the ground, Jamal said, "We were cold."

I was devastated that two-and-a-half-year-old Shamail had suffered a burn. He and his anxious brothers had been waiting nearly an hour for Abdullah and me to arrive. I was angry at myself for not being there to keep my children safe…

Absentee mom, I failed
To prevent harm
To my child.
Sweet children, I failed
When you needed me.
How do I choose:
Provide for you
Or care for you?

Fortunately, the camp guardian introduced us to a woman who agreed to watch the children, cook meals, and do laundry at the camp while we were gone. We didn't know if she was reliable, but we didn't have much choice at that point. Naima, who lived nearby, turned out to be a good laundress, an average cook, and an acceptable babysitter. Abdullah also discovered that she was honest. He accidentally left a hundred dollar bill, our only remaining hard currency, in his jeans pocket. When she discovered the money as she was washing clothes, she handed it to Abdullah and returned to her work. She was a poor woman, for whom that money would have been at least three months income. When we finally moved out of the camp into a small apartment, we asked Naima to continue working for us, and she agreed.

A month later, we moved into a small apartment in a pleasant neighborhood of Salé. The place was clean and secure, though cramped for our family of seven and a dog. The size was offset by the small walled garden at the front entrance. Each day after returning home from work, I ran my hand through the short hedge of rosemary that lined the front walk, letting the heavenly aroma fill the air.

"Salaamu alaikum! Is anyone up for a walk?" I called out to the family as I opened the front door. I smiled at Naima and nodded approval at her preparations for dinner.

The kids were sprawled on the living room floor, reading and playing with their toys. Jamal and Yusuf jumped up as one, "Yes!" Jubair, Taha, and Shamail agreed happily.

"Pick up your toys," I reminded them. They scurried to comply.

Opening the gate of our front garden, the older boys led their brothers onto the street, chattering as they rolled along like a mob of puppies. All the villas in the neighborhood were hidden from the street by walls that hosted masses of green vines laden with colorful flowers. The sweet fragrance of jasmine floated on the air, an invitation to reverie. As I kept an eye on my boys, I was simultaneously drawn into the luscious world of plants. That world encouraged me to grow and bloom, and I accepted the invitation.

The moist sea winds along the Atlantic coast of Morocco nourished palm trees, fruit trees, flowers, vegetables, and the delicious fresh mint that Moroccans added to their sweetened green tea. Under the blessing of the North African sun and winter rains, local farmers grew fresh produce and hauled it daily to the markets, where vendors displayed it in artful splashes of reds, oranges, yellows, and numerous shades of green.

"Ummmmmi!" Taha was crying. "Jubair took my stick!"

"Jubair, give him the stick," I admonished. "Let's look for another stick so you can each have one."

I noticed that Shamail had grumpily sat down on the ground. I was going to have to carry him. "Jamal! Yusuf! Jubair! Come back."

They grumbled a protest.

"We have to turn around now," I said. "Dinner will be ready by the time we get back."

The reminder of food spurred the kids to quickly reverse course. I picked up Shamail, hoisted him on my shoulders, and shepherded my kids home.

While my connection with the earth helped me stay grounded, my work and interaction with students and teachers at the ALC strengthened my confidence. I felt satisfaction in earning money for the family and developing relationships with people outside the home. From my students, I learned to listen more carefully and ask better questions. From my Moroccan friends, I began to acquire the skills of human connection and community that I had not absorbed in my childhood. I felt that I was at last starting to become an adult in the social sphere of life. Though I knew I had much more to learn, it was a new beginning for me.

Unfortunately, I was losing ground on another front. Because Abdullah's security in Morocco would always be at risk, we had concocted false identities – stories about who we were, why we were traveling, and how he and I had met. His freedom depended on both of us playing our parts convincingly in this false history, so I never told anyone about my real childhood, my youthful adventures, my education, or my own spiritual path. If anyone asked, I supplied details from our cover story. The burden of this constant charade was that my real self was hidden beneath a persona constructed of truths, partial truths and outright lies. I presented myself as a simple, happily married, American Muslim woman who was devoted to her children and supportive husband. My relationships with friends were based on this fiction…

> *They see only*
> *My mask,*
> *Not who I was or am or could be.*
> *They can't see*
> *What I've seen*
> *Nor feel my anguish,*
> *Nor hear my own voice.*

After several months of working long hours at the language center, Abdullah and I became more financially stable. We found a larger apartment with three bedrooms, a large living room, and a spacious balcony, as well as a garage, back yard, and small ground level room. I registered the younger children for a local private school where they would learn to read and write in Arabic and French. I was still homeschooling Jamal and Yusuf in English, though I struggled to find the time to check their work as I was now teaching a full course load. I came to rely heavily on Naima to do the housekeeping, childcare, and cooking, and we invited her to live in the downstairs room.

Things did not go well at this apartment. First, our well-loved dog, Mike, was stolen. Abdullah and I came home from work one day to discover that the front gate had been opened and Mike had disappeared. Naima and the kids had not gone outside of the compound, and the gate was usually locked, so someone else had to have opened it. Furthermore, Mike would have come back home unless he had been restrained or injured. That day, and for days afterward, Abdullah, Jamal, and Yusuf combed the area, searching and calling for Mike and listening for his answering bark. There was no sound from our faithful friend. After a couple weeks of fruitless searching after work each day and on weekends, we had to accept that Mike was gone.

Then, Naima left unexpectedly, taking all her belongings with her, and I didn't know why. Abdullah set about immediately looking for a replacement for her. It was a few months later that I ran across Naima in the souk. When I stopped to chat and see how she was doing, she hunched her shoulders and wouldn't look me in the eye. She was clearly ashamed about something that she would not reveal. Feeling her discomfort, I too was ashamed of whatever had happened to make her leave my home. I could find no words to utter to this humble woman, and we parted quickly. I knew she hoped never to see me again.

In the meantime, Abdullah had found a young woman to be our housekeeper. Attractive, married, and an excellent cook, Layla seemed intelligent and energetic. Since she came from a traditional family, her father visited us to make sure the position would be acceptable for his daughter. I immediately liked the old man, who was straightforward, honest, and religious. He wore the brown wool djellaba and white prayer cap of a traditional North African man, and I was surprised that I could communicate with him fairly well. Born and raised near the border with Algeria, Abdul Haqq spoke the dialect I had learned in that country. He was reassured by the fact that Abdullah and I were Muslims, and he agreed to Layla's employment in our home.

Layla's strongest skill was in cooking delicious, traditional Moroccan dishes that delighted the whole family. I had to teach her what I expected in caring for the children, and she seemed to catch on quickly. She was an adequate laundress and housekeeper, good enough for me but not necessarily for Abdullah, who expected spotless floors, a sparkling kitchen, and a neatly arranged household at all times. She learned to meet those expectations and develop a tentative relationship with me as well, teaching me to cook some simple Moroccan fare. I was relieved that the children and household were in good hands while I was working.

I came home tired after a long day at work, ate dinner quickly, and began getting the younger kids ready for bed. As I shepherded them to the bathroom to wash up, I turned in time to see Layla and Abdullah exchanging a long glance full of meaning. I finished putting the little kids to sleep, checked in on Jamal and Yusuf, and then turned out the lights on my way to bed. But there would be little sleep for me.

What followed was my angry confrontation of my husband, his vicious recriminations, and a stream of volatile abuse, like so many other fights that we had had in our tumultuous life together. I was so tired of this. It had to end. Sobbing, I retreated to the living room and collapsed on a mattress on the floor. Abdullah, angry that I refused to return to our bedroom, emerged and hurled parting abuse. At that moment, I hated him so much that nothing could have forced me to sleep with him. Exhausted and despairing, I fell asleep on a pillow drenched with tears.

In the morning, I got ready for work without speaking to him and took a bus to work for my early class. When he arrived at the language center later in the day, I avoided him and focused on my teaching. Work was something I could do with the part of my brain that wasn't in emotional turmoil.

When I returned home from the language center, I found that in my absence, Abdullah had destroyed a treasured book he had given me at our marriage. Torn pages and chunks of the broken binding were scattered all over the bedroom, and he was sulking in bed. I was so shocked I couldn't speak. This wasn't just an ordinary gift. It was my mahr, the token Abdullah had given me to seal our marriage in 1975, according to Islamic custom. Usually, the Muslim groom gives his bride money, jewelry, or other possessions which become her own personal wealth. However, I had felt that the spiritual bond between us and our love of Allah were more important than any material goods. Thus, I had asked him only for this book of spiritual guidance as the mahr. For over ten years I had cherished that symbol of human love and devotion to Allah, even when I felt weak in my faith and trapped in a loveless relationship. I felt numb as I gazed wordlessly at the tatters of our life littered on the floor. In a single furious onslaught, he had repudiated our faith , our marriage, and me.

Abdullah began talking as if he were trying to keep me from leaving him. I wondered why he bothered, since he had made very clear how he felt about me and our relationship. Silently listening to him, I realized that he considered me as a potential threat who had to be managed, since I knew more about his life, circumstances, and identity than anyone else. I sensed that in his eyes, I might defect from his side and choose to reveal his identity at any time. How little he knew me.

My numbness dissolved into tears of despair, but I remained silent, not trusting myself to speak. When I couldn't bear to listen to any more promises, I nodded, for the sake of our children. At least, for now. My gaze returned to the remains of the mahr littering the floor around our bed like pieces of my heart. Fallen tears spotted a fragment of a page at my feet.

"I'll get you another one," he promised without apology.

Silently, I turned away and retreated to the bathroom, the only private space in the apartment. Washing my face at the sink, I paused as I glimpsed my flushed, distraught face in the mirror. I heard the children coming home from school, calling to each other as they dumped their backpacks on the floor. But my mind was still occupied with the latest of the losses I had experienced in my marriage to their father...

My mahr is gone:
His gift of love,
Seal of our union,
The pledge of our hearts,
Gone,
The treasure thrown to earth in shreds.

During the years that Abdullah and I had corresponded across prison walls, I had come to love him as my spiritual companion in Islam. Leaving the country in 1980 and setting foot for the first time in the Muslim world, I had been filled with hope for both the blossoming of our marriage and my growth in Islam. Six years later, those dreams were battered beyond recognition. Now, I could not depend on Abdullah for spiritual support, as he seemed increasingly remote from our religion. Although I still loved Islam, my spiritual life wavered, like a distant light flickering and disappearing behind dark clouds. For periods of time, I prayed daily and fasted, trying to hold onto my religion. However, without a solid footing in my relationship with God, I felt myself slowly sliding downhill, away from the peace of oneness.

In Morocco, religion was central to the lives of the people, and I admired the way they expressed reminders of peace, blessing, and surrender to God in their everyday conversations. But without a command of the local dialect, I had little hope of establishing human relationships which could potentially support me in my spiritual crisis. Thus, even though Moroccans were warm toward me, I felt isolated from my brothers and sisters in Islam.

I still had a spiritual connection with the natural world, which had always been central to my life. I immersed myself in the life-giving rains of the Moroccan winter, entranced by palm trees waving in the wind. The giant storks nesting in trees by the river gave me a sense of peace, and the sweet scent of lush gardens along the coast comforted me. The air itself welcomed me.

I felt that Abdullah, too, experienced at least some serenity in places far from the city. In our first years in Morocco, he frequently took the family on day trips to the forest north of Salé, where he and the older children would play hide and seek while I watched the little ones and prepared a picnic lunch. On longer vacations, we took camping trips to the mountains near Ifrane and to the Mediterranean beach at Saidia. He was almost always relaxed on these occasions, and as a result, my own stress would lessen. In the beautiful surroundings, I imagined that our marital problems were just the normal stresses of two very different people living a married life together.

Such experiences gave me false hope and fed my denial about the reality of my relationship with Abdullah. But underlying my life with him – as well as my childhood and youth – was a constant current of depression. Sometimes, that current dove underground and I was able to ignore it, convincing myself that all was well. Other times, it emerged above ground as a raging torrent, devastating all hope.

As I write these words many years later, I understand much that I didn't know back then. I didn't know then that I constrained my grief, anger, and fear – and the resulting depression – behind a wall so that I could think clearly, play my part convincingly, and do whatever was necessary to survive. Though depression often seeped out of cracks as pressure built, I was still able to put one foot in front of the other, like a beast of burden pulling a heavy load. But this state left me feeling dull and empty inside, interfering with my spiritual life. At its worst, it left me devoid of emotion and unable to express my love to my children, despite my dedication to them. It also made me blind to the emotional stresses they were experiencing in the family.

I wanted to leave Abdullah, the source of so much pain for me, but I felt my suffering shouldn't be the cause of the breakup of the family. Committed to my children, my marriage, and my husband, I believed in the importance of marriage in ensuring a stable home for our children. I also strongly felt my sons needed their father. But the strongest influence on my decision to stay was not apparent to me at that time. The seeds of our mutual love and respect, seeds that were sown in the early years of our marriage, bore durable but asymmetrical fruit: though our personal relationship was damaged beyond repair, our soul connection to each other was steadfast. I know this now because I still feel that kinship with him.

In recent years, I've realized that my unquestioning idealism regarding marriage and the traditional family was patterned on my father's unconditional loyalty to my mother, his abusive wife. He seemed oblivious to the damage she inflicted on his children. And perhaps he, like me, had a deeper connection with his spouse that contributed to his decision to stay in the marriage. Ironically, as a teenager, I rebelled strongly against him, but in my marriage, I became just like him, loyal to a fault.

On the heels of this crisis, we moved into a large, two-story, stucco house in Hay Chmaou, some distance from Salé. Our house stood alone on the coast, far from any other habitations except for a rough shack that was home to a lame shepherd, his wife, children, and a few sheep. From the second story, we had a breathtaking, panoramic view of the ocean and the rugged coast. A couple hundred yards out to sea loomed a large, angular rock penetrated by a keyhole through which the surging waters of the Atlantic poured endlessly. A narrow footpath led down the cliffs to dark, sea-soaked, boulders where an occasional fisherman waited to hook dinner. On hot days, poor young men gathered there, daring each other to dive into the dangerous, often fatal waters. Because of the area's remoteness and lack of police presence, it was also frequented by rough men who engaged in various illegal activities along the shore. It was a wild, lonely place that both soothed and unsettled me.

To provide security for our family, Abdullah began raising and training Doberman Pinscher dogs to stand guard over our house. Highly effective in working with animals, he began to train dogs for resident foreigners in Rabat and Salé. Eventually, he built a walled kennel next to the house and offered boarding for his customers' dogs. Meanwhile, he and I continued to work full time as English teachers at the ALC in Rabat.

In 1988, my mother wrote me that she and my youngest sister were planning to come to Morocco to visit us. My painful memories of growing up were still repressed, and I felt only anticipation at being with my mother and Karen. I happily planned trips we would take to the coastal countryside, the ancient cities of Morocco, and the handicraft markets. Catching my enthusiasm, the children cleaned their rooms and colored special pictures for their grandmother and aunt.

When Abdullah returned from the airport with Mom and Karen, the kids besieged them with hugs and kisses.

"Hold on!" I laughed. "Let them come inside and sit down!"

Jamal and Yusuf led our guests into the living room while their younger brothers followed closely, talking all at once.

Taha ran ahead, "Nana, look at the picture I made for you!"

"Oh, that's beautiful! Is that you in the picture?" asked my mother.

"Karen, I can swim!" interrupted Jubair, who at eight years old was a good swimmer.

"Me too!" said five-year-old Shamail hopefully.

I could see that my mother was exhausted after her long trip. "OK boys, Nana needs to rest now. Why don't you show Karen around?"

While I helped my mother get settled in the guest room, the kids grabbed Karen's hands and took her for a tour of the back yard and beyond. I caught up with them as they approached a natural feature a hundred feet away from the house that impressed the children and terrified me. We referred to it as "The Hole," a fifteen-foot deep, vertical pothole in the porous, pockmarked rock. About two feet in diameter, the gap was just the right size for an unwary child to trip and plunge into the cave below, where chaotic waves smashed against rock. I made sure the children stood clear of the hole at a safe distance while Karen inspected it. Then I brought them away from that danger to gaze at the ocean. From the cliff edge, we watched the vast waters of the Atlantic rise and fall like the breathing of a sleeping giant, her exhalation creating spray that plastered our faces with salt.

One day Karen and the boys set out to explore a ruined fort along the coast, while I drove Mom on a short trip to Khemiset in search of handmade rugs. There was much to talk about as I drove — news about relatives, my mother's conservation activities, Moroccan culture, the grandchildren. Along the way, we stopped for a drink of water and a snack of bread, goat cheese, and dates that I had brought. During a pause in our conversation, my mother turned to me. "Aisha, I love you. You know, I've always loved you."

Startled, I stared at her. "I love you too, Mom," I mumbled, the words feeling strange in my mouth.

I was nearly forty years old, and as far as I could recall, my mother had never — not in my childhood, adolescence, or adulthood — told me that she loved me. And I realized that I didn't feel anything like love for her. Of course, we had a long history together, but our relationship didn't have any emotional depth. I didn't feel for my mother anything like the love I had for my brother, or for each of my children, or even for Abdullah early in our marriage. She was like a distant relative who had come for a visit. Why had she told me this so late in my life? Was this a sort of apology? For what? My childhood memories of her were tweaked, but they remained firmly buried. I was left puzzling over her words.

Much later in life, deep shamanic healing work showed me the cause of both my depression and my fractured relationship with my mother. Peeling the layers of my young life back, I discovered that my dark moods started much earlier than my conscious memories indicated. When I was about three years old, my mother began to harshly reject me, refusing to interact with me unless it was necessary to keep up the pretense of normality in front of other people. She fed and clothed me but didn't love me. Trapped in her own hell without mental health treatment, she had no interest in or energy for a young child.

During her visit to Morocco, I was perplexed by Abdullah's reaction to her. One night after the rest of the family had gone to bed, I saw him making his eyes bulge in a myopic, baleful expression that was unlike any I'd seen on his face before.

"What are you doing with your eyes?" I asked.

"I'm doing like your mother," he responded, intensifying the hostile expression, which reminded me of her darkest, most frightening countenance. "I can't stand her."

Disconcerted, I blurted, "Why?"

He refused to reply, and I knew he would not say another word. I could see why he might not like my mother. She was often impassive, distant, and aloof. But why did he imitate this facial expression? I couldn't guess.

Looking back on that moment, I see that they were so alike, my husband and my mother. Both were highly intelligent. They were consumed with an inner, volcanic anger which they concealed thoroughly from outsiders, but with which they controlled and intimidated their immediate family members. And yet, at times, they both seemed to rise above their demons to celebrate a child's birthday, enliven a family outing, or plan holiday fun. Both were well respected by people outside the family, and they made positive contributions to their communities.

Fortunately, during my mother's visit to us in Morocco, she and Abdullah kept a lid on whatever tension existed between them. The kids took Karen and their grandmother to their favorite haunts, and I organized field trips to Marrakech and historical sites. We were experts at denial and pretense, and the visit ended without mishap.

For my fortieth birthday, Abdullah threw a large, lively costume party at our house, inviting our friends from the language center, local Moroccan acquaintances, and Abdullah's friends from the running club and the dog club. There was good food, music, and dancing, and the guests arrived in an amusing assortment of improvised costumes. I dressed as a black cat, with black tights, a long T-shirt, and cat's whiskers painted on my face with mascara. As the party heated up, Abdullah provided alcohol to select friends while offering soft drinks to Muslims. For those inclined to hashish, one of his Moroccan friends passed joints in the back yard.

It wasn't the alcohol or hash that called to me but the pounding music and the lively crowd. My body responded with wild dance, jumping and writhing away my worries as I celebrated my four decades on the earth. I immersed myself in the shouts, singing, acrobatics and sweat of the partygoers as Abdullah tended the sound system, producing waves of loud dance music that enveloped the house. What a blast! Finally, winded, I pulled myself out of the throbbing mass of guests and stumbled outside to breathe the cool night air.

Walking a short distance away from the house, I stopped to clear my head and smell the salty sea breeze swirling around me. Above me hung the deep, starless sky. The dark waves of the Atlantic slammed repeatedly on the rocks below, the reverberation of which made my feet hum, connecting me to the endless, living ocean. Beyond the lights of the house, the black night embraced me, and I raised my hands to feel the moist air flowing above me and through my lungs. For a while, I was an integral part of the rocky shore, the night sky, and surging waters. For a while, I felt whole. However, this healing was not to last.

For months, Abdullah had seemed to be unstable. He spent money we could not afford and became careless at work. He bought a big, expensive motorcycle and rode around Salé with Layla seated behind him, her long hair flowing. He ignored my requests to discuss our finances, and he stopped consulting with me on work or family matters. Finally, he stopped talking to me altogether.

When he ran out of hash, he would fall into a rage, and the children, would run away and hide in the bamboo thickets between our house and the shore. At these times, Layla would quickly go to her family's home to ask her brothers to buy more hash for him. If I were home, I'd collect the kids from the stand of bamboo, and together, we'd take our dog Diamond for a long walk. We hoped that Layla would soon return with hashish to calm Abdullah.

I knew the situation was becoming critical, but I didn't know what to do about it. If he wouldn't listen to me or even talk to me, how could I help him? More importantly, how could I protect the children? One evening, in a rare, calm moment, Abdullah sat down with me to talk. Silently, I waited to hear what he had to say.

"I've been thinking about marrying Layla, now that she's divorced," said Abdullah, looking at me for my reaction.

If I was surprised, it was because he had finally decided to talk to me. It was obvious he was not happy in his relationship with me, but we both had a responsibility to our children. Perhaps with Layla, I thought, he would be happier, smoke less hash, and settle down. Perhaps two wives could manage him better than one.

"Will this make you happy?" I asked him. "Is it what you really want?"

He looked at me softly, a look I hadn't seen for years. "Yes," he replied.

In that moment I had a glimpse of the man I had married. But regardless of what he said, I knew I could only wait to see how this played out. This, I believed, was our last chance to save what remained of our marriage and keep the family from falling apart altogether. "All right then," I said.

Unfortunately, the calm I thought I had seen in Abdullah's eyes was fleeting, and his marriage to Layla did not improve the situation. He was fired from his job at AMC, accused of mismanaging an important exam. Worse, because I was his wife, I was judged guilty by association and lost my job at the language center. This precipitated a financial crisis for our family. When he and I sat down to discuss our financial state, Abdullah revealed to me that he had not paid the rent for many months and now owed thousands of dollars in back rent. Looming over our heads was a lawsuit brought by the owner against Abdullah. He had almost nothing in his checking account, and I had only enough in my account to pay a month's worth of family expenses.

Moving into action, I immediately got full-time work as a bookkeeper for an agriculture project at Mohammad the Fifth University, as well as a part-time job tutoring at the American School in Rabat. I became the sole wage earner for the family. Because our car had developed mechanical problems that we couldn't afford to fix, I commuted by bus, big taxi, and on foot for hours each day to my jobs in Rabat.

Working to support the family was not only a financial necessity but also my method of managing depression. While my mind was fully occupied with work, that shadow rarely slipped out of its locked compartment. But after I returned home at the end of the day, my fatigue cracked open the gate to that dark place and I descended into the neighborhood of despair. I had given my heart to a man who was drowning in his own chaos. Now, bereft of my husband's love and my faith in God, I plunged into the deep vat of my own unspoken traumas. The dark thoughts did not flee when sleep came to me but fueled disturbing dreams. Dreams of powerful waves washing over me, taking me away. Of undertow carrying my limp body out to sea,

Although I had finally realized the children and I would be better off without Abdullah, my depression left me without energy to do anything but go to work. I became suicidal, walking along the shore in the evenings, trying to get up the nerve to fall into the surf and let myself be taken into the ocean's arms. Walking along the coast one night, feeling hopeless beyond all reason, I was so overwhelmed with torment that I even deluded myself that the children would be all right with Abdullah and Layla after I killed myself. As I turned toward the ocean, I chanced to glance back toward the house. Behind me a couple hundred feet was Jamal, trailing me. He waved to me and began to run toward me.

I waited. "What are you doing out here?" I asked.

He answered honestly, "Abu sent me to follow you."

"Why?"

"He was worried about you."

I could see Jamal was worried too. I wondered what he thought might happen to me, but I wasn't going to discuss it. "Let's go back. It must be time for dinner," I told him.

On the way back to the house, my depression was brightened with an edge of anger. If my husband was so concerned, I thought, why hadn't he come to me himself? Instead, he had sent a child to do what he should have done. I seethed. The anger sharply brought me to my senses. Neither Abdullah nor Layla would be able to care for my children without me. Even

now, the children were largely unsupervised and at risk while I was at work.
I had to find a solution immediately.

I was especially worried about Yusuf, who had learned to make gunpowder by studying an old encyclopedia and seeking the advice of knowledgeable old Moroccan men. He used the black powder to blow up rocks and power homemade rockets, including one that flew a couple kilometers along the coast, startling the local shepherds. I was impressed with his ingenuity but worried sick about the danger of his experiments. Knowing he would continue while I was at work, even if I forbade him, I asked him to wait until I was home to work with the gunpowder and rockets. He agreed, and I hoped he would keep his promise.

Meanwhile, both Yusuf and Jamal, in their early teens, needed educational opportunities that weren't available to us. Unlike their younger brothers, who had attended local schools since the age of five, the older boys weren't literate in Arabic, though they could speak the language fluently. Moroccan schools had no way of addressing the needs of second language learners, other than to put them in first grade. Instruction in English was available only at the private, prohibitively expensive American School. Reluctantly, I decided to send Yusuf and Jamal to stay with my mother in the States, where they could attend high school.

The departure of my oldest sons for the faraway U.S. was painful for them, for their younger brothers, and for me. I mourned alone, trying to stay strong for the family. Jubair, Taha, and Shamail cried, asking me to take them to America. Even Abdullah was subdued. Although our family had its problems, it was tightly knit after years of traveling and living together in foreign lands, dependent on each other for survival. The break created by the sudden absence of Yusuf and Jamal left a hole in the family that could not be filled.

Energized by the need to protect my younger children, I resolved to ask my American friend Ouarda Mehdaoui to help me and the children to leave Abdullah, quickly and quietly, before he could stop us. It wasn't the best plan, since she was a good friend of his, but I had no one else I could ask.

Unfortunately, it was shortly thereafter that Abdullah announced that he was going to leave Morocco before the landlord's suit against him came before the court.

I was floored, "You said you were negotiating a settlement with the landlord!" I cried.

"Not gonna happen," he responded casually. "No way I'm going to pay him."

He was again burning bridges behind him, destroying the possibility of his returning to Morocco. We had been in this country for three years, and it was a good place to live. "Where will you go? What's your plan?"

"I'm leaving for Tunisia as soon as the car is fixed at the end of the week."

"What?!"

"And I'm taking Layla and the kids…"

"No!" I objected. "Leave us here while you find a place and get settled. We'll move to an apartment, and I'll keep working."

Abdullah looked at me grimly, "It's already decided. They'll come with me. Luka and Diamond, too. You'll keep working until the end of your contract, so we'll have money to travel and to start over in Tunisia."

I crumbled. For months I had known I needed to somehow evade Abdullah and leave Morocco with the children. Under the impression that Abdullah had made arrangements with the landlord, I thought I had time to come up with a plan. But this was not to be. I had never been separated from my children, and the thought filled me with dread, especially in these circumstances.

Abdullah read my face, "It won't be long," he said. "Only three months. Since we can't go through Algeria, we'll travel through Spain, France, and Italy and take the ferry to Tunisia. You'll fly to Tunisia in August to join us."

I noticed that he had obviously planned his getaway carefully, without consulting me. Prior to this, we had always discussed each major decision and mapped out our plan of action together. Now, he was embarking on a risky journey without my input, putting the family in jeopardy. I knew Layla could not manage the children, organize the traveling, set up and break camp quickly, and keep to a tight budget, let alone support Abdullah in his security concerns. Above all, she could not keep him grounded. She didn't even know he was anything but a wealthy American professor. Meanwhile, the children would be vulnerable without my presence.

Within days, he packed the car, moved me to a small apartment in Rabat, and left in the dead of night with Layla and the children. Abdullah knew I was deeply unhappy in our marriage and sensed I was getting ready to leave him. His preemptive action prevented me from leaving him and allowed him to avoid the court order for his non-payment of rent. Traveling with the family would help him to prevent suspicion while traveling. Since he had the children with him, he ensured I would send him money from my earnings for the next three months. And at the end of the summer, he knew I would follow him to Tunisia.

Sick at heart and alone in Rabat, I blamed myself for indecisiveness, for not foreseeing this turn of events, for not insisting the children stay with me in Morocco. I missed the children terribly and worried about them. But I never thought of going to the U.S. embassy for assistance. I was still blindly loyal to this man, even though I no longer loved or respected him. Deprived of my children – temporarily, I assured myself – I kept working, longing for the day when I could rejoin them in Tunisia.

Free time was something I hadn't experienced since the birth of my first child over fifteen years ago. Now, with time on my hands, I visited friends in Rabat. Sometimes, I visited a friend who was a talented artist. She and I were both hard-working mothers, and we both had rocky relationships with the men in our lives. When I left Rabat, she gifted me with one of her paintings, a portrayal of a Moroccan mother and child.

Another friend often joined me for lunch under a tree on the campus of the university. A foreign graduate student, he was the first male friend I had had for many years. I was delighted to have a friend with whom I could relax and be myself, without having to measure my words. We came from different cultural backgrounds, and I enjoyed learning about him, his studies, and his hopes for the future. Sometimes in the late afternoon we would go for a walk on the beach. Other times, we returned to his simple dorm room, where the books and papers on his desk invited him to resume studying for the evening. We got along well, but I wasn't interested in a deeper relationship with him. I constantly thought of my sweet children, who needed me, and I looked forward only to the day when I would return to them.

Ouarda and her husband had invited me to visit them for lunch at their lovely villa in a rural area outside of Rabat. For one afternoon, I entered their pleasant world. While their toddler ran in energetic circles around us, we sat in the garden, talked about our experiences in Morocco, and ate delicious couscous with a topping of savory chicken and vegetables. When it was time for me to go, I walked through gardens of flowers and trees toward the high wall surrounding the house and grounds. A gatekeeper waited to let me out, wishing me "Ma salaama" as he closed the heavy gate behind me.

The fragrant garden I had just left contrasted starkly with the bone-dry fields outside the compound and the dusty, rural road where I stood waiting for a big taxi. Such taxis — old, well-used Mercedes imported from Europe — had fixed routes and carried as many as seven people at a time packed into both the back and front seats. I waited a long time, daydreaming of my children...

> *Wish I had a bicycle.*
> *Jamal and Yusuf walked ten miles to buy a small old one,*
> *Rode everywhere, proud of their bike,*
> *Taught Jubair, but he lost control,*
> *Crashed into a moving truck.*
> *My God how worried I was:*
> *Concussion and dislocated knee.*
> *Back home, goofy boy Taha*
> *Practiced before a mirror,*
> *Sad faces, crying real tears,*
> *But when he saw I saw,*
> *Ran off laughing.*
> *And Saturday morning cartoons:*
> *Shamail broke out giggling,*
> *Inspector Gadget*
> *Saving the day.*

Still no taxi. I sighed, slumping against the Mehdaoui's villa wall. At least I hadn't had to flag down a taxi to take the kids to school every morning. Their school owned a van that came around and picked up all the children who lived at a distance. When the bus pulled into our yard and the driver honked the horn, Taha would burst out the front door, running and skipping to the vehicle. Jubair, still favoring his leg, would greet the driver and climb gingerly into the van. And Shamail, heedless of the driver's impatient honking, walked slowly in a dignified manner that earned him the nickname, Al-Mudeer, or school principal. Jamal and Yusuf would be starting their home school lessons, trying to get all their work done in the morning. Afterward, they'd take an excursion to the souk, where Yusuf searched for materials for his chemistry experiments and Jamal chatted with old men drinking tea in the shade.

I missed them all so much. My heart trembled as I thought of my five lively children, now so far away from me. My eyes let loose a stream of tears, salty like the seas that separated me from my loved ones. There was no sign of the taxi, and no place for me to sit down. I leaned back on the solid steel gate and rested one foot while standing on the other. I wiped the tears from my face. Looking up the dirt road I saw no cloud of dust that would indicate an oncoming vehicle, but I did see an old dog meandering toward me. As it got closer, I realized it wasn't old. It was sick, with frothy saliva dripping from its mouth. Rabies!

Alarmed, I turned and pounded on the gate, yelling for Ahmed's gatekeeper to open it. No reply. In vain I searched for hand holds on the nine-foot-high villa gate, a smooth slab of steel, or the smooth concrete walls on either side of it. There was no way to climb to safety, and there were no other houses nearby. I knew that running from the dog was the one thing I must not do, since that would invite an attack. I dared not pound again on the gate for fear of startling the unpredictable dog. Frantically, I yelled for help again and again, as the deadly dog wobbled closer to me. No one answered.

I was trapped. In the face of mortal danger, I thought of my children. I wanted to survive and return to them, but I knew my fate was uncertain. I might live. Or I might be bitten by the rabid dog and suffer a horrific, painful death. The menacing animal was coming closer. With no way to escape, I could think of nothing else to do but to make myself invisible. It was an old trick that I'd used many times as a child, not always successfully.

Standing very still, I turned my face away from the dog, not looking at him. I emptied my mind and slowed my breathing as best as I could. Slowly the unsteady, panting, slobbering dog approached. As he approached, I could hear his shuffling step and labored breathing. I was motionless for endless minutes. When the dog was within ten feet of me, it paused. I held my breath and didn't move a muscle. Then, out of the corner of my eye, I saw him veer away from me, staggering across the road and heading toward the river below.

I remained still for a long time, and then gradually allowed myself to breathe deeply. When the taxi finally came, I shook my head, roused myself, stepped into the visible world, and flagged it down.

10

DEFEAT IN CARTHAGE

1989-1991

"Assuredly, no one man has been blessed with all God's gifts. You, Hannibal, know how to gain a victory; you do not know how to use it."

Marhabal, Hannibal's commander[26]

The shimmering, sun-warmed Mediterranean called to me, awakening my longing. I had missed this beautiful sea, her deep teal shades splashing toward shore, wave after wave. I hadn't known how much I craved living with her changeable moods. On the sandy beach, my feet thanked the earth and my heart opened to the sky and sea. I whispered a prayer of gratitude.

In that instant, Jubair, Taha, and Shamail threw themselves into my arms crying "Ummi! Ummi!" Luka and Diamond, tied up in the shade, barked and tried to join us. Like the waters of the sea, my tears flowed. My lonely months in Rabat were over, and now we were a family again, united under the welcoming sun of Tunisia. Talking all at once, the children grabbed my hands and pulled me down to the shore, where they showed me the treasures they had gathered, the new swimming skills they had learned, and the underwater discoveries they had made. We were home.

Abdullah had seemed tired but glad to see me when he picked me up at the airport. My own emotions were ambivalent. I was relieved to finally return to my family, but I resented him for taking me for granted, separating me from my children, and expecting me to earn cash to cover his mistakes.

---

[26] *The History of Rome*, 22.51. Titus Livy.

I didn't trust his warm, affectionate demeanor. But I was here now, and I would see what tomorrow would bring.

Abdullah told me about the trip across Spain, France, and Italy, which had been stressful. Despite his driving nearly nonstop, the family had run out of cash in Italy. Then, he had difficulty receiving the money I had wired to Genoa from my bank in Morocco. Not only was the transfer late in arriving it was also delayed by the Italian bank. When he finally received the money, he had to spend nearly all of it on fares for the ferry from Genoa to Tunisia. Now that I was here, we had the money from my last paycheck, but it wouldn't last long. It would be critical for Abdullah and me to get jobs immediately.

While Abdullah went off to buy some groceries, Layla and the children gathered around to tell me about their trip across southern Europe.

"Spain was really green!" exclaimed Jubair. "And there was a really big beach with nobody on it!"

Taha piped up, "The campground in Italy was nice! I helped Abu fix the car. And we played soccer with some people, and they taught me to count in Italian — uno, due, tre, quattro, cinque…"

"But we were hungry," said Shamail with a pained expression. "We…"

Taha interrupted, "Abu took the dogs away in the car and left them somewhere, but they came back."

"What? Why?" My jaw dropped. Those dogs were precious to my husband.

"No food for dogs, just a little food for us," Layla replied. Then she went on, speaking rapidly. "Abdullah was *ahmak*! At camp, he beat me bad and I run away. But he come, he catch me, he beat me more. I stay. Afraid. He crazy!"

A lump rose in my throat, and I felt my heart skip a few beats. I saw that he had knocked her front tooth out, and I hugged her. Later, I learned that she was pregnant.

"And Abdullah beat Jubair," she added.

"Because I was playing in a box," said Jubair. "I didn't know it was a box for dead people." Before embarking on the ferry, my family had camped near a cemetery, where Jubair discovered the discarded casket. I cringed and my eyes filled with tears. I had never imagined the trip would have deteriorated to this extent. But the family had more to tell me.

"We had to hide in the car," stated Shamail, with Taha and Jubair clamoring to speak.

"What?"

"No money for tickets," explained Layla. "Money for Abdullah and me, not the kids."

"You mean on the ferry? But how, where did you hide?" I asked the children. The camping van was compactly designed, with tiny appliances and minimal storage space, sufficient only for a weekend trip.

"I had to lie down under the back seat," replied Jubair.

A chill crawled up my back. The storage compartment under the seat couldn't have been big enough for him, I thought. He was a tall nine-year old.

Jubair continued, "Abu took everything out and put me in there. He didn't put the seat all the way down, so I could breathe. But I was scared."

"And Shamail and I had to be in the closet," said Taha, my lanky seven-year-old. A shadow crossed his face. "Shamail went in first, and then I went in. My legs and arms hurt. I was crying."

"Oh my God!" I exclaimed. The interior width of that closet was only a foot wide. I suppressed a sob, thinking of how cramped and frightened the kids must have been.

"I was really hot in there," said Shamail. "I couldn't see anything."

Later, I learned that the children were so uncomfortable that they started knocking on the walls of the compartments so Abdullah would let them out. He refused and threatened them. Fearfully, they remained quiet. But five-year old Shamail had become overheated in the tiny closet and had passed out. He was unconscious when Abdullah finally retrieved him from hiding.

My shock at the horrors the family had experienced shifted to fierce anger. Because of my husband's actions in Morocco, he had decided to leave the country abruptly, though ill-prepared for the journey. As a result, Jubair, Taha, Shamail, Layla, and even the dogs had been endangered in the nearly disastrous journey to Tunisia. I thanked God the family had made it safely to the North African shore. But I could see that Layla and the children were traumatized by all that had happened.

After a while, my anger gave way to grief that Abdullah had been reduced to making choices that hurt the family. He wouldn't have intended that. If I had been with them on the trip, I thought, I could have shared the stress with him. I could have helped make decisions, keep the children safe, and squeeze every penny out of the food budget. In the past, working together was how we pulled through tough times. But it was clear that times had changed.

I struggled to corral my vacillating emotions for the sake of the children, who needed me to take control of the situation. I cleared my throat. "What about the customs guards?" I asked. "Didn't they look inside the van?"

"Diamond and Luka in car," replied Layla. "The guards see dogs. They afraid. They don't open door."

After the customs guards had gone and the boat was under way, Abdullah let the children out of the hot vehicle, and they all went up to the deck of the ferry.

Shamail, who had been listening solemnly, spoke up, "We went up on top of the boat and I could breathe there. I saw the ocean. At night we had a little room to sleep in."

"Yes, we had a small room," explained Layla, "but only two beds. And only food for two people. We all ate the food, and all of us hungry."

"No!" I sobbed As I processed the total nightmare my children had suffered, my self-control weakened and tears rolled down my face, The kids were visibly distressed by my anguish, so I struggled to brighten my mood. "Alhamdulillah you are safe," I said, bringing a smile to my face and trying to soothe the anxiety I saw in their faces. With that attempt, my love for them finally broke through my emotions. I hugged the children and Layla, comforting them. "Allah has brought us here now, to this beautiful beach," I said. "Let me change my clothes and we'll take a walk together."

The sunshine, sea and fresh air began to heal the family. I spent time with the children trying to make up for my long absence. I knew they needed to regain their trust that I would always be there for them. In the meantime, our financial situation was critical, and the money I had brought from Morocco had already been spent on necessities. Just in time, Abdullah obtained a full-time English teaching position at the British Council in Tunis.

Not far from our camping spot on the beach, we rented a small, walled villa in the town of Carthage. Within the property walls there were two buildings. The main house, where the children and I lived, was a square stucco structure with two bedrooms, a basic kitchen, a bathroom, and cool stone floors. Behind the main house, there was a small cottage where Layla lived. Abdullah slept alternately in one house or the other. Between the houses grew a large tree with thick, spreading branches that was perfect for the kids to climb. They spent hours playing on and under the tree, building forts and imagining themselves as warriors and heroes.

Our house was just a short distance from the pristine beach of Carthage, where daily we swam and played in the water, flew kites, collected shells, and walked the sandy shore.

Taha was excited, "Ummi, I caught a crab!" He held up a small crab that was waving its claws in the air.

"Wow, Taha, how'd you do that?"

"I put some bread on a string and threw it out there near those big rocks," he replied. "I just went out to see if there was a crab on the string."

Shamail joined us, "The water is so clear I can see the fish swimming around! And an octopus! And things like flowers under the water!"

"Cool!" I smiled. "I think the flowers are probably coral."

"And I stepped on a sea urchin!" he cried. "But I got the needles out of my foot by myself," he added proudly.

I frowned, "Let me look, just in case. When we get back home, I'll put some medicine on your foot." There was the potential for an overlooked urchin spine to fester.

Jubair ran up to us, "Ummi, I saw a shark out there!" He pointed toward the rocky shelf. "But it was small. My friend said it wasn't dangerous."

"Uh, kids, I think you better not swim out there, just in case."

"I love this beach!" Taha leaped his joy like a little goat.

"Me too," I laughed. "Now I'm going for a swim!" The kids knew they couldn't catch me, so they just watched as I swam out into the gentle waves and turned on my back to kick and glide. Finally, I coasted to a halt and floated motionless under the Mediterranean sky, breathing softly.

The beach in Carthage was not the only local attraction for my family. The children and I were fascinated by this town that was a living museum, with Roman ruins interwoven among residential areas. There were layers of history dating back to as early as 1400 BCE, including an ancient harbor where Phoenician ships once moored. Residents lived in homes built in traditional Arab architecture or classic French styles, or a mixture of the two. Even the paved streets were named after historical heroes of Tunisia. Here, history was a living legacy that school children, as well as adults, proudly claimed. My kids loved exploring the area and taking me to see their latest discoveries — mysterious Latin inscriptions on a crumbling wall, an empty rectangular pool in a roofless building, or the ruins of small rooms arranged around a courtyard.

"We found something, Ummi!" said Jubair. "It's a big place. It's round on one side, and has, like, lots and lots of stairs! Come see it!"

Taha and Shamail agreed, "Yeah, Ummi, come on!"

Off we went, the children running ahead of me through the streets toward a section of the historical area I hadn't yet seen. Out of breath, I slowed as they continued to run uphill.

"It's here!" called Jubair. When I caught up with the boys, I found myself at the top of a hill looking down on semicircular rows of stone "steps" that lead to a flat, open area below.

"This is a Roman theater!" I exclaimed. "See, these steps are actually seats, where the people would sit to watch a play. The actors would be on that platform down there. They'd have to speak really loud for everyone to hear, I think." Looking at the stone seats, I thought they were in too-good shape for being so old, though the place seemed to be in the style of an ancient theatre. I later learned that this was a restoration of the original theatre, and it was often used for public plays and concerts. Regardless, I thought it was an excellent place for the kids to burn off some of their energy, so I directed them in races down and back up the stairs. Meanwhile, I sat in the top row, imagining a Roman crowd in the theatre laughing and commenting on a comedy enacted nearly two thousand years earlier.

Centuries before Roman theatergoers enjoyed plays there, the city of Carthage had been the center of the republic called Carthage, which covered North Africa from Morocco to Libya. In wars between this vast state and the Roman Empire, the great Carthaginian general, Hannibal, distinguished himself as a master of military tactics and strategy, as well as a shrewd student of human behavior. Key to his success was the intense loyalty he inspired among his troops. His most famous campaign was the seemingly impossible invasion of Italy, in which he marched his troops and war elephants over the Pyrenees mountains from Spain into France and then over the high Alps into Italy. Hannibal and his troops occupied southern Italy for fifteen years as they waged war against Rome.

Before moving to Tunisia, I had known nothing about this history, which every school child in this country knew. Later, toward the end of our family's sojourn in Tunisia, I would have occasion to recall the charismatic Hannibal again.

Early one morning, I walked down to the beach so I could be alone and reflect for a few minutes before the children woke up. I was deeply grateful that my little ones were safe, and I had been reunited with them. As I murmured thanks to the Compassionate One over and over, the gentle morning sea breeze carried my words aloft. I felt a tentative peace in my heart.

Abdullah and I had begun to take walks together along the beach, and I realized he was reaching out to me, trying to salvage our relationship. I felt an odd incongruence of hope and distrust. I would wait and see what developed. I was not going to plunge into a renewed relationship with him without careful discernment.

Now, as I stood at the water's edge, I knew I was longing for something beyond what my husband could offer me. Longing for true peace and true love, I reached out for a renewed relationship with the Creator. Standing on the wet sand at the water's edge, with gentle waves lapping my feet, I felt a deeper calm descend on me like a prayer...

> *By the will of Allah*
> *I stand:*
> *Grains of sand*
> *Stick to my feet,*
> *Time pauses,*
> *My gratitude surges,*
> *And instantly*
> *Love returns,*
> *Over and over.*

And yet, I knew how weak I was spiritually. In the past few, faithless years, I had lost nearly all contact with my true center. Tears of disappointment came to my eyes. I knew the spiritual path was for all kinds of weather, but I had lost my way. With great longing, I wanted and needed to return to that path. As the tide tickled my toes and the sun rose in the east, I prayed for strength and guidance in doing so.

When I began teaching part-time at the British Council, I gained confidence and direction in my career. I enjoyed the work and valued what I learned from my students, who loved to speak English. We engaged in wide-ranging conversations about social issues, difficult choices in life, women's rights, raising children, the goals of education, scientific discoveries, and much more. These classroom relationships inspired me to become a more effective teacher for my students. When my employer sponsored me to take professional training toward an English as a Foreign Language teaching qualification, I was determined to make the best use of it.

Now that Abdullah and I were back on our feet financially, I decided to enroll Jubair, Taha, and Shamail in a local martial arts class. Although we lived in a nice neighborhood, there were nearby neighborhoods where rough kids could make trouble for my sons, so I wanted them to have some training in self-defense. It wasn't long before I learned that the Tae Kwon Do classes were well worth the money.

One afternoon, Jubair, Taha, and Shamail all ran into the house, breathless.

"A man attacked Shamail!" Jubair cried.

I stopped what I was doing and knelt next to five-year-old Shamail, "Are you all right? What happened?"

He nodded. "I ran away, and he couldn't catch me."

Jubair explained, "The man was crazy. Shamail was sitting on the curb and playing with his cars. Taha and I were playing football with our friends. Some other kids started teasing the man, and he tried to get them, but they all ran away."

"Then the man tried to get us, and we ran away," added Taha. "But Shamail didn't see him at first."

"Oh no!" I cried, looking Shamail over for cuts or bruises.

"The man tried to hit Shamail, but he blocked the man, just like we learned in Tae Kwon Do class," Jubair said. "He blocked, ducked under the man's arm, and ran the other way!" Jubair was proud of his little brother, and so was I.

With regular martial arts classes, the boys became more confident in their abilities to defend themselves. At home, Abdullah would supplement the techniques the boys learned in class with real world strategies. One day, nine-year-old Jubair wanted to demonstrate to his father some new moves he had learned in class. Layla and I watched as he got into position.

"OK, come at me," Abdullah told Jubair.

Jubair moved in with a kick and punch, which I expected his father to parry. Instead, Abdullah suddenly reacted with fury. He turned on the boy, threw him to the floor and pinned him down, yelling, "You think you can beat me, you little punk? Huh?"

When he pulled his arm back to punch Jubair, I intervened. "Abdullah! Stop! Leave him alone!" I stepped up to him, staring hard.

My husband glared at me and let go of Jubair, who ran off. My adrenaline had surged, and I wasn't afraid of him. I scowled and then stalked away. When I went to check on Jubair, I found that he was having an asthma attack. I gave him his medicine and together we went down to the shore, where he — and I — could breathe better.

Sadly, the summer's enchantment was over. Our house, designed to be cool in hot weather, became damp and chilly in winter. Heavy clouds moved swiftly over the horizon to release floods upon the earth, bringing lush, green life to the summer-parched vegetation but also gloom to humans longing for sunlight. I still went for walks along the beach, sometimes with one or more of the kids, but most often alone. My husband, immersed in his own thoughts, no longer joined me. The joy we had all felt in the magical Carthaginian summer had washed away with every heavy raindrop dripping from the sky.

The fragile hope that I had felt when Abdullah and I tried to restore life to our relationship, now faded. He appeared to be spiraling into depression, though I couldn't be sure what he was feeling, since he wouldn't talk to me. I reinforced my defensive barrier and squashed the hope that had started to grow, throwing myself into my work and family responsibilities. Layla's pregnancy was showing now. Although she was receiving routine obstetric care and would give birth in a local hospital, she worried about being so far from her mother and sisters, who would ordinarily have assisted her in her pregnancy, delivery, and recovery. The children, sensing the rising tensions, tried to be quiet and not attract attention from the adults.

The pressure was exacerbated in mid-January of 1990, when the peace of the night was broken by the sound of automatic gunfire nearby. There were multiple rounds being fired, back and forth between two or more positions. Since the gun battle seemed to be coming from the direction of the presidential palace, we worried that this could be the beginning of an attempted coup. Political violence would be dangerous for foreigners like us as well as for Tunisians. Abdullah ordered all of us to lay on the floor of the living room, well below the level of the windows. After a while, silence descended. Abdullah went outside but was unable to discover what had happened. The next day, we learned that the home of an official of the Palestinian Liberation Organization had been attacked by an opposing Palestinian faction. Three PLO officials were killed, and two hostages were taken. Eventually, the hostages were released, and the assassin was arrested by Tunisian police.[27]

Although we were relieved that the violence was not due to a broader problem that might lead to riots or revolution, our feeling of safety in Carthage had been shaken. Unfortunately, such conflict was not new. Our Tunisian friends told us that just four years earlier, in 1985, Israelis had bombed the PLO headquarters on the coast south of Tunis, killing fifty people and wounding over sixty, many of them women and children.[28]

But foreign attacks were probably the least of the problems facing the Tunisian government in 1990. In private spaces, there were whispered rumors that Muslim fundamentalists were fighting government forces in the western part of the country. The radicals were said to be escaping across the border into Algeria and receiving aid there. This was not the sort of news that appeared in the newspapers in Tunisia, and it would have been risky to discuss it openly because of the thorough infiltration of society by government intelligence operatives. As in other countries we had visited – Algeria, Iran, Turkey, Pakistan, Morocco – the government of Tunisia exercised authority over the press and carried out repressive policies to control the people.

As Abdullah became more remote from the family, Layla and I got to know each other better. On the days when I wasn't working and the boys were at school, she and I would walk together to the souk to purchase groceries. As we chatted, we browsed the colorful displays of fruit, vegetables, spices, grains, and dairy products. Layla was an expert at bargaining, expressing

<hr>

[27] https://www.upi.com/Archives/1991/01/15/Three-PLO-officials-killed-in-Tunisia/7833663915600

[28] https://www.nytimes.com/1985/10/02/world/israeli-planes-attack-plo-in-tunis-killing-at-least-30-raid-legitimate-us-says.html

mock outrage balanced with sardonic wisecracks. The vendors seemed to enjoy the interaction as much as she did.

These excursions away from the house helped us discover in each other an unexpected friend. Walking back from the souk one afternoon, Layla said, "I wish my mother were here, and my sisters. The baby is coming soon."

"Don't worry," I replied. "You'll be fine at the hospital. And when you and the baby come home, I'll help you."

Layla looked at me. "You are my baby's other mother."

"Yes," I agreed. "And you're the other mother of Jubair, Taha, and Shamail."

We smiled at each other with sudden recognition of a shift in our relationship. I realized that much of what Abdullah had told me about her seemed designed to prejudice me against her. She seemed to have come to a similar conclusion about me. Together, we learned that we could depend upon and help each other. Little did we know that the alliance we slowly forged would soon be necessary for the survival of our family.

By February, Layla was heavily pregnant. Our trips by foot to the market ceased, and Abdullah stepped in to buy groceries. When I was home, I would help clean the house, wash clothes, and cook meals. Then one day, Abdullah announced that the baby was on its way, and he was taking Layla to the hospital.

"Is Layla going to have the baby?" Shamail asked anxiously.

"Yes," I smiled. "She'll be home soon."

"I hope it's a girl!" Jubair said.

"Yeah, we want a sister!" added Taha, leaping around.

When Abdullah brought Layla and her healthy baby girl home, the whole family celebrated. The boys were excited about their new little sister, Noor, and they vied with each other to hold her. I helped Layla get started with nursing, and when she was resting, I tended the baby. The miracle of new life brought joy to the family.

Gradually, I began to feel stronger in my spiritual life and less isolated than I had been in Algeria, Iran, and Morocco. My Arabic was improving. Not only did I have an ally at home, I also felt more connected with my colleagues and students. The latter were educated Muslims who respected Islam and practiced the religion in their own way in this moderate Islamic society. Some of the women wore hijab, and others did not. Even the most devout women or men saw their religious choices as personal, and they did not pressure others to make the same choices. I learned that some of my students, both female and male, were feminists who strongly supported equality in education, the workplace, and home. They didn't view these positions as conflicting in any way with Islam.

Inspired by these thoughtful Muslims, I envisioned myself integrating into this society and renewing my spiritual path. The prayer I had breathed on the beach months earlier was quietly being answered. When Ramadan came that spring, I felt centered and grateful for this special time when Muslims celebrate the revelation of the Qur'an to the Prophet Muhammad. Like Muslim adults everywhere, I fasted from sunrise to sunset, with nothing to drink or eat. At work, I felt tired and very thirsty in the afternoon, but I persevered. The children weren't required to abstain, and they ate their usual meals, though at times they tried fasting for a few hours. The family looked forward to the end of each day, when we would break the fast with dates and milk, followed by delicious food prepared by Layla. Sometimes after supper, we would all go for a walk, joining countless residents celebrating Ramadan in the streets.

One day, Abdullah interrupted his silent gloom to tell me that he had gone to the U.S. embassy to apply for a passport for Noor.

I couldn't believe it. "Why, Abdullah? Why?" In our eleven years overseas, he had always known that he could not walk into any U.S. consulate or embassy and remain a free man. We had long agreed that if it was necessary to conduct any business at an embassy, I would be the one to do it. When he had removed pages in our family's passports so that we could leave Algeria in 1986, he understood the repercussions. We knew that we must not show those altered passports to any U.S. official anywhere.

"Noor needed a U.S. birth certificate and passport," he said. "I had to show them my passport."

"But you knew you couldn't show your face there! Noor's mother is Moroccan, so she is a dual national. You could have gotten her a Moroccan passport, at least for now."

He shrugged, "I had to get an American passport for her."

"Well, you always told me that we'd have to declare our passports 'stolen' one day, and then we'd apply for new ones. Why not do that first? And then apply for Noor's passport?"

He just shrugged.

I was floored. Fleetingly, I wondered if Layla had somehow threatened him to ensure her daughter received U.S. documentation. Again, he had not consulted me before taking this huge step. Now he had jeopardized his and the whole family's security. I asked, "What did they do when you showed them your passport?"

He seemed resigned, "They asked about the missing pages. They took the passport. They want you to bring in yours and the children's passports."

"Why didn't you talk to me before you did this? We could have considered alternatives. Now you'll be arrested," I said angrily, "and Noor, Jubair, Taha, and Shamail — your children — will be left without their father!" I paused to consider the ramifications, shivering. "And maybe they'll arrest me, too."

He didn't reply. I found it hard to believe that Abdullah, always so meticulous in his planning, hadn't thought about the danger of going to the embassy. Was he so depressed he wasn't thinking clearly? Was he tired of being on the run? Was there something he wasn't telling me? I had no answers.

Meanwhile, we had more important things to consider. "What's next?" I asked him. "Are you going to try to make it into Libya? Further south into Africa?"

"I couldn't go far without papers," he said. He wasn't even going to try to keep his freedom. This seemed so unlike him, so unlike the proactive man I had known for the past seventeen years.

"Well then, what?"

"Maybe they won't find out who I am," he replied. He had always had incredibly good luck and considerable skill at eluding the authorities. But his luck had finally run out, and he seemed unwilling to try to evade capture.

"That's not realistic," I replied. "Abdullah, I just don't understand. What's going on?"

But he remained silent and turned away from me. I couldn't help him if he wasn't willing to help himself. He had boxed himself in and given himself up for his daughter's U.S. citizenship. Whatever his reasons, I would have to gather my courage and take my passport and the boys' passports to the embassy. And then we could only wait to see what the Americans would do.

At the U.S. embassy, a clerk accepted the passports from me without comment. I asked when we could get new passports, and she looked down at the papers in front of her and replied that they would have to wait for word from Washington. I felt trapped and uneasy, not only about my husband's situation, but also about the children's and my security. We were now at the mercy of the massive, unknowable bureaucracy of the U.S. government.

One Saturday afternoon, I had cleared the lunch dishes away and Layla was nursing the baby. Abdullah would be coming home soon, after his last class.

Taha ran up to me, "Ummi, come see the fort I'm building in the tree!"

"OK, just wait until I clean up the kitchen," I replied absent-mindedly. I couldn't stop worrying over Abdullah's dilemma and our future.

Shamail ran up to me. "Ummi, Layla needs a cloth for Noor. She spit up! All over!"

Jubair headed toward the front door, saying, "Ummi, I'm going to play football with my friends. In the street out front."

I nodded to Jubair and then handed a clean diaper to Shamail, who ran to give it to Layla. He loved watching his baby sister.

"UMMI!!!!" Jubair yelled, slamming the front door open. "Abu says come quick!"

Alarmed, I rushed outside to see three men bustling Abdullah into a dark, unmarked car. He shouted to me, "They're police! Call John Bryant!" Two of the men hopped into the backseat of the car on either side of Abdullah, slamming the doors behind them. The third jumped into the front seat next to the driver, who gunned the engine and drove away with my husband. All of this had happened in the space of a few seconds. Stunned, I silently watched the disappearing police car.

Our van was parked in front of our house, where Abdullah had left it after arriving home from work. Feeling numb, I opened the driver's side door and stood there, gazing at the keys, which were still in the ignition. The palms of my hands came to rest on the driver's seat. It was still warm, where my husband had sat just moments earlier...

> *So suddenly*
> *He's gone.*
> *Oh my love!*

It was April 20, 1991, and Tunisian police had arrested Abdullah at the request of the U.S. Embassy. I turned back toward the house, telling Jubair, "We'll all talk about this together."

First, I called John Bryant, our boss at British Council. He was flabbergasted that one of his most popular teachers — and a likeable family man — had been arrested. He promised he would find out why Abdullah was arrested and where he was taken.

Then, I faced the fearful, uncomprehending faces of Layla and the children. None of them knew Abdullah's story. They didn't know the real reason why we had traveled and lived in the Middle East and North Africa. The older boys, Jamal and Yusuf, may have remembered visiting Abdullah in prison in the U.S., but Jubair was only an infant when he, his older brothers, and I first traveled overseas to join their father. Taha was born in Algeria and Shamail in Iran. This nomadic life was all they knew. They believed what we had told everyone we met — that Abdullah and I were just ordinary American Muslims traveling the world and working as English teachers. The children had visited the U.S. with me twice, but they never wondered why Abdullah didn't join us on these trips.

The arrest of their father and the seriousness with which I now spoke caused their chatter to cease. They studied my face intently. Layla, who knew no more than the children, was anxious and tearful, holding her infant daughter tightly.

"Abu used to be in prison in America before you were born," I said simply, in English and then Arabic for Layla. "He escaped from prison, and he got on a plane and flew to Libya. Then Jamal, Yusuf, Jubair and I came to Tunisia, where Abu joined us. Jubair was a little baby then."

"What about me?" asked Shamail.

"Shamail and Taha, you weren't born yet," I said. "Since Abu escaped, the American police have been looking for him, so we traveled to Algeria and Iran and Morocco. And now here to Tunisia. The police have found Abu and they want to take him back to prison in America."

"But he said he was a professor in America," blurted Layla, her face betraying a sudden understanding of the lies he must have told her. "What do we do?" she cried. The children began to whimper, and I hugged them to me.

Squeezing the kids, I said, "Don't worry, we're still together, and I'll figure this out, inshallah." I reached out for Layla's hand, reassuring her. Though I was far from confident, I knew that now more than ever, I had to be the rock of our family, strong and steadfast. Silently, I prayed to the One for help.

After making inquiries, John called to tell me that Abdullah had been taken to the prison in Tunis, and the U.S. embassy was pressing for his extradition. He had been assigned an English-speaking lawyer and there would be legal proceedings to determine his disposition. Evidently, Abdullah admitted to Tunisian police that he had escaped from a U.S. prison, but he claimed he had been unjustly incarcerated in the U.S. because he had defended a mosque from attack by American police. I already knew that he had never told me the real story of his crime, and I was sure he had invented this new account to win the sympathy of the Tunisian government.

Ironically, not only was Abdullah's claim certainly untrue, the American consul's description of his past was also false. She asserted that Abdullah had been imprisoned because he was an "Islamic terrorist." But in 1972, when he was convicted, there were no violent Islamic radicals in the U.S. In the Muslim world, various political and religious movements had been common from the inception of Islam, but it wasn't until the 1970s that radically conservative, oppressive, and brutal "religious" ideologies began to impact the Middle East. This infection didn't reach the U.S. until two decades later. In any case, the Tunisian government believed the consul's lie. Considering their own troubles with armed rebels on their border, Tunisia didn't want to have another presumed terrorist in their country.

Less than a week after Abdullah's arrest, the police pulled up in front of the house and requested that I go with them. With the trauma of Abdullah's arrest fresh in their minds, Layla and the children were hysterical. I struggled to keep myself together…

> *Wild agitation scrapes my guts,*
> *But I bind it up.*
> *Sweat drenches me,*

Quickly, I called John Bryant and asked him to look for me if I didn't return home. Then, slowing my breathing, I tried to feel a calm center within me and made my face betray nothing. I stepped outside and walked toward the police car.

I persuaded the police to let me follow them in the family car with our large Doberman. They agreed, if I allowed a policeman to accompany me. I had Diamond sit in the front passenger seat. On high alert, he stared steadily at the frightened cop in the back seat, growling if the man moved even an inch. Diamond couldn't have helped me if I were arrested, but he did make me feel safer on the drive to the police headquarters.

I followed the police car to a large concrete building in the government area of Tunis. The police led me to a large office on one of the upper floors. They stood guard while I was interrogated by three English-speaking Tunisian men who worked with the International Criminal Police Organization, also known as Interpol. One of them sat at a big desk in the center of the otherwise unfurnished room, and I was told to sit in a chair six feet away, facing him. The man at the desk asked most of the questions, which I answered truthfully.

"Are you aware that your passport has been altered?"

"Yes."

"Who altered your passport?"

"My husband."

"What's your husband's name? Are you aware that it's illegal to alter a passport?" At first, the officer seemed mostly concerned about passport violations. Then he began asking about Abdullah.

"Did you know that your husband was a fugitive?"

"Yes," I answered, hoping that my status as his wife protected me from accusations of harboring a fugitive. At that time, I believed the law in the U.S. did so.

"What sort of drugs was he smuggling?"

"None. He doesn't have any drugs." That question surprised me. I was glad they hadn't asked if he had ever smuggled drugs.

"What Muslim organizations does he belong to?"

"None. He's a teacher. At British Council."

The three of them appeared to confer over a piece of paper on the desk. Finally, the interrogator told me I was free to go, but I was forbidden to leave Tunis until they notified me. One of them escorted me out of the building, and I walked slowly to the car, feeling a slight trembling in my legs. I got in the car, gave Diamond a hug, and drove away.

At home, I collapsed in the arms of my children, who kissed and hugged me, crying. Layla brought me hot mint tea as I tried not to shed tears in front of my precious family, who loved me and needed me to be strong. I needed them, too, so very much.

Waiting outside the central prison in Tunis, I stood in a long line of dusty, worried women who hoped to visit their loved ones. I reviewed the things I needed to discuss with my husband – the interrogation by Interpol, the lawyer's request for Abdullah's original trial transcript, my letter to his friend Sandy asking her to obtain the transcript, and John's efforts to get the British consulate to intervene. There was so much to talk about in so little time. The prison allowed him two ten-minute visits a week. Layla and I alternated visits, taking a different child each time. We were also allowed to take a basket of food to Abdullah, which was vitally important to him, since he reported the prison food was inedible, and there wasn't enough of it for all the men crowded together in the cell. Evidently, the government had been cracking down on dissenters, activists, and armed rebels, and as a result, the prison was overflowing.

As we waited, I talked with Jubair to keep him from getting bored. At the same time, I listened to the women in line gossip about me, not imagining that I spoke Arabic. "Miskina, poor thing! She's a foreigner, but her husband is in prison. Like our loved ones," one of them said.

And then it was our turn. Jubair and I stepped toward the window. I passed the basket of food to an officer, and he passed me the empty basket from the previous visit. And then, there was my husband, his face framed by the plexiglass and bars of the small window between us.

"Abu!" cried Jubair. "When are you getting out?"

Abdullah looked relaxed and pleased to see us. I wondered how he could keep his cool considering his uncertain position. "Jubair, how's it going?" he asked. "Are you taking care of your mother and brothers? I love you!"

"Me too, Abu!"

He turned to me with love in his eyes, "Habiba...."

I felt a murmur of the enduring stream that had carried our love throughout a tumultuous life together. "I love you," I whispered, and I meant it. But there was no time for following that current. We had vital things to discuss. I told him about my meeting with the lawyer and his request to see the transcript of Abdullah's trial in 1972.

Abdullah was again the confident, take-charge person I knew. He asked me to call Hasan in Tehran to see if the Iranian authorities would request the release of Abdullah to them. He also instructed me to meet with the Libyan ambassador to request asylum. In case those strategies failed, he wanted me to write a letter to the Tunisian president, Zine El Abidine Ben Ali, pleading with him to refuse Abdullah's extradition to the U.S.

When I received the full trial record, which I had requested an American friend to send, I immersed myself in reading it. It was a grim and revealing experience. The eyewitness account of what happened the day of the murder bore no similarity to the stories Abdullah had told me. The transcript did not support his story about defending a day care center from police attack. Nor did it support his claim that he had been arrested while returning money to the bank that his friends had robbed. And there was, of course, no support for his latest tory about resisting a police assault on a mosque. Instead, the transcript clearly described how he, in the company of some friends, had killed a police detective during an attempted getaway from an ill-conceived bank robbery in New York. If the Tunisian court saw this transcript, it would only serve to support the American request for Abdullah's immediate extradition.

However, one section of the transcript was similar to my husband's account. During the phase of the trial dealing with mitigating circumstances, an expert psychologist testified about his interview of Abdullah, who had been administered a so-called truth serum, Sodium Pentothal. He said that while Abdullah was under the influence of the drug, he had questioned him about his experience in Vietnam. The psychologist reported that the accused had reacted and spoken in a manner consistent with PTSD. This testimony was accepted by the court as evidence of a mitigating factor, which eventually resulted in a life sentence rather than a death sentence. Abdullah's version of the truth serum interview was the same, except that he said he had programmed himself to act as if he were reliving the trauma of combat during the psychologist's examination. He told me that he had not actually been traumatized by the war, but he hoped a diagnosis of PTSD might help him avoid the death penalty.

Setting aside the trial transcript, I processed what I had learned. I imagined my husband as a 23-year-old veteran of the Vietnam War, angry, unemployed, and high on drugs most of the time. He and his friends concocted an ad hoc plan to rob a bank, and it went terribly wrong, costing a police officer his life and Abdullah his freedom. It was no surprise that he didn't want to tell me the shameful truth. But the transcript also revealed other facts that directly contradicted what he had told me about his early life. Although he did grow up in Georgia, he had neither attended nor graduated from the Citadel. Going directly into the army after high school, he was sent to the war in Vietnam, where he reached the rank of platoon squad leader — a non-commissioned officer — not a lieutenant or a captain as he had told me on different occasions. And although he had often expressed pride in his military service, he did not receive an honorable discharge. Around the time of his arrest, he was reported as AWOL from the army.

During our seventeen-year marriage, I had discovered occasional discrepancies in his accounts of his life. But now I realized that much of the picture he had painted was untrue. The issue was much deeper than his need as a fugitive to present a false persona, for he had been telling me a mixture of truth, half-truth, and falsehoods from the moment I met him. Of all the things he had ever told me about his life, I'd never know what was true. Suddenly, I had to confront the reality that I didn't know him at all.

I reflected on something he had told me a couple years earlier. I had asked him about the emotional impact of an event in his past, and he abruptly cut off the discussion, saying, "You'll never understand me. I live by different rules than other people." The implications of that harsh statement shocked me, but I think it was the closest I ever got to understanding him. And although I was angry with him, I was even angrier with myself for being such a fool, especially when my blind faith in him had endangered my children.

When the lawyer asked whether I had received the transcript, I told him I had not. Shortly thereafter, the final hearing was held before a judge.

Standing at the back of the courtroom, I saw Abdullah and his lawyer in the front, facing the bench. The judge spoke loudly to everyone in the room, but I couldn't understand any of the Arabic legal language. However, I perceived a certain finality in the judge's voice, and there was no discussion. I knew, then, Abdullah had not been granted a stay of extradition. He never saw me as he was taken away.

Tunisia had been under some international pressure to allow Abdullah to return to Iran or seek refuge in Libya. In addition, the British government had received an asylum request on behalf of Abdullah. Even Amnesty International had begun to make inquiries about his case. A short, positive article about Abdullah had been published in a Tunis newspaper, and among Tunisians there was support for Abdullah, a fellow Muslim seeking refuge from the U.S. In the end, however, the President of Tunisia rebuffed internal and external pressures, rejected my plea that he refuse extradition, and bowed to the greater pressure of the United States government.

The next day, Taha and I went to the prison to visit Abdullah. After waiting in line, we stepped up to the window, as usual, but the guard told me he wasn't there.

"But where is my husband?" I asked.

"I don't know. I only know he isn't here."

I turned to Taha, "Abu isn't here. I think they moved him to another place."

Taha was outraged, "But it was my turn to see Abu today! Jubair and Shamail had their turns already, today was my turn!" He began to cry.

"Let's see if we can find out where he is," I replied, picking up the basket of food Layla had carefully prepared for Abdullah.

At the U.S. consulate I angrily complained that my husband had been moved without notifying me, and I demanded to know where he was. An apologetic American employee of the consulate came into the waiting room and told me he was terribly sorry, but U.S. marshals had already taken him by plane back to the U.S.

"You took him back to the U.S. without letting his children see him?" I shouted. "What kind of heartless people are you?" The man cringed and apologized again, and I knew I was yelling at the wrong person. He was only the messenger.

I stormed out of the embassy, closely followed by Taha, who was howling in grief. Back in the car, I tried to collect myself so I could drive. I hugged Taha and whispered, "It's going to be all right. I'm here. I'm sorry they took Abu." My words were insufficient. Taha's face was covered with tears and snot. I handed him a tissue.

"When are we going back to America?" he asked. "I want to see Abu."

"I don't know, Taha. I just don't know."

Back at our house, the news of Abdullah's removal from Tunisia and extradition to the U.S. was met with shock and disbelief.

"Ay, ay!" Layla cried. "I'll never see him again. My little girl will never know her father," she sobbed.

Jubair's tear-streaked face reflected his shock, "But how can they just take him away like that?"

Shamail was sniffling, "He was going to take me to the carnival! He promised!" As he burst into tears, he repeated, "He promised. He promised."

"I didn't have my turn to see Abu," Taha protested, as if someone could fix this for him.

But I couldn't fix it. I couldn't take away my family's pain. I couldn't bring Abdullah back. I couldn't change what had happened. We were now on our own. I was in charge, and I'd have to lead on.

"Let's bring some cookies," I suggested, "and take a walk on the beach." I didn't know what else to say or do. Perhaps the sand and sea would help to ease our pain.

Now that my husband was gone, I reflected on the irony that the final stop of our long journey was in Tunisia, the historic land of the Carthaginians and of their famous general, Hannibal. Like him, Abdullah was talented and skilled in maneuvering people and situations to his benefit. Like the Carthaginian leader , Abdullah was charismatic, gathering loyal friends and family around him, including me. He was outrageously lucky, taking big risks and having very fortunate outcomes time and again. He knew how to emerge victorious when the obstacles seemed overwhelming. But unfortunately, like the military commander of ancient Carthage, he ultimately didn't know how to use his victories to his best advantage.

Abdullah had spent eleven years traveling with his family and teaching English from North Africa to the Middle East, all the while eluding the U.S. authorities. This was an extraordinary feat. But when it came to doing what was needed to ensure his long-term status as a free man, he failed. His defeat saddened me. There was still part of me that loved the intelligent, spiritual man I had met years ago, a person with so much potential to make something of his life. But that time was long past. The wild, exhausting ride of our years together in Muslim lands was over, and I was overwhelmed not with grief, but with relief.

John was on the phone. "Aisha, I'm wondering if you can come to the office?" he asked. "Something has come up that I'd like to talk with you about."

On the drive from Carthage into Tunis, I reflected on the family's present and future. Following the chaos of Abdullah's arrest, legal maneuvering, and extradition, I had resumed teaching my students at British Council. The work was fulfilling, but more importantly it brought in necessary income. For six months, I had made every effort to keep my family financially and emotionally stable after the earthquake that wrenched Abdullah away from us. We were feeling reasonably comfortable in this moderate Muslim country, and all of us were beginning to acculturate into Tunisian society.

Returning to the U.S. was not an option for me. I refused to turn up destitute on my elderly mother's doorstep and ask for shelter for me and my three youngest children. She had already taken on the responsibility of supporting Jamal and Yusuf and helping them get through high school and enter college. I didn't want to burden her any further.

Another major reason not to return to the U.S. was the rampant racism that my young children would face every day if we lived in that country. They were completely unprepared for the devastating reality of being Black in America, and I would not be able to protect them. In Tunisia, they blended in with all the other brown, black, tan, and olive-skinned children. Sometimes, other kids taunted them about being Americans, but I knew that when my children became fluent in Tunisian Arabic, they would be indistinguishable from Tunisians.

I reflected on the spiritual vacuum in the U.S. and the corresponding materialism that reduced the meaning of life to financial transactions. This new religion measured human worth not by good character but by material wealth. When I moved overseas to Muslim countries, I discovered that Islam still moderated human obsession with wealth and clearly advocated good deeds and brotherhood of all nations and races. Although governments in this part of the world were generally corrupt, individual

Muslims had a basic kindness and generosity that made me feel more at home than I had ever felt in the U.S.

Recalling my first, uncertain steps when I set foot in Tunisia in 1980, I recognized how much I had changed during the eleven intervening years. No longer hesitant, I was determined to continue living in the Muslim world, because I knew my sons and I could thrive there. As an independent, professional woman, I could support my family here. And I wasn't going to run back to a place I no longer called home.

"Hi John," I greeted the man who was as much my friend as an employer.

"Hi, come on in, Aisha," John smiled. "Could you close the door behind you?"

As I settled into a chair opposite his desk, he continued, "I've just got a notice from the Tunisian government. I know you've been planning to continue working here, and I'd love for you to do that, but the government has rescinded your work permit."

I was at a loss for words.

John continued, "Unfortunately, they want you and your family to leave immediately."

"I don't see how we can leave immediately," I objected. "Jubair is in the middle of treatment for his allergies, and I will have a lot of arrangements to make."

"I'll ask them for an extension for humanitarian reasons," John replied. "Meanwhile, British Council will arrange for air tickets for you, Layla, and the children, in accordance with Abdullah's contract. And we'll ship your belongings to you. But you'll have to show your tickets to the police to verify your travel plans. Do you know where you'll go?"

I paused. I had assumed we could stay in Tunisia, and I could keep working. I'd hate to take the kids back to the U.S., that soulless land. My flushed face must have betrayed the surge of anger I felt toward the U.S. government.

"I know this is all very sudden," said John. "You can let me know when you decide. Aisha, I'm here to help you in whatever way I can."

It didn't take me long to decide. We would go to Morocco, where I was sure I could get a job at one of the language centers or schools. It was not expensive to live there, and I knew my way around the Rabat-Sale area. More importantly, Layla's family had already become family to me and the children. Morocco would be our home.

However, there were two problems with going to that country. First, I didn't know if I would be held liable for Abdullah's debt to our former landlord. Although my name wasn't on the lease, I didn't know how these things worked in Morocco. To be safe, I would have to avoid owner of the property.

More worrisome was the likelihood that when the Tunisian authorities saw that I was flying to Casablanca, they would warn their counterparts in Morocco. I desperately wanted to avoid having the Moroccan police expel me from the country as a suspected terrorist. To address this issue, John and I came up with a plan. He would buy Layla and Noor tickets to fly to Morocco. For the boys and me, he'd purchase tickets to London, which I would show to the police as evidence of our destination. Then, I would return them to John, who would exchange them for new tickets to Morocco. The hardest part of this subterfuge was that I had to lie to everyone else. I couldn't afford the truth to leak out to the ever-present secret police. My colleagues at British Council assumed the kids and I were returning to the U.S. via London, and it was easiest for me not to correct them. As far as Layla and the children were concerned, the boys and I were going to England. And that's what we told our neighbors and Tunisian friends, too.

Finally, the U.S. embassy issued new passports to Jubair, Taha, and Shamail. Layla was happy that baby Noor was also granted a U.S. passport and birth certificate. I received a new, short-term passport, which I would have to renew earlier than usual. I believed this was one way that the U.S authorities could keep track of me as the wife of Abdullah Khalid. But it didn't bother me, as I had no plans to do anything illegal. I was living on my own terms now.

The next couple weeks were busy. Jubair completed his series of allergy shots. Layla and I purchased new travel clothes for the kids, packed suitcases, and filled trunks that John would ship to us later. All three kids were in a fever of excitement.

One night, after everyone had gone to sleep, I carried a hefty stack of papers into the back yard. Lighting a match, I burned the transcript of Abdullah's trial. I wondered if, after years on the run with Abdullah, I was being paranoid about security. But if the wrong person were to read the transcript, he or she could make trouble for me in Morocco. I didn't want more problems. I just wanted to work and support my family.

The big day finally came. At the airport, Jubair scrutinized the departures billboard – reading both the French and Arabic. "Hey Ummi! I don't see London on the board."

Keeping our real destination secret until the last minute, I had not yet told the family. Now was the moment of truth. "Well, there's been a change in plans," I declared. "We're all going to Morocco."

"What?" cried Taha. "I want to go to England, not Morocco."

Jubair was surprised and puzzled. "Why are we going to Morocco?"

Shamail looked at me and Layla questioningly, but he didn't say anything. He seemed to accept the change as confusing but normal adult behavior.

"I'm really sorry I couldn't tell you where we were going," I apologized. "We needed to go somewhere I could work to support you. I can't work in England, but I can work in Morocco."

Jubair pressed me, "But why did you tell us we were going to England?"

"Why?" Layla asked, echoing Jubair.

"If I had told you, the police in Tunisia might have found out," I explained, looking around to make sure no one else was within earshot. "And they would have told the police in Morocco we were going there. And then we would have had a lot of trouble." Their faces showed shock and hurt, not just that I had changed the plan, but that I had lied to them.

"We wouldn't have told the police," Taha protested.

"I know you wouldn't mean to," I responded. There was no way they could understand this, and I deeply regretted having betrayed their trust. "I'm sorry. Now let's catch our flight."

As the plane rose into the air, Layla busied herself with the baby, and Taha and Jubair rummaged in their backpacks for snacks. But Shamail and I looked down on the vast Mediterranean, which sparkled a bon voyage display of millions of stars...

Old friend,
I'll miss your precious waters,
Your sudden temper,
Your sweet breeze.
We may not meet again
In this land
From which I'm banished,
But drops of my tears
Remain with you
Along your shores
Washed by your waves
Always.

II
STARTING OVER
1991-1994

"Our steps invent the path as we proceed; behind us they leave
no trace, only the void. So we shall always look ahead and
trust our feet. They will take us as far as our minds will
believe..."

Tahar Ben Jelloun[29]

Leading my family down the stairs from the airplane onto the tarmac, I breathed the scent of the Atlantic, mixed with the stench of melting asphalt and the odor of grimy Casablanca. This city was not my favorite place. But it was in Maghreb, the land that had welcomed us before and would hopefully embrace us again. I was overcome with gratitude. We were still together — except for Abdullah, whose absence was a raw wound in the family — and we were in the Muslim world. Jubair, Taha, and Shamail gathered around me, waiting. Layla, with Noor in her arms, looked at me questioningly. I took a few steps and stopped again, letting my fervent prayer of thanks to Allah waft over the blessed land. With tears brimming in my eyes, I smiled at Layla and the children, "Alhamdulillah! Morocco!"

Emerging from the airport terminal, we were enveloped in the blare of taxi horns, calls of street vendors, and the excited chatter of travelers returning to their families.

Layla's sharp eyes spotted a taxi parked a hundred feet away. "Come!" she said. "There they are!"

---

[29] *The Sand Child,* Tahar Ben Jelloun, 1985.

Layla's brothers were running toward us to help with the luggage. Giving the boys hugs, they exclaimed, "Aisha! Jubair! Taha! Shamail!" The oldest brother turned to me, "Aisha, Are you well? Not bad? We didn't know you were coming, too. Welcome to Morocco!"

We piled into the taxi and began the two-and-a-half-hour trip to Sale. I dozed, but soon enough the exclamations of the kids woke me, and I saw we were crossing the Bou Regreg River into Salé. As the taxi navigated a maze of traffic, I felt a sense of homecoming. On the dusty streets of Salé, beat-up cars veered haphazardly around the donkey carts full of vegetables or cactus fruit. Boys darted out into traffic to chase a deflated, lopsided ball. Women wearing colorful jellabas and head scarves scuffed their plastic slippers along the edge of the street, their bulging shopping bags in hand. A shopkeeper called across the street to a friend, who responded cheerfully. On a corner, a fight broke out, but it was quickly snuffed out by half a dozen men intervening to calm the hot-tempered youths. This gritty area of the city was noisy and vibrant.

I didn't recognize that we had arrived at Layla's family compound until our driver pulled the taxi up to a steel door surrounded by a high concrete wall. Standing there was a little girl, who broke into excited chatter as we all piled out of the car.

"Sweetheart!" Layla said to the girl, giving her a kiss. "Go get your mother."

Shortly, Layla's older sister emerged smiling from the doorway, and then, the whole Abdul Haqq family was there, led by Layla's father, a dignified, authoritative man with a time- and sun-worn face and large, sad eyes. Next to him stood his wife and their adult sons. Finally, their youngest daughter and a daughter-in-law appeared.

Spontaneously, all the women present burst into the joyous, high-pitched, warbling sounds of zagrouta that Moroccan females make in times of celebration. Then the family broke ranks, and the women smothered us in hugs and kisses, repeatedly exclaiming expressions of gratitude to Allah for our safe arrival. The men shook hands with Jubair, Taha, and Shamail, and chatted with them as if they were adults. I was moved to tears at the warm, loving welcome.

We all adjourned to the living room, a small room with benches around the edge and a low, round wooden table in the center. A couple of framed verses from the Qur'an were the only decoration on the green concrete walls. As we sat around the table, Layla's sister served traditional green tea with

Moroccan mint from a shiny metal teapot, pouring the hot liquid in a long stream into small, decorated glasses.

Abdul Haqq spoke first, "I'm sorry about Abdullah." Layla had evidently told her family about our husband's arrest in Tunisia. "He is a good man. I was always happy to see him. The government..." he paused, weighing his words. His family was respectfully silent while he spoke. "Everywhere, in America and in Morocco, too, government people do what they want for their own purposes. And because of that, the people suffer. But Allah is all-knowing."

I knew that poor Moroccans were often the targets of heavy-handed treatment by the police and the courts. Many young men ended up in prison, and not all of them had committed crimes. Perhaps Abdul Haqq believed Abdullah was innocent, too. Speaking simply to make sure I understood, he continued, "No one will know Abdullah is in prison. We will tell people Abdullah is working in America. We'll say that Aisha and Layla are waiting for him to bring them to America."

"Yes," I agreed. "This is best." I knew that people would identify with this story, since most Moroccans knew men who had left the country to work in France or elsewhere. They would periodically send money home to their families, planning to eventually be reunited with their loved ones.

"Do you understand me?" Abdul Haqq looked around at his wife, daughters, sons, and spouses, who nodded in response. "Good," he said. Then he rose and left the room. The Abdul Haqq family would keep our secret.

A few days later, I put on my best work clothes for the first day of my job search, and I caught a bus to Rabat. I felt nervous. I had listed the schools and institutes that I knew taught English in Rabat, but there was no guarantee that they would need another teacher. And if a school did need a teacher, it could probably only offer me a few hours of work each week. I might have to cobble together several jobs to make ends meet. And of course, a large employer of English teachers, the American Language Center, was out of the question since Abdullah had been fired from that school, and as a result, I was not welcome there. But I tried not to think about the possibility of not getting enough work to take care of my family.

My first stop was the British Council, which was housed in a small, three-story office building near the center of Rabat. I found my way to the office and inquired about a teaching position, telling the receptionist that the Director at British Council in Tunis had recommended that I apply here.

"One moment," the secretary told me. She made a call and then turned to me, indicating a door, "The director will see you now."

Surprised, I walked into the director's office. A slender, dark haired young woman stood up, smiling. "Welcome! My name is Mary. You're Aisha, aren't you?" She shook my hand. "John Bryant called from Tunisia to tell me you might be on the way to Morocco."

"Thank you. Yes, I was teaching at British Council in Tunis," I said, handing her my résumé and the letter of recommendation from John.

"Please have a seat," she said, indicating a chair in front of her large desk. Sitting down, she briefly scanned my papers and then turned to me. "How did you like teaching in Tunis?"

"I loved teaching there," I said. "The students were interesting people and eager to improve their English. I think I learned as much from them as they learned from me."

We chatted a bit about my experience in Algeria and Iran, but she had obviously made her decision. "We have a full-time opening for an experienced teacher, and I think you will be a good fit here," she said.

I tried to not let my smile split my face. "Thanks, that's great!" I replied. Whatever John had told her must have been convincing.

"Can you come Monday for orientation, paperwork, and signing of the contract? You'll get your class schedule then, too. There will also be some teacher meetings next week that you should attend, and you'll have time to prepare lessons. I know time is short, but classes start the following Monday."

"That's fine!"

Mary smiled and continued, "On your CV, I see that in Tunisia you were studying for the DELTA exam. Are you interested in continuing your studies?"

"Oh, definitely. If I can."

"I'm happy to hear that!" she exclaimed. "We can take over sponsorship of your program and help with training."

I was ecstatic. Not only would British Council give me a full-time position in Rabat, but they would also support me in my professional development. At this critical moment in my career, I was getting a major boost from my new employer.

At the door to the Abdul Haqq compound, I called out to Layla and the kids, "Salaamu alaikum! Guess what? I got a job!" The kids ran to me, cheering exuberantly while Layla gave me a hug and thanked God for this blessing. "I guess we can start looking for an apartment now," I told her. Do you think you and your father can find us a good place to live, with a rent I can afford?" Since Abdul Haqq was well known and respected in the area, I hoped he could negotiate a decent price on the rent.

She smiled broadly and nodded.

A week later, when I arrived home from work, Layla was waiting for me. She had good news. "Aisha, we found a good apartment! It's not far from here," she said. "Come see!"

"OK, let's go," I responded, dropping my bookbag inside the door.

The small, two-bedroom walk-up flat was on the fourth floor of a new building on a main street of Salé just a couple blocks from the Abdul Haqq home. It was sunny and clean, with a modest kitchen, bathroom, and separate toilet. The living room had one section divided from the rest by a half-wall. That section would be the boys' room, while Layla and Noor would have the larger bedroom, and I would take the small bedroom overlooking the street. Best of all, I could afford it.

"It's perfect!" I told her. "And a good price!" With my salary, I could pay for rent and our basic expenses, and I could pay Layla for keeping the house clean, shopping, cooking, and watching the children while I was at work. I felt strongly that she needed independence in providing for herself and her daughter. I also knew that, as single mothers with young children, we needed each other, and our blended family needed stability.

This was a very unusual arrangement in Morocco for a couple reasons. First, since Layla was part of my family, she wouldn't ordinarily have been paid for her work in the home. And second, women didn't live alone in this traditional society. Young people, female or male, would live in their parents' home until married. When a woman married, she would go to live with her husband's family. If a woman's husband died or divorced her, she would usually return to the home of her father, who would support her. But Layla and I didn't fit this mold, and Abdul Haqq would not object if I chose to support his daughter. There were already nine family members to feed in his household, with only his and one son's income to support them.

Although I was Muslim, I was also a foreign woman who was used to being independent, and the Abdul Haqq family – and most Moroccans – didn't expect me to conform to all the usual norms of their society. Layla's mother jokingly framed my family's situation in traditional terms, saying, "Aisha is like the man, going to work and paying the bills. Layla is the woman, cooking and taking care of the children. It's a good deal, no?"

I signed the lease and paid one month's rent. That left me rather short of cash, as we still needed to buy basic household things for the apartment. Fortunately, the nearby souk was a plentiful source of cheap items – everything from old radio parts to used clothing, and even pre-owned dentures, which unsettled me. Layla and I purchased used cooking pots and utensils, which we would soak in hot, soapy bleach solution. I bought new but cheap straw-stuffed pallets for the kids and me. Layla bought a mattress for herself and negotiated a deal on several large, colorful pillows which we could use as seats in our living room. Meanwhile, her father found a sound, used refrigerator, and arranged for the shop to deliver it to the door of the building. When it arrived, Abdul Haqq's sons, God bless them, carried it up four flights to the apartment.

The next day, I went off to work early and Layla set about cleaning and arranging the apartment. When I returned home late in the day, she was cooking dinner, and the kids were playing with their Legos. "Hey fellas, keep those Legos in your room. I don't want to see any toys on the living room floor."

Shamail ran to me, saying, "Look what I made!"

Taha made a whooshing sound. "This is a rocket!"

Jubair showed me an ingenious Lego vehicle with lots of moving parts.

I admired their handwork. "Wow, that's pretty cool!" After a while, I wandered into the kitchen. "Mm, that smells great, Layla!"

"Chicken tagine," she said. "My father bought a chicken. He slaughtered it here. Then he did a little prayer."

"A prayer?"

"Yes, for the new home. He put a little chicken blood in each corner." She pointed to the four corners of the apartment. "Don't worry it's just a little blood." She seemed hesitant, not knowing if I would approve.

This was not an Islamic practice. I gathered it was an indigenous ritual intended to keep evil away, but I didn't have a problem with it. "Oh, that's good!" I replied. "I'm glad your father did this for us, for our new home." I figured that this was how they did things in Morocco, and if it made Abdul Haqq feel at ease, I was all for it. I added my own prayer…

Oh Allah, thank you
For shelter and security.
Ya Allah! So many times
You saved us from the worst,
And now you've brought us.
Home.
I give thanks
For Your compassion,
For the gift of prayer
For the gift of our being
Alive
In this world.

Now, we had a clean, safe apartment, and my job brought in enough income for us to live simply. Since we lived near Layla's family, my kids often played in the family compound with Layla's niece. Sometimes the young men of the family took my boys to get haircuts and go to an Indian movie dubbed in Arabic. Every Friday, after Abdul Haqq returned from the weekly services at the mosque, we visited the family for a midday dinner of Moroccan couscous with chicken and seven different vegetables cooked in a delicious broth. Layla's father took on the role of the boys' grandfather, teaching them about avoiding misdeeds, acting honorably, respecting adults, and taking care of each other and their mother. He and Shamail became especially close, and they could often be found in a quiet corner of the compound playing checkers.

For the most part, our life in Morocco was predictable and uncomplicated. But still, I couldn't fully relax. I was keenly aware of the possibility that Moroccan authorities might be informed of my expulsion from Tunisia as the wife of an "Islamic terrorist." Though this was unlikely, the two countries did share a culture, language, and family ties, and a casual remark could travel a long way over the "Arab telephone." I was relieved when my work visa was approved by the appropriate government agency without any issues. However, the fact remained that if certain people came to know I was in the country, I could be in trouble.

In addition to my own concerns, all of us had to be careful about dangers in the streets of this rough, impoverished neighborhood. Some street kids threw rocks whenever they saw Taha and Jubair and hurled verbal abuse as well. If a shopkeeper on our street saw the attack, he would scold the young aggressors and warn them, for such fights were bad for business. The bad boys would flee, not wanting to risk angering the man, since if he banned them from his store, their mothers would beat them.

Sometimes, however, an attack was not by known delinquents but by a stranger who was inebriated or mentally ill. Once, after stepping off the bus as I arrived home from work, I saw a grimy, wild-haired, barely clothed man headed my way, throwing grapefruit-size rocks at anyone who came near. The usually busy street was empty, and shopkeepers had lowered security gates over their store fronts. Cars were dented and at least one window smashed by the man, who was obviously delusional. I managed to get into the doorway of my building and run up the stairs before he saw me.

Another time, a drunk man grabbed Taha and tried to rob him of the money I had given him to buy milk for the family. Unable to escape the man's grasp, Taha, ever the prankster, suddenly looked at the ground with wide eyes and exclaimed, "Look! Twenty dirhams!" The man let go of Taha to dive for the money, except there was none. My crafty son escaped and ran. His ruse had succeeded, and the man was left empty handed, thank God.

As I had done in Tunisia, I enrolled the boys in the local Tae Kwon Do club. The youths at the club – and the teachers – were tougher and more serious than those at the club in Carthage. This was training for the real world that waited just outside the door. Shamail was in a class with younger students, but Jubair and Taha, who were tall for their age, trained with the older youths. Initially, they came home sore and bruised, but they kept going back. They learned not only Tae Kwon Do but also some street fighting.

After I arrived home from work Saturday afternoon, Layla announced, "Aisha, let's go to the beach tomorrow. We can get my friend to take us in his taxi." She was restless, having been taking care of the home and kids all week.

"Good idea! We can cool off in the sea," I agreed. I didn't work on Sunday, and the weather was very hot now that it was August. "Hey boys! Want to go to the beach tomorrow?"

As one, Shamail, Taha, and Jubair said, "Yay! Yeah!"

"OK. Empty your knapsacks and put a towel, flip flops, and an extra shirt in the knapsack. Put your swim shorts and a shirt on top – you can wear them going to the beach."

Layla and I made lunch to take with us, and she put it in the refrigerator.

"We'll take Noor to my mother tomorrow morning, and the taxi will meet us at the door of the school," she told me.

I chuckled, "Really? You've already arranged this?"

She nodded, with a sly look.

We arrived early at the beach to avoid the most intense rays of the sun. Layla and the kids were black from the North African sun, but my white skin would burn badly if I didn't protect it. Over my swimsuit I wore long, cotton pants and a long-sleeved shirt. After putting down our blanket and beach umbrella, I got out the tube of Desitin that I generally used for minor burns or babies' diaper rash and slathered the stark-white zinc oxide ointment all over my exposed face, hands, and feet.

"Here I come!" I yelled to the kids. I didn't care that I must look like a ghostly apparition to other beachgoers. Running to the shoreline, I splashed into the waves, where Layla and the kids were already playing. "Oooeeee!" I plunged into the icy waters of the Atlantic and was immediately knocked over by a powerful surge that smashed me into the sandy floor of the sea…

Atlantic:
Awesome immensity,
This oversalted ocean,
Insulting human tongues,
Freezing fragile skin,
Slamming unwary ones with
Power
Massive beyond imagining,
Daring tiny us
To sink into her embrace.
Exhilarated with fear and joy,
We tremble, held by our Mother,
Who's stronger by far
Than her barefoot spawn.

Summer was over. The kids had arrived home after their first day of school.

"Ummi, here's a list of things you have to buy for me," Jubair said. "The teacher said I need them. And I need books."

"My teacher gave me a list, too!" Taha kicked his tattered knapsack with its broken shoulder strap.

Shamail shoved his list into my hands. "My friends showed me the shop where we can buy our notebooks and books. Can we go there now?"

I glanced at the list, written in Arabic. I would show it to the shopkeeper. "Yes, let's go now. And please bring the shopping baskets." We always brought along our woven straw baskets when we went shopping, since there were no plastic bags or even paper bags at the market.

"And if we can afford it, we'll get new knapsacks. Your old ones are a mess," I said.

The boys grinned in anticipation. I had enrolled them in a local private school, where they would study in Arabic and in French. With low school fees and no more than thirty students per classroom, it was a reasonable alternative to the public school with its large, noisy classes and unruly students.

At the private school, I hoped my kids would get the extra support they needed, since there was no one at home to help with their homework or read stories to them in Arabic. Though I continued to improve my spoken use of the language, I had acquired only elementary Arabic literacy and grammar. My command of French was even more limited. Though Layla was a native speaker of Moroccan Arabic, she had unfortunately dropped out of school in fourth grade and could barely read.

We all settled into the comforting routine of work and school, and the autumn turned into winter, when people rejoiced at the onset of the life-giving rains. Muddy puddles appeared in the open lots and dirt roads surrounding our apartment building. The farms along the coast exploded with life, as fields of mint, parsley, cilantro, lettuce, and cabbage turned lush shades of green. The cool temperatures were comfortable during the daytime and occasionally freezing at night. Sitting around our portable butane heater in the evenings, the kids did their homework and I planned and prepared lessons. Layla retreated to her room, where she bundled up with Noor under layers of thick blankets and watched shows on the small television she had bought.

One night, after the rest of the family had gone to bed, I reflected on the changes in my life. It was seventeen years since I accepted Islam and fell in love with Abdullah. Now, that era was over, and I was on my own, responsible for my three youngest children, Layla, and Noor. We had adjusted and moved on with our lives. I still had some anger at Abdullah, but I didn't dwell on it, for I was focused on supporting the family and raising my kids.

When I thought about my husband, I had to admit I was grateful to him. It was he who introduced me to Islam, and it was he who brought me to the Muslim world, where I now felt very much at home. The love that I had felt for Islam from the beginning of my journey was mirrored among the Muslims I met here. Even as our marriage was collapsing, he and I usually leaned on each other for support in difficult times. But overall, the stress of living with him was intense.

Since being freed of Abdullah's presence, I felt I was becoming a fuller version of myself. Pondering the years of our marriage, I understood that I had made three critical mistakes. First, I had given up my power to him, thinking that this was what a good Muslim wife must do. My resulting powerlessness in our relationship damaged me and prevented me from protecting the children as I should have. Perhaps it had even harmed Abdullah by giving him more power than he could handle. Another major error was to take his word at face value, despite clear indications that he was not telling me the truth on many occasions. My tendency to minimize this problem and make excuses for discrepancies in his reports only encouraged this behavior. The worst mistake, of course, was not trying to leave him earlier, despite the seeming impossibility of doing so. Although I had thought about it frequently, I had been unable to formulate a concrete plan that would enable me and all our children to escape safely and successfully. But in the end, consciously or unconsciously, Abdullah had made the decision for me. By deciding to walk into the U.S. consulate on that fateful day, he had taken the first step in leaving me, Layla, and our children. Perhaps, that was his final gift to us.

"Ummi, come look!" Jubair ran to our apartment window overlooking the street,

I joined him and watched a crowd of people passing by, celebrating. "What are they singing about?" I asked Jubair, whose Arabic was fluent now.

"God and the Prophet and the awliyya," he replied. "It's a holiday today. Of course, every day in Morocco is a holiday," he laughed.

"What are awliyya?"

"Something like famous holy friends," he translated roughly.

I understood. Throughout the year, Moroccans celebrated moussems, in which they honored different saints, holy men or women. We watched as men dressed in traditional white robes and turbans drummed, played stringed instruments and horns, and sang praises of God and the friends of God. Behind them, crowds of people followed, clapping and singing joyfully. The parade proceeded slowly along the street toward Salé and soon disappeared from sight.

It wasn't until years later that I realized that a moussem was a Sufi celebration, and the awliyya were revered mystics of ages gone by, many of whose small, whitewashed tombs dot the countryside of Morocco. While modern, puritanical Muslims, such as the Salafis or Wahabis, deny the existence of saints, Muslims from Morocco, and many other countries, still hold fast to this anchor of their spiritual lives. The daily remembrance of God is heard in conversations throughout Morocco, as it is built into their language and social interactions. And after prayers, the devout may be observed repeating the Name of the One quietly in the Sufi fashion. Their religion is not a political statement but a personal relationship with Allah; they embrace moderate Islam and shrug off extremist rants.

"Step back, boys! Quick! Come over here next to me! Now!" I yanked my children back from the edge of the rectangular field, where a line of fifteen manned horses was charging at top speed. The riders, exotic and fierce in their turbans and flowing white robes, guided the huge animals with their knees as they lifted old fashioned rifles to their shoulders.

PPPOWW! In unison, the riders fired the guns as they rode, the terrifying boom echoing across the valley. As thundering hoof beats shook the earth, the unearthly horsemen were obscured by the acrid smoke of gunfire. Without a pause, the riders rapidly reloaded the muzzle-loading weapons and hauled on the reins, bringing their animals to a sudden, dramatic stop just before the end of the field, where hundreds of onlookers stood. This was tbourida, a sport requiring expert skill and horsemanship. It was the centerpiece of the saint-day celebration in a rural area north of Rabat.

"Expert riders," I thought. "But a single mistake could end up with a horse and rider plowing into a crowd of people and killing someone!" No other spectators seemed to be concerned in the least, however.

The show was over, and the kids wanted to see the rest of the moussem, which was set up like a country fair, with tables of food and cheap souvenirs.

"Come on, Ummi," Taha tugged on my arm. Jubair led the way, and his younger brothers pulled me along from one vendor to the next.

When passing a table loaded with trinkets, I stopped, saying, "Wait, let's look at this." Among the strings of beaded necklaces and bracelets on the table, one small item caught my eye. It was a necklace of tiny glass beads, with blue stones on either side of a pendant in the shape of a golden sun. From the center of the sun, a mischievous face smiled out, appealing to me. It was cheap enough and I bought it. Then the boys pulled me away, guiding me to their goal, a vendor selling bottles of Fanta out of an ice chest. Laughing at their silent plea, I treated them to their favorite soda.

I've worn that necklace occasionally throughout my life, but it was only recently that I understood what it meant. In my studies of Sufism, I learned about Shams of Tabriz, the spiritual friend and mentor of the famous Persian poet and mystic, Jalaladin Rumi. Together, the two men communed, prayed, meditated, drummed, and whirled in mystical ecstasy. My necklace was a symbol of Shams, the famous Sufi whose name means "Sun."

The light of that moussem was counterbalanced by a very different saint-day I attended, which displayed a different side of Moroccan beliefs. The celebration took place near the tomb of the saint, a whitewashed adobe building with a rounded roof situated on a knoll overlooking the fairgrounds. When I arrived, a small parade of white-robed devotees was coming down the hill from the tomb, drumming, singing loudly, and whirling. In their midst, a woman was whirling wildly, her very long hair sweeping the earth and sky as she turned her head and body with feverish energy. Watching her, I felt a sense of awe and fear. I'd never seen anyone so entranced, so consumed by a state I couldn't understand. When the procession was over, the disciples of the saint seemed to melt away.

This moussem felt dark and strange. There was a man surrounded by a large crowd who watched as he poured boiling water into a crock, lifted it to his lips, and drank it down. His mouth was evidently not burned, and he continued talking normally to the crowd. I was deeply unsettled, hoping that it was merely a magic trick. I stopped watching and quickly moved away from the crowd, but there were other disturbing sights – a man walking on coals, another reclining on sharp nails, and one playing with a cobra – all for the benefit of paying spectators. Uncomfortable, I left the fair.

This reminded me of an earlier encounter with an herbalist who turned out to be much more than a healer. I had been shopping in the Salé souk, not the touristy area but the narrow lanes where Moroccan residents would buy cheap clothes for their kids, plastic sandals, dented aluminum pots, and the like. As I walked deeper into the souk, the cold symptoms that had been bothering me all day worsened, and I knew it was not a cold but the flu. Aching, coughing, and fatigued, I decided to look for an herbalist shop where I could purchase a remedy for my symptoms. I asked a shopkeeper, who directed me to a booth where herbs hung in bunches.

The herbalist – like so many people in Morocco – didn't know the standard Arabic I spoke. But she understood when I demonstrated my symptoms – coughing, shivering, and runny nose. She began to grab bundles of herbs and put them into a large paper bag. As I waited, I looked deeper into her shop. Hanging from the low ceiling were dead, desiccated creatures – a snake, a couple frogs, and other shriveled up animals I couldn't identify. This was not just an herbalist but a practitioner of the black arts. I shivered, as much from this sudden realization as from my fever. When she had filled the bag, she stated her price, and I put some coins in her palm. In response, she gave me the blackest, most evil look I'd ever seen, accompanied by a threatening grin. I realized I had misunderstood her, and I hastily emptied the contents of my change purse into my hand and offered it to her. She picked out what she needed and sent me on my way. I hoped she hadn't sold me some dangerous herbs.

Back home, I showed the herbs to Layla, who smelled and examined them carefully. I was relieved when she verified that they were commonly used for cold and flu symptoms, including fever. She also let me know that black magic was alive in Morocco. Then, as the children listened with wide eyes, she told us stories about curses on a wayward husband's mistress, spells to make a man lose his virility, or rituals to bring catastrophe to an enemy. Then she told the gruesome story of the infamous Aisha Kandisha, an immortal, terrifying demon who lured men with her beauty as she walked along the oceanside at night. After she had bewitched and possessed the unlucky man who encountered her, she revealed her horrendously ugly form. Her victim was rendered sterile, dull, and listless. Layla obviously believed the story, and now, so did my children.

During the past year in Morocco, I had come to appreciate our quiet life, marked by the rhythm of the seasons, holidays, and daily routines of work and family. By now, I was fairly certain that neither police nor government officials had noticed that Abdullah Khalid's wife was back in Morocco, and I was relieved not to be constantly vigilant.

During spring break, I took the boys by big taxi to visit my friend, Rachida, a German woman who, like me, was a convert to Islam and the mother of five children. Widowed, she lived with her kids on a farm outside of Khemisset.

"Salaamu alaikum!" Rachida greeted us. "Would you like to go to the hot springs of Oulmes? I can drive us there." The spring of Oulmes was originally the source of the Moroccan brand of carbonated water that we often drank.

"Sounds good!" "Yeah!" "Let's go!" A couple of her kids and my children and I were up for an adventure. We piled into her ancient, tank-like Mercedes, with Rachida at the wheel.

After a short drive, she slowed the car and pulled alongside a field. "We're here," she said.

Walking across the large open area, we came to a steep ravine that divided the flat, agricultural land from more hilly terrain. At the bottom of the ravine, a fast-moving river rushed among rocks from which young men dived and swam. On the other side of the river, a steep cliff rose up the mountainside, and from the top of the rock face a spring burst forth. The abundant spring water of Oulmes cascaded down to a row of small bath houses built into a ledge of rock, and from there, the water flowed down to the river.

While Rachida took the kids to swim in a shallow pool, I crossed a footbridge to the hammam. I opened the door of one of the baths and entered the narrow room, which was big enough for one or two people. A long, stone tub was filled with fresh water from the constantly flowing waterfall. On this cool day, I was pleased to discover that the water was indeed warm and mildly carbonated. I removed my clothes, lay down in the tub, and soaked my body in the comfortable heat of this miracle of nature. Alhamdulillah!

Reluctantly, I emerged from the warmth. I hadn't come prepared with a towel, so I dried off with my T-shirt, wrapped it around my wet hair, and then put my pants and jacket on over my damp skin. As we all walked back to Rachida's car, we felt refreshed, rejoicing in our perfect spring afternoon.

In this beautiful land, we had so much to be grateful for. My children had adapted quickly to our new life. They had become fluent in Moroccan Arabic, made friends in our neighborhood, and learned to avoid troublesome people. They were adequate students and were learning French as well as standard Arabic. Our family was stable, emotionally and financially, thanks to Layla's and my efforts and the support of her family.

For the first time in my life, I had a full-time job that was challenging and satisfying. As part of my training through British Council, I learned to teach English more effectively and passed both the written and practicum DELTA exams. Now that I had received certification, I continued to grow as a teacher, gaining competence and confidence. I could see myself doing this as a lifelong career in Morocco or elsewhere in the Middle East.

"Aisha, come look!" Layla called from her bedroom. Her favorite Mexican soap opera — translated into Arabic — was on TV. I wandered into her room and made myself comfortable on the bed, paying attention to the action on the screen. I didn't particularly like soap operas, but their predictable plots and simple, conversational Arabic helped me improve my listening comprehension. And watching the show with Layla was also a way to bond with her, away from childcare and household chores.

"Who's that?" I asked her. There seemed to be a new character in the show.

"That's her boyfriend. But he isn't nice. No good for her," Layla explained.

"What about the other man? The one she wanted to marry?" I asked.

"Oh, he's in love with another woman now…"

As my Arabic improved, I learned to talk about and better understand the everyday lives of our Moroccan friends, family, and neighbors. At times, I even caught myself thinking or dreaming in Arabic. But the Arabic that I spoke was a mixture of modern standard Arabic, Algerian Arabic, Moroccan Arabic, and a bit of French. I could make myself understood to people who had been educated in standard Arabic, but not those who spoke only the Moroccan dialect, Darija. Though Layla spoke the latter, she knew some of the standard language from watching TV shows, and like most Moroccans, her speech was peppered with French words. In addition, she used English words she had learned in her time living with our family. Together, we had unintentionally developed fluency in our own pidgin language, which combined all these influences. And this common language brought us closer together.

Layla was a caring mother to Noor as well as to Shamail, with whom she had a warm relationship. She often took him on shopping trips or visits to her family or friends. However, she was clearly indifferent to Taha and treated him as a nuisance. With Jubair, she was sharp and disagreeable. Both boys complained that she was mean to them when I wasn't around.

Layla and I had come together to preserve the safety and well-being of our children. Without each other, our lives as single mothers would have been very difficult. Our arrangement was necessary for both of us, but my view of it changed when I came home from work one day, tired and out-of-breath from climbing the four flights of stairs to our apartment. As I opened the door, I saw Jubair lying in his bed, gasping for air, holding his throat, and crying. Layla appeared to have just released him as she turned toward me. Taha and Shamail were bawling as they ran to me and hugged me.

"Layla sat on Jubair's chest and was choking him!" Taha cried. "He couldn't breathe!"

Angrily, she yelled, "He was bad. He didn't do what I said."

Jubair sat up on his bed, still breathing roughly. He couldn't speak.

"Layla," I said firmly. "You will not beat the children. Ever. If you have a problem with Jubair, Taha, or Shamail, you tell me, and I'll deal with it."

She shrugged and turned away, retreating to her room.

This serious incident marked a turning point in our relationship, and my faith in her judgment was shaken.

During a break between classes, I walked over to Hassan Tower to stroll the broad plaza that was dotted with the ruins of an ancient mosque. I needed time alone to think about my family's future. For the first time in years, I felt free from the cloud of depression that had followed me throughout my life. Despite the usual challenges of living, I felt content here, supported by the moderate Muslim culture. This was my real home, a place where I could be myself, and take charge of my life and my family.

Though I would always be a foreigner in Morocco, I felt welcomed here. I was embedding myself in the culture of the people and becoming more fluent in Arabic. After years of spiritual malaise, I could again find solace in daily prayer and fasting in Ramadan. And coming out of my lifelong isolation, I was making friends among Moroccans and foreigners alike. Alhamdulillah, I was where I wanted and needed to be.

Though money was tight, it was sufficient to cover our basic expenses. I could see myself teaching at British Council for the long term and enjoying the work. In a couple years, perhaps I'd be able to take on greater responsibility, earning a pay increase. Perhaps I would eventually move the family into a better, safer neighborhood. After the family's unexpected loss of Abdullah and our precipitous departure from Tunisia, the children had settled down. Layla had also adjusted, and after the incident with Jubair she was trying to follow my rules. All three kids enjoyed the familial support of the Abdul Haqq family and spent hours at their house each week. They had also made friends at school, in the neighborhood, and in their Tae Kwon Do club.

When I considered the children's future, however, I knew that they were not receiving the education that they needed, as English-speaking, American citizens. When they grew up, they would need skills to pursue careers anywhere in the world, but a Moroccan high school certificate or a college degree would not help them get jobs outside of Morocco. Even within the country, education did not guarantee good jobs, and unemployment among young people was very high. While knowing Arabic and French would undoubtedly be useful to my children in the future, they needed to study in English, the international language and their native tongue. However, here in Morocco, I couldn't afford the only private schools that taught in English. And with my full-time job, I couldn't home-school the children.

I now had to consider the option that I hadn't wanted to consider, leaving Morocco. If we returned to the U.S., the kids would get free public education, but they would have to work hard to catch up. With Jubair in 7th grade and Taha and Shamail entering 5th and 4th grades, delaying our return would make it even harder to close the gap between them and their classmates. Although the three of them would probably do well enough in American math classes, they would have to study English reading and writing from the ground up, probably in a bilingual class. It would be daunting, but since they already spoke English, it seemed feasible.

The real problems they would face wouldn't be academic but social. Culturally, they would be different from other American kids their age, never having been exposed to American TV, cinema, music, slang, cultural attitudes, and behaviors. Worse, my sons would suddenly be plunged into a white, Judeo-Christian world where, despite claims of equal rights, being Muslim was seen as objectionable, and being Black could assign an individual to the lowest rung on the ladder. Although they had experienced prejudice from some Arab kids who didn't like Americans, it was minor compared to what they would face in the U.S.

Living in America would be tough for me, too. Since I had almost no reserve funds, I would have to get a job immediately. And I knew that no matter how hard I worked, I might not be able to support my kids on my income alone. My siblings could not help me financially, and my mother was facing the problems of declining health and resources. Abdullah, of course, had no income. I would be venturing into a capitalistic world with no back-up plan or safety net.

Equally important, I knew that a return to the U.S. would put my spiritual life, my practice of Islam, and my connection to Muslim culture in jeopardy. The support that I had felt from the people and the culture of Muslim countries would suddenly disappear, and I would be on my own to try to continue my practice of Islam. Would I be able to feel my connection to God when all around me was a world of materialism? Would I get so caught up in survival that my spiritual life fell by the wayside? I didn't have a good feeling about this.

Then I considered the most important reason to return to the U.S. I had recently received word from Karen that Jamal and Yusuf had been hanging out with bad friends, getting in trouble, drinking, and smoking weed. I was dismayed, realizing that my mother had kept this news from me so that I wouldn't worry. If I had known my older sons were at risk, I would have returned much earlier. Tears welled up in my eyes as I thought about our three-year separation. During that time, they had needed me, but I had been far away, unavailable.

And so, I decided to leave Morocco. Despite the difficulties we would face in America, it was probably best for all my sons. The cost of returning to the U.S. would be high, but the cost of staying here was greater. As painful as this decision was for me, I would leave the Muslim world.

Dear Mom,

I hope you're doing well. The kids and I are doing fine. I've already told British Council I'll be returning permanently to the U.S. this summer. Now I need to start looking for a job. Could you xerox and send my enclosed résumé and cover letter to the colleges and English language schools listed below, and any others you might know of in the Northeast? Thanks for offering to put us up. Hopefully, it won't be for too long...

I broke the news to Layla. "My sister wrote to me that Jamal and Yusuf are having problems. They need me."

"Will you go back to America?"

"Yes," I answered. "But I don't like the idea of living there. Morocco is so much better."

"You're not happy about going to America?" Layla looked at me quizzically. "Why? It's your home."

"It's not my home now," I replied. "My family is there, but they live very far from each other, and they don't see each other often. Not like your family here. And in America it's all work, work, work. Most people just believe in work and money. It's not a friendly place. And life is very expensive."

"I can help you in America..." Layla began.

"Layla, I'm really sorry, but I won't be able to take you and Noor to America," I said with regret. "As a teacher, I won't earn much, and it will be hard to afford an apartment that's big enough for me and the children. In America, they don't like it if there are too many people in a small apartment, like here." I looked around our cozy, two-bedroom flat, which was home to all six of us.

Layla was crushed. "But Noor needs to be with her brothers," she objected, tearfully.

"I know. The boys need her, too." I was sure my sons, who cherished Noor, were going to object to being separated from her. I felt like a heel, but I also knew I couldn't support all six of us in the U.S., let alone, possibly, Jamal and Yusuf.

I thought about the situation. Abdullah's friend, Sandy, had visited us recently. Perhaps she could work with Abdullah to help Layla and Noor come to the U.S. "Look, I'll help you write Sandy and Abdullah. We can ask them to start working on the paperwork you'll need. Noor has an American passport, and you should be able to get a visa as Abdullah's wife. Hopefully, they can get together money for your airplane tickets. But that will take time, and the boys and I must return this summer so I can look for a job. Then we'll see what happens."

LETTER, MAY 1993

Hi Mom,

Just a quick note. Thanks for sending out all those résumés! Since we haven't had any responses, I think it's best for me to return to the U.S. and continue my job search on the ground. If you can get tickets for any available date in late June or early July, that would be great. The kids and I can't wait to see you. Thanks so much for doing this for us. Let me know the details. You can give me a call at British Council Monday, Wednesday, or Friday between 2 and 4 PM Morocco time. We'll see you soon!

In June, my mother called with the news that Professor Michael J. Connolly of Boston College wanted to talk to me about a potential job teaching freshman English to college students whose native language wasn't English. He could call me at British Council to interview me. On the appointed day, I was in the middle of teaching when the Director came to my classroom and said the call from the U.S. had come in. Another teacher immediately took over my class.

Mary could see I was nervous. "Don't worry, you'll do fine," she said. "You have plenty of experience and excellent teaching skills. Good luck!"

She was right. At the end of the interview, Prof. Connolly asked me to come in for a second interview when I got back to the U.S. After I hung up the phone, I sat for a moment, stunned. A second interview! I had a good chance of getting this job. Perhaps this was a sign of good things to come, inshallah. I murmured a prayer of thanks.

The rest of the summer was a whirlwind of finishing up my classes, visiting friends, buying new clothes for the kids, and packing up our belongings. But while the kids were in a fever of excitement, I was quietly grieving…

Maghreb,
My heart breaks to leave you,
Sunset edge of Muslim lands.
Generous, you accepted my lonely soul,
Giving me heart and hope,
Embracing me,
And now under your sky,
Nourished by sun and rain,
I pray to the One:
Guide me on the way,
Give me strength to depart,
Though my heart
Cries to stay.

As we had done so many times in the past thirteen years, we moved to another foreign country. The U.S. was both familiar and alien to me, but it was virtually unknown to my three youngest children. Our arrival was softened by the pleasant stay with my mother in rural Rhode Island, where we could enjoy sunshine, green fields, and rocky shores along the Atlantic Ocean. The boys often walked up the road to see the llama a farmer kept in his field. Sometimes my mom and I took the kids to the beach, where they could swim and collect shells. The water was cold, and the beach was rocky, but they didn't mind. As I looked out on the Atlantic, feeling its power and beauty, I recalled standing on the opposite side of the ocean, experiencing the same emotions. I had come full circle.

Within days of our arrival, I drove to Boston for an appointment with Professor Connolly. As my previous manager at British Council had predicted, the interview went well, and I was offered a position as a lecturer teaching three courses a semester. The campus, with broad, well-kept lawns, granite stone classroom buildings, and a large, modern library was a world away from Morocco. But it was now my new teaching home.

I had so much to do in so little time — search for and move into an apartment in Boston, order textbooks and develop syllabi for my classes, and register the kids for school. On the advice of another teacher in my department at B.C. I looked for housing in neighboring Brookline, which was known for its well-rated schools and good bilingual education. I rented a small, reasonably priced, two-and-a-half-bedroom apartment. Our neighbors were a mix of blue-collar Americans and immigrants from Russia, China, India, and other countries. Jubair, Taha, and Shamail made friends quickly. They joined pick-up games of soccer, learned to play basketball, and found their way around town.

When school started in September, the boys were busy with classes, homework, after-school activities, and their new friends. I was fully occupied with teaching my regular courses during the day as well as an evening class once a week. It was a struggle to make ends meet, keep the household running, cook dinner for the children, and attend parent-teacher conferences. I tried to monitor the boys' homework, not very successfully. Although our life was often chaotic, we managed to remain cohesive as a family.

In less than a year, Abdullah and Sandy had secured a visa and airfare for Layla and Noor, who flew from Morocco to the U.S. During spring break from work and school, the boys and I went to visit them at Abdullah's mother's home. After a joyful reunion, we drove several hours to the upstate prison in New York where he was incarcerated. As we traveled, the cityscape gave way to suburbs and then endless hills, farmland, and forests.

"So big!" Layla exclaimed. "And so many trees! And farms!"

I heard the awe in her voice and felt her homesickness for Morocco. But she was also a strong woman, dedicated to giving her child a good life in this strange land.

"How do you like living in the U.S?" I asked.

"It's OK. But I want my own place. And a job." I gathered there was conflict between Layla and Abdullah's mom. I knew she hoped to move in with me and the boys, but there was no room for them in our crowded apartment, and my income was barely covering all the bills. I was already looking for another part time job to help make ends meet.

From the back seat, the sound of Noor giggling made Layla and me smile.

"Mooo, mooooo!" cried Shamail, accompanying the story book he was reading to her.

"Noor, look!" Jubair said, pointing at an animal grazing in a field. "It's a horse!"

Finally, I saw the signs to the prison ahead and slowed. I pulled the car into the parking lot. "We're here," I announced. Turning off the engine, I got out to stretch my legs.

"Is this where Abu is?" asked Jubair. He and Taha and Shamail, still in the back seat, looked at me expectantly. Layla, who now held Noor on her lap, awaited my answer.

"Yup. I know it's taken a long time, but we're finally here. This is the prison where Abu is," I replied. "Come on, let's go inside. We must register and then wait for them to bring him to us."

The prison, built in a rural area in upstate New York in the middle of vast, empty fields, was the definition of isolation. Most of the prisoners, I guessed, were urban dwellers from New York area and maybe Albany. Most were Black. They must have felt they'd been sent to an alien moon to serve their sentences. The visiting room, like those in so many other prisons, was well-worn but relatively clean, like a high school cafeteria, but with guarded exits. Uniformed men watched the prisoners and the visitors, monitoring them for any forbidden actions.

Layla and the kids didn't seem to notice their surroundings. Their eyes were on Abdullah, who had just arrived at our table wearing the same brown uniform and white kufi that I recalled from fourteen years ago. It had been a long three years since we saw him last in Tunisia. Now he was here, back in the New York prison, as if he had never been free, traveling Muslim lands with his family. Despite the failure of our relationship and my bitterness toward him, it pained me that he was caged like this.

"Salaamu alaikum!" he greeted Layla as she rose to meet him. His eyes twinkled as he held Layla close and kissed little Noor on her curly hair. He talked softly to Layla, and she said a few words and shrugged.

He turned to me, giving me a hug which I didn't welcome. "Aisha! You look great!" I stiffened. I had come here so the family could see him, but I had vowed to never again fall prey to his charms. "Hey, are you OK?" he asked, pulling back from me. I looked him in the eyes, unsmiling. He backed off. "Oh, well, OK then." He tried to reminisce with me about old times, but I wasn't in the mood for nostalgia. I reminded myself of the pain I had suffered.

Turning to Jubair, fourteen years old, and Taha, twelve, he exclaimed, "Whoa, guys, you two are both taller than me! And Shamail, last time I saw you, you were this high!" He held his hand at waist level. Shamail frowned, disliking the description. Uncomfortable, the kids were unsure of what to say to their father. But as Abdullah chatted with them, they gradually loosened up, telling him about school, sports, and our neighborhood in Boston.

"Hey, where are Jamal and Yusuf?" Abdullah asked.

Jubair replied, "Oh they're in college now. Jamal lives in New Hampshire, and Yusuf is in Massachusetts."

"Wow," Abdullah looked uncertain for a moment. I wondered if he realized that not only the older sons but also the rest of us had moved on with our lives and left him behind. But he caught himself and resumed his lively conversation with Layla, Jubair, Taha, and Shamail. I felt they needed this time to reestablish family ties, so I just listened, patiently waiting for the end of visiting hours. Though I had harshly established my safe boundaries with Abdullah, I also felt pulled by sympathy for him. I felt the dissonance of the dreams we had shared of a life free together, and the chaotic mess that we had made of that opportunity. And that past had led us to our present, opposite paths...

He doesn't belong here:
A talented man, a father,
Not in the right place.
That place he surrendered,
And we,
Just visitors
Related by blood and love,
Will soon return to our place,
Leaving him
Stranded in unreality.

Finally, it was time to leave, and Abdullah hugged the kids, and we said our goodbyes. The guards shepherded the visitors toward the exit, while the prisoners headed for their own door into the interior of the prison. Taking one last look at his family, Abdullah returned to his life deep within prison walls. Feeling deeply sad, the rest of us returned to our lives on the outside.

Exhausted by the visit, Layla and the children fell asleep. I fortified myself with coffee and drove the superhighway, putting mile after mile behind me. I felt sorry for Abdullah, but my relationship with him was finally over. I hadn't spoken many words with him during the visit, but he understood my message. I didn't know what lay in my future, but it would be mine, not his.

I put the driver's window down and rejoiced as the wind ruffled my hair and cleansed my face. I inhaled deeply, feeling the center of my being, feeling Allah within me. I let my breath out…

> *I carried it all these years:*
> *An untold burden.*
> *Now fallen by the roadside,*
> *It has tumbled down an embankment*
> *And returned to earth*
> *Nourishing*
> *Spring blossoms.*
> *And my life is renewed*
> *And I leap up*
> *And I am flying*
> *And I am free.*

EPILOGUE
1993-2026

Whenever I think about it now, I'm deeply grateful we survived the aftermath of coming back to the U.S. – the culture shock, emotional turmoil, adolescent defiance, depression, and the rest. Abdullah's absence left a huge vacuum which I couldn't fill as the boys entered adolescence. Doggedly, I struggled to hold the family together, meet with the boys' teachers, counselors, and family therapists; work at Boston College and other part-time teaching jobs; and do graduate studies in linguistics at Boston University. My spiritual life faded away in the intense stress of surviving those difficult years.

I was grateful for the support my family gave us. My sister, Karen, was strongly supportive, as my children and I went through our seven years of hell. Karen and I laughed together whenever we could and consoled each other when we couldn't. (We still do this for each other.) My brother, Gerry, and his wife and daughters were supportive and provided my kids with a model of a healthy, generous family. Gerry has passed away, but his memory enriches me. My mother loved to visit with her grandchildren, and they enjoyed visiting her at her home near the sea. She and I had never had a typical mother-daughter relationship, but in her last years, she and I got to know each other a bit better. When she died in 2004, I felt that a friend had passed.

As a single parent, I found that raising a family in Boston on my teacher's salary was impossible. I finally gave up my teaching career and looked for work in other fields. Because I had taken some computer programming courses and done independent study in computational linguistics, I was hired as a linguist for a software company. I felt incredibly fortunate to be earning a living wage, and I was eventually able to buy a used car and a two-family home forty miles outside of Boston. In 2004, I earned my Ph.D. in applied linguistics from Boston University.

Both Layla and I filed for divorces from Abdullah. Occasionally, the kids and I visited her and Noor, or they visited us. Layla took classes to improve her English, and she remarried. With Sandy's help, she made sure her daughter received a good education in the U.S. In high school, Noor was an excellent student with a talent in the arts, but her heart was set on helping others. After graduation, she plunged into a pre-med program and then medical school. She is now married and practicing medicine as a general surgeon.

During our years overseas, my children learned that the wide world was a place to experience and explore, making friends wherever they went. They developed a facility for acquiring new languages and other skills that were required in our ever-changing environment. After a rocky start in America, they put those abilities to use teaching themselves building construction, electronics, computer software and hardware, and more.

Early in his career, my oldest son, Jamal (River), taught technical mountaineering skills in New Hampshire and guided clients on high altitude expeditions in Alaska and Ecuador. On a long solo motorcycle adventure, he made a monumental seven-thousand-mile trip from New England to Tierra del Fuego, the southernmost tip of South America. Married and the father of three boys, he now stays closer to home, working as a skilled carpenter and team lead on commercial and residential construction projects. He enjoys taking his wife and kids hunting, fishing, camping, canoeing, and rock climbing.

Yusuf (Forest) moved beyond his childhood fascination with rockets and plunged into physics, mathematics, and engineering. His published research is focused on advanced mathematics and algorithms for radar imaging. Interested in visiting places he hadn't already seen, he has traveled throughout the U.S. and to Thailand and Cambodia. Married with two children, Yusuf is an accomplished cook and dedicated gardener who raises all the flavorful fruit and vegetables his family needs.

When Jubair (now Zia) was seventeen, she taught herself to program and design websites. Since then, she has expanded into software architecture and management. She started and ran her own small business, developing websites and web apps for clients. Later, she moved into a corporate job designing software architecture and managing a team of developers. A few years ago, she took a break from her busy career and traveled to Morocco, where she visited with the Abdul Haqq family as well as other friends. The parent of five children, Zia and her kids can often be found trekking through a wooded park, stargazing, playing computer games, or enjoying exhibits at the Science Museum.

As a teenager, Taha became a self-taught whiz in electronics, robotics, and eventually computer hardware and software. He was reading college engineering textbooks with keen interest. In the U.S. Army, Taha was deployed to Afghanistan, and subsequently, he did contract work in that country as well as Kuwait. On vacations, he traveled to India and the Philippines. Back in the U.S., he put his technical skills to work in software development and IT operations, with a focus on cyber security and data analysis. He and his wife have two children. He's enthusiastic about teaching his kids robotics, electronics, climbing, and scouting skills.

Shamail was a natural businessman and computer geek from the time he arrived in the U.S. An expert at playing a certain online game, he built up his characters to a very high level and then sold them to other players for cash. Using the money he earned, he bought a new computer, promptly dismantled it, and then built it back up again. Then, at seventeen, he left home to join the Army, where he was a communications technician stationed in Korea and Iraq. Upon his return, he studied web and front-end development. Then he branched into all aspects of the software life cycle, becoming a full-stack software engineer. He and his wife have traveled to Türkeye and Malaysia, and they now live in Morocco with their young daughter, fulfilling their dream to live in the land and culture they love.

The patriarch of our clan, Abdullah, is still in prison, serving a life sentence. He has married a Muslim woman and returned to Islam. Behind the walls of the prison, he counsels young inmates, trying to guide them to positive choices. Jamal, Zia, Noor and I have visited and maintained contact with him. After much reflection, I decided to shed the anger and blame I long felt toward Abdullah and forgive him.

With my children grown and nurturing their own families, I have embraced my vital link with nature. In the peace of forests and remote waters, I savor my sacred connections with trees, plants, rocks, springs, and creatures. I also explore different dimensions of the natural world and build relationships with generous beings in those realms. This shamanic work has healed me.

Spiritually, I've come full circle from the moment in my twenties when I took my first tentative steps in Islam. I have returned eagerly to the daily prayers, like a thirsty traveler to a cold spring in the desert. Throughout the day, I may forget my connection to the One, but I keep trying to wake up. The path of Sufism – the mystical facet of Islam – leads me on this way with wonder and awe.

I still miss Morocco: the close human relationships, delightful food, color-drenched souks, and rhythmic music in the streets. The mountains, desert, and sea. The devotion to spiritual life. The call to prayer echoing from the mosque at dawn. And when my longing becomes unbearable, I recall the words of the incomparable mystic and poet, Jalaladin Rumi:

> *"Why do you weep?*
> *That source is within you,*
> *And this whole world is springing up from it.*
> *The source is full,*
> *And its waters are ever-flowing.*
> *Do not grieve, drink your fill.*
> *Don't think it will ever run dry,*
> *This is the endless ocean."*[30]

---

[30] *The Way of Passion, a Celebration of Rumi.* Andrew Harvey, 1994.

POSTSCRIPT

Salaamu alaikum Abdullah,

It's 4:30 AM and I'm awake. I check the time. Too early for Fajr prayer yet. Lazily, I reach out to pull the curtain open next to my bed. I look up and see the stars clearly, hanging near to earth, looking down at me. Startled, I sit up. And think of you.

It's surreal seeing the stars without my glasses. I'm very nearsighted, and there's no way I should be perceiving them as anything more than a faint smudge of dust. But now I admire the bright stars of my favorite winter constellation and remember a dark, starry night long ago, when I pointed it out to you. I was so young then, a different person than this older, weathered, and occasionally wiser person I've become. Despite my years, I'm not jaded but in love with the creation and its Creator.

I put my glasses on, but they make no difference. The stars couldn't be any clearer. Under those beacons of light, I realize that you and I have a soul connection that is still alive, even after all that has happened between us. Just as amazing as the steadily beaming stars, the spiritual thread between us has outlasted the firestorm of those years we were together. The tie is not love or affection but something deeper, longer lasting. There's no explaining it.

I've been shaken into consciousness. I splash cool, blessed water on my hands, face, and feet. Then, facing the qibla, I gratefully pray. Afterward, I ask Allah's blessing on your soul and mine. You and I are of an age that forces us to confront our imminent return to the One whose light is a star within us. May that light guide you and me on our separate paths home.

Peace, Aisha

ACKNOWLEDGMENTS

I believe it takes a village to create a writer. Many people have encouraged me to begin this account, continue writing, and plow through the tough spots. Foremost among them are my sister Karen Lee, and my adult children, River Jamal Lee, Zia Saidi, Taha Saidi, and Shamail Saidi, whose faith in my project inspired me from the beginning to the end.

My local writers' group and other readers have been enthusiastic about my memoir, even as I revised again and again. Their weekly support over the years has been vital to me. I give many thanks to Janice Campbell, Laurie Downey, Wendy Farrand, Janice Maves, and Bernie Monette for their helpful critique.

I'm also grateful to those who have supported my spiritual and psychological growth during times when I hesitated to continue writing: friends and fellow meditators Doug Bowen, Donna Nelson, and Fran Demaio; insightful shamanic guides Evelyn Rysdyk and Allie Knowlton; and teacher Andrew Harvey, who taught me to delve fearlessly into my spiritual depths.

I give special thanks to Kabir and Camille Helminski, Mahmoud Mostafa, Khadim Chisti, Rahima McCullough, and others of the Mevlevi Sufi path. They have helped me to experience prayer as an exchange of love with the One. Thanks to them, I feel at home in Islam again. Alhamdulillah.

THE AUTHOR

Aisha F. Saidi spent many years writing this memoir, changing focus and even abandoning it at times. With this final rewrite, she is looking forward to spending more time with her friends and family.

Her varied career springs from her love of language. As a teacher of English for Speakers of Other Languages, Aisha specialized in college level academic reading and writing. While earning a graduate degree in linguistics, she began working as a computational linguist, helping to develop speech recognition software and an aviation safety thesaurus for integration with text mining. She has also been a technical and proposal writer on web and software projects.

However, her most difficult and rewarding accomplishment has been to raise her five boys to adulthood despite the challenges. She is proud of them and of her grandchildren.

Aisha lives in a small cottage in rural New England, where she raises a few chickens, tends a messy garden, and wanders the woods and hills. She enjoys playing with her dog and visiting with family. For this quiet life, she gives thanks to the Spirit in All.